Also by Gregg Jarrett

*The Russia Hoax: The Illicit Scheme to Clear
Hillary Clinton and Frame Donald Trump*

*Witch Hunt: The Story of the Greatest
Mass Delusion in American Political History*

THE
TRIAL
OF THE
CENTURY

GREGG JARRETT

WITH DON YAEGER

THRESHOLD EDITIONS

New York London Toronto Sydney New Delhi

Threshold Editions
An Imprint of Simon & Schuster, Inc.
1230 Avenue of the Americas
New York, NY 10020

Copyright © 2023 by Gregg Jarrett

First Threshold Editions hardcover edition May 2023

THRESHOLD EDITIONS and colophon are trademarks of Simon & Schuster, Inc.

For information about special discounts for bulk purchases, please contact Simon &
Schuster Special Sales at 1-866-506-1949 or business@simonandschuster.com.

The Simon & Schuster Speakers Bureau can bring authors to your live event. For
more information, or to book an event, contact the Simon & Schuster Speakers
Bureau at 1-866-248-3049 or visit our website at www.simonspeakers.com.

Interior design by Silverglass

Manufactured in the United States of America

10 9 8 7 6 5 4 3 2 1

Library of Congress Cataloging-in-Publication Data

ISBN 978-1-9821-9857-2
ISBN 978-1-9821-9860-2 (ebook)

In memory of Joseph W. Jarrett,
a gifted trial lawyer and loving father

"Here, we find today as brazen and as bold an
attempt to destroy learning as was ever made in the middle ages,
and the only difference is we have not provided that they shall be
burned at the stake. But there is time for that, Your Honor.
We have to approach these things gradually."

—CLARENCE DARROW, SCOPES TRIAL, JULY 13, 1925

Contents

THE
TRIAL
OF THE
CENTURY

Discovering Darrow and the "Trial of the Century"

I don't know why I did it.

I was barely a teenager when, one summer day, I plucked a single volume off my father's densely packed bookshelf. The handsome navy blue jacket had the words *Clarence Darrow for the Defense* embroidered in rich gold lettering on the binding. The author's name—Irving Stone—was printed just below. It looked important, to the extent that one, to use that old line, can judge a book by its cover. I opened it and was instantly confronted with a full-page photograph of a rather austere gentleman dressed in a dark three-piece suit. He wore an unruly black bow tie tethered around a crisply starched white shirt. He had a full head of dark hair that was, at once, combed and slightly tousled. The right side of his face was draped in subdued shadows yet failed to conceal the deep creases embedded by time. His weary visage and sober countenance were appreciably softened by eyes that appeared to reflect a genuine benevolence.

Turning the page, I read a brief but poignant epigraph from the man: "I may hate the sin, but never the sinner." I remember pausing to consider the meaning of those words that, to this day, I have never forgotten. Intrigued, I kept going.

Over the next several days, I eagerly read about the finest American trial lawyer who ever lived. I did not understand it all, no surprise given my age. After reading the 520 pages, I returned to the start and began absorbing it all over again. I have revisited the book many times since then, always discovering something new. I have often considered how a gesture as simple as reaching for a random book that day ended up shaping the course of my life. Whether it was boredom or curiosity, I cannot say, but it was serendipitous. After I set the book down, I resolved to follow as best I could in this eminent man's profession by becoming an attorney myself. While I could never replicate Darrow's impressive accomplishments, at the least a legal education would be a worthy, useful, and productive pursuit.

I am also aware of my father's influence. Like Darrow, he was a trial lawyer of exceptional talent. I loved and admired him for his goodness, gentleness, and warmth of spirit. He cared deeply about fairness and honesty, a passion he passed along to his two children. My father and I often ruminated about Darrow and the positive impact a skilled lawyer might have on other people's lives. Occasionally, I would skip school to watch Dad try a case in front of a jury. I learned the art of cross-examination at our dinner table, usually as the recipient of penetrating questions. I discovered what it felt like to perch uneasily on the witness stand. My responses sometimes bent the rules of evidence and candor, as teenager answers are prone to do.

One day, my high school drama department announced plans to stage a production of *Inherit the Wind*. The play is a fictionalized version of Darrow's most famous case, the Scopes Monkey Trial. I had read about the trial in Stone's biography and found the story riveting. I was only a sophomore when I sheepishly auditioned and earned an exceedingly minor role as an anonymous press photographer. The part called for me to utter all of six words. But being in the company of Darrow, even a novelized one, was all that mattered.

Later, my father took me on a trip to London. We visited the Old Bailey criminal courts and spent hours observing cases tried by barristers in their white-powdered wigs. In London, we watched a one-man play with the splendid actor Henry Fonda portraying the life of Clarence Darrow. Fonda bore a striking resemblance to the image I had scrutinized at the front of Stone's book. The actor's mannerisms and cadence matched Darrow's words as they had flown across the pages. The experience fortified my affection for the great lawyer.

The more I studied Darrow, the more I admired his passion for the law, his abiding sense of justice, and his unyielding commitment to civil liberties and intellectual freedoms. I also found in Darrow the same human frailties and foibles that afflict us all. I identified with his flaws and failures, just as I struggled with my own. Despite devastating defeats that led to bouts of disillusion and anguish, Darrow persevered. Over time, he evolved into a heroic figure—a fearless iconoclast who despaired of the dangers of conformity, social control, and government intrusion. He dared to challenge traditional beliefs and defend controversial ideas when others would shy away. He upheld the right to individualism and self-determination.

As I consumed accounts of Darrow's courtroom exploits, I was consistently struck by his tenacious advocacy. He rarely backed down from a legal brawl and defended the indefensible with uncommon ability and ingenuity when no one else would, no matter how unpopular or infamous the cause. The lost and the damned became his treasured clients. He gave them what they so desperately yearned for—compassion and hope. He fought for their redemption because he understood their torment and guilt. He had experienced those struggles himself and was haunted by them.

Whenever possible, Darrow wanted to level the legal landscape, where power and wealth all too often prevail. He detested the unchecked authority and unlimited resources of prosecutors who cared more about netting convictions than rendering true justice. In Darrow, the needy, despised, and oppressed found a champion. Without him, they scarcely stood a chance. "I have friends throughout the length and breadth of the land, and these are the poor and the weak and the helpless, to whose cause I have given voice," he once said.

Darrow loathed ignorance. He was incensed by narrow-minded bigotry and racial hatred. Inside and outside the courtroom, he was an apostle for civil rights who despised the senseless prejudice of white supremacy and all forms of discrimination. I revered him for it.

More than anyone else, Darrow helped shape my perspective on crime, science, religion, labor, capital punishment, civil liberties, morals, and social consciousness. Yes, he was a liberal and a declared agnostic. I am decidedly neither, but that was irrelevant. Politics did not define Darrow. His *principles*, including standing up for the individual to challenge society on politics and religion, influenced his thinking. In turn, they animated my own. Many of his *values* became mine. They are philosophical, not political, beliefs. They embody the rights of fundamental fairness that place humanity, dignity, and equality above all else.

Darrow was a gifted and poetic orator. His ability to persuade came from an impressive mastery of language, gained as a lifelong bibliophile. Yet Darrow never lectured with the arrogance of certainty and flamboyance. His passion and convictions did not overwhelm his sense of empathy. He would remind jurors of our intrinsic imperfections. Charity and mercy were constant themes. So was decency.

This approach was instinctual to Darrow because he was an astute observer of humanity. Vital to his success in the courtroom was a keen understanding of his audience. He was always aware of whom he was talking to and mindful of their education, literacy, prejudices, and politics. Darrow would often alter the manner of his presentation to conform to the listeners' background. This was a central component of his genius.

Inside a courtroom, there might appear to be two markedly different Clarence Darrows. He could easily recite statutory and case law in front of a judge. He could conquer almost any legal obstacle by the sheer force of his intellect. But in front of a jury, Darrow was strikingly different. He would transform himself into an artful and intoxicating storyteller who could spin proverbs, fables, and local folklore to illustrate his point. Darrow never spoke down to jurors, nor did he talk over their heads. He was convincing because he was emotional, sincere, and authentic. Darrow was in touch with the pulse of society because, as he once said, he was eternally intrigued by the "motives that move men." Consequently, he understood them.

Of course, Darrow's courtroom demeanor and presentation included some calculation and theatrics. He was aware that sound and imagery could elevate his powers of persuasion. It was said that whenever he tried a case in a rural venue, he would ball up his expensively tailored suit and stuff it underneath the mattress of his bed the night before trial. He was constantly combating the accusation by his opponents, including at the Scopes Trial, that he was a fancy Chicago lawyer, which belied his humble beginnings.

Another insult hurled at Darrow was that he was an "infidel." The truth, as is often the case, was more nuanced. Darrow was never hostile toward Christianity. His many debates and lectures suggest the opposite. He was intrigued by the Bible and had an intimate knowledge of it, including being able to recite some passages by memory.

What Darrow abhorred were religious zealots who preached that the Bible was the only source of truth in the world. They demanded unyielding conformity of belief, depriving people of their individual liberties—including their right to think. Fanaticism to the point of obedience was Darrow's enemy, not religion. He fought to bring enlightenment to the human mind. Science and all avenues of education were indispensable instrumentalities. When prosecutors debased him as an "infidel" during the trial, Darrow replied, "I hate to be accused of such a foolish thing as infidelity because everybody in the world can be accused of that." The provocative quip prompted more than a few grins and chuckles in the audience. It was the last time the aspersion was cast.

Darrow approached man's belief in God as he did every other issue in life—as a practical lawyer. He could neither prove nor disprove the existence of a supreme being or deity who created all things. If Darrow could not see, hear, or touch a supernatural force, then he felt that he must by definition categorize himself as an agnostic. Ever the attorney, Darrow drew the line at the intersection of faith and proof. He did not discount the existence of God as atheists do, although a few of his compositions raised questions of measured doubt. During the trial, he explained simply, "I do not pretend to know where many ignorant men are sure—this is all agnosticism means."

The legendary Supreme Court justice William O. Douglas was among Darrow's legion of admirers. "What his religion may have been, I do not know. But he obviously believed in an infinite God who was the Maker of all humanity," Douglas wrote.

Irving Stone was also unconvinced that Darrow was immutably agnostic. For his biography, Stone interviewed many of the acclaimed lawyer's closest friends and colleagues who "believed him to have deep religious promptings." Clergymen who debated him about religion extolled Darrow's abiding grace. "Here is a man who lives by Christ's teachings," said one. Another minister remarked, "No one was a greater worker for the good of mankind and for God than Clarence Darrow." Still another theologian observed that Darrow "lived as close to the Golden Rule of Jesus as anyone I have ever known."

What defined Darrow was his conscience. He possessed an enduring sense of morality that derived its sustenance from his mother's teachings, even as his father expressed doubts over religion. Never once did Darrow object to the practice of Christianity or any other religion. On the contrary, he praised the many virtues of religions. But Darrow thought that living the values of a Christian life was more important than preaching it. He did this by helping those who could not help themselves. As Stone noted, Darrow supplied a "piteous heart" for those in need of pity.

One minister offered an insightful—and surprising—take on Darrow, even comparing him to Saint Francis. "He exemplified the Christian life," John Haynes Holmes, a Unitarian minister at Community Church of New York and sometime debate opponent of the prominent attorney, wrote about Darrow. "He had a heart that could exclude no man from its sympathy. There were no limits to Darrow's compassion. It reached everywhere, touched every life. . . . If religion is love, and it surely is, then Clarence Darrow was one of the most religious men who ever lived." Stone recognized the same qualities in the famed attorney. "Darrow was a Christian by example and precept, but by intellect he was an agnostic," Stone wrote.

The irony of a theistic skeptic who adhered to the teachings of Jesus should be lost on no one. Raised as a Unitarian by a father who graduated from a theological seminary, the son belonged to no organized religion as an adult. Instead, he infused his life with the same

Christian principles that Abraham Lincoln famously drew from the Bible when he counseled "with malice toward none, with charity for all." No man can be faulted for that.

This is why Darrow was the perfect lawyer to defend John T. Scopes in what became the most famous courtroom drama in twentieth-century America, the Scopes "Monkey" Trial. Scopes, an amiable public high school coach who substituted as a science instructor in Dayton, Tennessee, was charged with teaching evolution to his students. A new state law made it a crime to do so, even though the state-approved textbook contained a chapter on the well-accepted theory of evolution. Teachers across Tennessee were required to use the book, and students were encouraged to read it. But faculty members were forbidden from teaching the chapter because lawmakers had determined that such material "denies the Story of the Divine Creation of man as taught in the Bible." In essence, Scopes was being prosecuted for doing his job.

The Scopes Trial became the trial of the century. Long before attorneys such as F. Lee Bailey and Johnnie Cochran became celebrities, Darrow was an American icon and a household name. With his unmatched intellect, beguiling mix of charisma and wit, and eagerness to reach out to the public through the media, Darrow became one of the most prominent personalities of his era and a larger-than-life figure. His cases invariably became newsworthy and often impacted public sentiment. Through his courage to take up objectionable causes, he became the conscience of America. In Tennessee, academic freedom was at stake.

Darrow's commitment to the principles of the First Amendment remains timely today. Almost one hundred years after the Scopes Trial, questions about free speech persist in higher education and social media. "I would place no fetters on thought and actions and dreams and ideals of men, even the most despised of them," Darrow said. And he meant it. In the Scopes Trial, Darrow defended the right of free thinking in the classroom and advocated the benefits of science exploration. He believed that progress was dependent on uninhibited expression.

Darrow's devotion to free speech is particularly relevant amid today's struggles over partisan censorship in political discourse, polarizing disinformation campaigns, accusations of classroom indoctrination, a sometimes punitive "cancel culture" under the guise of social justice, and, for example, the movement on college campuses to adhere to a particular orthodoxy that excludes diversity of opinion and opposing views. Conformity of thought supplants robust debate. Predetermined narratives are rigidly reinforced as ethical boundaries are erased. This is the antithesis of what educational venues should represent—the free exchange of ideas and information, however unpopular they may be. Beyond intellectual institutions, there is evidence that technology companies suppress disfavored speech. Under contrived or contorted standards, dissent is mislabeled and denounced as misinformation.

All of this would infuriate Darrow. He would fight mightily against any such restrictions on the human mind and exposition. Almost a century ago, Darrow battled to allow a single schoolteacher to share with his students a lesson plan not pulled from the Bible. Today, most educators can face severe discipline for teaching the opposite. Both sides of that coin, Darrow would argue, are dangerous and destructive in a society founded on fundamental liberties.

Through his conscientious work in the Scopes Trial, Darrow became a pivotal figure in the transformation of American law and education, defending the disenfranchised and paving the way for divergent voices to be heard. He was the guardian of lost causes, a tireless advocate for ordinary working citizens.

The acclaimed play and film *Inherit the Wind* was the first time a Broadway production focused so squarely on the virtuosity of a trial attorney—the character clearly inspired by Darrow—defending a disfavored cause. Other literary and cinematic portrayals of lawyers battling against the system and injustice were to follow, from Atticus Finch to Perry Mason to those in John Grisham's many bestselling books. These are mainly the result of Darrow's exploits in the Scopes Trial, which were scrutinized with fascination by a worldwide audience.

Unlike some of the films and novels, Stone's book and Darrow's 1932 autobiography, *The Story of My Life,* offered inestimable insight into the attorney's popular appeal, including his efforts to arouse public opinion. More than most, he understood the power of the press. Through his adept use of the media, he mobilized civic attitudes in a way that advantaged whatever good or noble cause he adopted. By becoming a regular source for "copy," which he certainly was at the Scopes Trial, Darrow played a preeminent part in the media's increased influence.

Darrow was an adroit student of the law and the Constitution. Drawing inspiration from Thomas Jefferson, he understood the Framers' desire to create a religiously neutral society that would permit free expression of faith or doubt, unimpeded by government dictates advancing sectarian doctrines and suppressing any secular opinions. Just as people should be permitted to exercise religion freely, they should be allowed to learn science freely, Darrow argued. Darrow's defense of Scopes posed a vital question: If science was to be excluded by law, where was man to gain his wealth of knowledge? As the great lawyer cautioned, "Scopes isn't on trial, civilization is on trial."

In urging the judge to throw out Tennessee's law as injurious to cherished constitutional rights, Darrow's ominous warning to the court was as compelling then as it is now. "They passed a law making the Bible the yardstick to measure every man's intellect, and to measure every man's learning," Darrow told the judge. "Every bit of knowledge that the mind has, must now be submitted to a religious test. . . . If men are not tolerant, if men cannot respect each other's opinions, if men cannot live and let live, then no man's life is safe.

"Your Honor knows the fires that have been lighted in America to kindle religious bigotry and hate. If today you can take a thing like evolution and make it a crime to teach it in the public school . . . tomorrow you may ban books and magazines and the newspapers. Ignorance and fanaticism is forever busy and needs feeding. Always it is feeding and gloating for more."

Although Darrow's thesis was vindicated long after his death, the battle he fought in a rural Tennessee courtroom is still being waged elsewhere today. The Supreme Court's belated decision notwithstanding, evolution remains a topic of fierce dispute and deliberation. In some public schools across America, biology teachers are quietly discouraged from even mentioning Darwin's cornerstone theory despite its inclusion in textbooks universally.

Consequently, Clarence Darrow's intrepid defense of academic autonomy, scientific empowerment, intellectual growth, and freedom of expression matter now more than ever. This makes the Scopes Monkey Trial, instead of the case of O. J. Simpson or the Lindbergh Baby or the Chicago Seven . . . the *real* trial of the century.

Gregg Jarrett
JUNE 2022

1

"Hell Is Going to Pop Now"

More than two thousand people gathered outside the Rhea County Courthouse in Dayton, Tennessee, in the eastern part of the Volunteer State, on July 20, 1925, on a muggy summer afternoon, in a clash for the ages: a battle over what children should be taught in public schools.

As the crowd started taking their seats in bleachers set up around the courthouse square on that hot Monday afternoon—men sweating, women trying to cool themselves off with fans—the heat mirrored the tension between two prominent men, both titans in American life, as they readied to battle in intense, personal combat.

The tension built through the crowd with whispers and comments and even occasional laughter over what was about to take place. The stakes could not have been higher. Even the enormous shadows of the courthouse and its bell tower could not alleviate the oppressive heat. The impressive brick courthouse, at the heart of this town of eighteen hundred people, conjured images of Italian architecture, a rarity in this part of Tennessee.[1]

Under that bell tower, Clarence Darrow, the most brilliant lawyer in America, a celebrated defender of free speech, and the underdog, stood in one corner. In the other stood William Jennings Bryan, a three-time presidential candidate who shattered the calmness and the complacency of the Gilded Age with his soaring rhetoric championing farmers, evangelical Christians, and many of those left behind by the rise of industrial capitalism. The buzz continued to build through the crowd, much as it would forty-five years later when two undefeated heavyweight champions representing different strands of American life—Muhammed Ali and Joe Frazier—clashed in Madison Square Garden. Of course, Dayton was a vastly different stage from the Garden. Dayton appeared to be the personification of quiet small-town life where things moved at a deliberate pace.

As Darrow got ready to face Bryan on the stand, the crowd intensely listened to the legal maneuverings under the blazing Tennessee sun. More than a few residents of this sleepy little Tennessee town could be pardoned if they raised their eyebrows at the language used by buttoned-up attorney Dudley Field Malone as he watched Bryan take the stand to be questioned by Darrow. Malone, one of Darrow's cocounsels, turned to John Scopes, the teacher at the center of this storm, and let down his stuffy persona to comment, "Hell is going to pop now."

Heading outside on that hot Monday afternoon, Clarence Darrow knew that everything was riding on this last piece of the trial. Over the weekend, he'd come up with a plan to turn things around. A lifelong baseball fan, Darrow knew it was the bottom of the ninth—and he needed a home run.

Arthur Garfield Hays, one of Darrow's cocounsels, sprung the trap that Darrow had designed. Hays had won national attention during World War I when he helped German Americans who were accused of opposing the federal government. Like Darrow, Hays was used to taking on the crowd—and he did just that, with a surprising request to the judge.

"The defense desires to call Mr. Bryan as a witness," Hays said, cheerfully admitting that "we recognize what Mr. Bryan says as a witness would not be very valuable." But, Hays explained, "There are other questions involved."

Due to the heat and his fears that the courtroom floor would collapse with so many people on it, Judge John Raulston had ordered the trial moved outside for Monday's proceedings. The politically ambitious Raulston, one of the leading Republicans in the area, also wanted as large an audience as possible. Thankfully, a convenient place was already set up that could hold the proceedings. Under the courtroom windows stood a platform that had been constructed for Independence Day festivities earlier in the month. With one of the most high-profile cases in American history under way, the platform would serve as the stage for a dramatic confrontation.

With thousands of people sitting on the bleachers, straining to hear every word and scrambling for the shade offered by a few maple and oak trees, Judge Raulston was puzzled by this maneuver.

Over on the prosecutors' side, grumpy Ben McKenzie quickly pushed back, insisting, "I don't think it is necessary to call him."

But Bryan, plump and wiping the sweat off his ample face, had no objections, provided he could put Darrow, Malone, and Hays on the stand if needed. Indeed, the famous fundamentalist and veteran politician was eager to take the stand to go face-to-face with his nemesis Darrow. With decades of experience in garnering attention for himself, Bryan had been champing at the bit for days to take on Darrow.

Raulston asked Darrow if he wanted Bryan sworn in. Darrow answered with a simple no.

"I can make affirmation," Bryan, his coat off and wearing a bow tie, insisted. "I can say, 'So help me God, I will tell the truth.'"

Also in his shirtsleeves, his suspenders keeping his sweaty shirt in place, Darrow declined that offer as well, saying, "I take it you will tell the truth, Mr. Bryan."

Darrow's move to put Bryan on the stand was a last-ditch effort to force the great fundamentalist to concede publicly that not everything in the Bible—which was, after all, man's creation—should be accepted literally. At the least, Darrow thought he could make Bryan look foolish for believing that the Bible should be taken literally—and hopefully sow some doubts about the prosecution's case. Having dealt with Raulston for a week, Darrow knew that the judge would never allow the jury to hear this testimony. But sitting in that courtroom, seeing the sign telling the jury and citizens READ YOUR BIBLE DAILY, which Darrow requested be removed, he had no other options. He needed to turn this case around—and thought putting Bryan on the stand could help in the court of public opinion.

Darrow dug in and got ready to swing.[2]

Darrow was employing a "proffer"—a legal technique of offering a preview of what an expert will tell the jury if permitted. A proffer is a standard procedure, but the testimony must be relevant to the case and assist the jury in evaluating a material fact.

During the first week of the case, Raulston had already said that the jury didn't need any help from experts. The jurors were equipped to decide the matter on their own. But the judge reluctantly allowed the proffer of Bryan's testimony to appease both the defense team and Bryan himself despite the objections of the rest of the prosecution. Raulston had no intention of ever letting the jury hear Bryan's testimony despite all that.

After the many disappointments at the end of the previous week, Darrow needed to reverse things. Some of his cocounsels were already waving the white flag. Just as he had so many other times during his legal career, Darrow faced overwhelming odds as he stood alone to take on popular opinion.

Even if he was going to lose in the court of law in Dayton, Darrow could make his case to the world. Putting Bryan on the stand allowed Darrow to claim more of the spotlight to present his views, especially with reporters from across the country writing about the trial and a large crowd eagerly watching.

The Great Commoner, as Bryan was known across the nation, strode confidently to the witness stand in a common Tennessee town, but in a trial that can only be described as extraordinary. What followed was the most remarkable courtroom confrontation in the history of American jurisprudence.

With only a trace of humility, Bryan was more than willing to hold himself out as an authority on the Bible. Darrow even taunted him about it, labeling Bryan a "profound Bible student" who "has an essay every Sunday as to what it means." Piling on the sarcasm, Darrow said a "Tennessee jury who are not especially educated are better judges of the Bible than all of the scholars in the world."

With Bryan now on the stand, Darrow started his examination by showcasing Bryan's expertise on the Bible: "You have given considerable study to the Bible, haven't you, Mr. Bryan?"

"Yes, sir, I have tried to."

Darrow reviewed Bryan's recent columns and speeches on the Bible. "You claim that everything in the Bible should be literally interpreted?"

"I believe everything in the Bible should be accepted as it is given there; some of the Bible is given illustratively." Bryan offered an example: "For instance, 'Ye are the salt of the earth.' I would not insist that man was actually *salt*, or that he had flesh of salt, but it is used in the sense of *salt* as saving God's people."

Bryan recounted how he had studied the Bible all his life, lectured on its many meanings, and written extensively about how it must be interpreted. Did any mortal man know more than he did about the Bible?

Continuing to press Bryan, Darrow turned his attention to the Old Testament, starting with the story of Jonah. While Darrow said a "whale" swallowed Jonah, Bryan countered that a "big fish" had eaten the prophet.

"You say, the big fish swallowed Jonah, and he there remained how long—three days—and then he spewed him upon the land. You believe that the big fish was made to swallow Jonah?" asked Darrow.

"I am not prepared to say that. The Bible merely says it was done."

"You don't know whether it was the ordinary run of fish or made for that purpose?"

Bryan responded by playing to the crowd: "You may guess; you evolutionists guess."

"But when we do guess, we have a sense to guess right," Darrow fired back.

"But do not do it often."

Darrow continued to push Bryan about the seeming absurdity of a "big fish" swallowing a man who then survived in the gut of the fish for three long days. To Darrow and his prominent theologians, the story was an obvious parable with a moral lesson to be drawn. The Bible was filled with them. But to the obstinate and fanatical Bryan, it was a literal event that he described as one of God's miracles.

Darrow and Bryan quibbled over miracles and matters of the imagination. Realizing that Bryan's ego and his obstinacy could harm their case, the prosecutors objected, insisting Darrow was being "argumentative." Undeterred by this, Darrow kept his focus on Bryan and turned to another miraculous event recorded in the Old Testament. Bryan proved equally emphatic about another poetic passage of a supernatural event drawn from the tenth chapter of the book of Joshua.

"The Bible says Joshua commanded the sun to stand still for the purpose of lengthening the day, doesn't it, and you believe it," Darrow said.

"I do."

"Do you believe at that time the entire sun went around the earth?"

"No, I believe that the earth goes around the sun."

While the prosecutors tried again to cut Darrow off, Raulston noted that Bryan was clearly happy to testify and let him continue. As much as he had ruled in the prosecutors' favor through the trial, now Raulston was inadvertently giving Bryan enough rope to hang himself.

"If the day was lengthened by stopping either the earth or the sun, it must have been the earth?" Darrow asked.

"Well, I should say so."

"Now, Mr. Bryan, have you ever pondered what would have happened to the earth if it had stood still?"

Bryan replied no and insisted that the "God I believe in could have taken care of that."

Darrow asked if Bryan "ever pondered what would naturally happen to the earth if it stood still suddenly."

Bryan answered no.

"Don't you know it would have been converted into a molten mass of matter?"

Bryan's irritation with Darrow's questions was starting to come through as he shot back, "You testify to that when you get on the stand, I will give you a chance." Bryan said he wanted to "hear expert testimony on that."

"You have never investigated that subject?"

"I don't think I have ever had the question asked."

"Or ever thought of it?" Darrow asked, starting his effort to build an impression that Bryan was a fool who never used his brain.

"I have been too busy on things that I thought were of more importance than that."

Sweating under the hot Tennessee sun, wiping a handkerchief over his brow, Bryan was growing noticeably uncomfortable. Darrow's questions were vexing, and the self-described expert on the Bible had offered precious few answers that were satisfying or even reasonable. Many had assumed that Bryan would be an impressive figure on the witness stand, but his responses were not.

He had never considered the metaphysical implications of certain events recounted in the Bible—mythical stories that defied both science and common sense. He had simply accepted them as factual when many were clearly not. Bryan had never bothered to study the realities of space and time, cause and effect, and the physics of objects and their properties. He had confidently embraced a narrow—and seemingly naive—view of religious thought. He compensated with bluster for what he lacked in knowledge. His explanations appeared implausible, if not wrong.

And Darrow was just warming up. There were more blistering questions to come.

With Bryan faltering, the legend of Clarence Darrow, the best lawyer in America, continued to grow.[3]

===

Larger-than-life heroes and personalities dominated the 1920s. Through the new medium of the movies and newsreels, the public's epic figures could be seen in every town square. Over the radio, these personalities inhabited most living rooms across the nation. In their homes, Americans could listen to Babe Ruth shattering home run records in the Bronx and Jack Dempsey cleaning out the heavyweight division. They witnessed Ernest Hemingway, F. Scott Fitzgerald, and William Faulkner changing the English language with their novels and Coco Chanel redefining fashion. They listened to Josephine Baker, Duke Ellington, and Louis Armstrong usher in the Jazz Age. They even listened as politicians and legal legends debated their versions of truth.

===

There was no more unlikely place for hell to pop than Dayton, Tennessee.

Nestled in the gentle hills that gradually rose to become the mighty Smoky Mountains, Dayton seemed somewhat isolated from the rest of the world, linked to more metropolitan settings by railroad tracks headed to Chattanooga, Knoxville, and Nashville. Despite the front porches and welcoming exteriors, Dayton was not the typical Southern small town. The Civil War's ghosts, memories, and legacy did not linger here. Founded in 1877, as Northern troops headed home after a dozen years of Reconstruction following the war, Dayton was even named after the city in Ohio, showing the city had no ties to the Old South. Instead of the plantation past, Dayton looked forward to a future spurred by businesses and commerce.

Even in the 1920s, the booms and busts of the business cycle remained present. Facing a major economic downturn, leaders from Dayton decided to push this unlikely town to the nation's center stage for a few days via a challenge to the state law prohibiting the teaching of evolution in public schools. The trial had garnered attention all over the country and had already been dubbed the Monkey Trial.

Residents of Dayton, unaccustomed to the glare of the limelight, knew that the Scopes Trial had resulted from a conversation at a small table right across Main Street from the courthouse. At Robinson's Drug Store, a handful of local businessmen had met to think about ways to bring more attention to the town, which had been struggling in recent years. This humid Monday would determine if those business leaders had made a winning bet—or if Dayton would continue to be overlooked even as the country enjoyed unprecedented prosperity.

After weeks of preparation and another week of previous proceedings, the crowd knew the protagonists both by sight and reputation. Most of these men commanded respect, but all eyes were on two of the most legendary figures in American history. Clarence Darrow and William Jennings Bryan had been on the public stage for decades, generating more than their share of love, hatred, and respect.

Dubbed the Great Commoner by allies and enemies alike, Bryan, now sixty-five and a fixture on the national political scene for almost three decades, spoke for the forgotten masses, namely farmers left behind by the economic prosperity of the Gilded Age. Three times he sought the presidency and three times won the Democratic presidential nomination, but fell short in the general election against William McKinley in 1896 and again in 1900 and when he took on William Howard Taft in 1908. Even after an uneven stint as Woodrow Wilson's secretary of state, Bryan remained a powerful force, flexing his muscles at the 1924 Democratic National Convention. His brother Charles was on the ticket as the vice-presidential candidate after it took 103 ballots to nominate John W. Davis. However, the Davis-Bryan ticket fell short against Calvin Coolidge.

William Jennings Bryan remained politically active, though his attention had shifted in recent years to real estate development in Florida and, primarily, to religious and social issues. Increasingly alarmed by the technological and social changes spreading across the United States after World War I, which he had opposed America entering, and the influenza epidemic, Bryan called for people to return to traditional Christian values. With the 1920 census showing more Americans living in cities than on farms, he helped lead the crusade against the nation's changes. Bryan was instrumental in passing the Eighteenth Amendment, prohibiting the sale of alcohol.

As the Roaring Twenties continued to pick up steam, Bryan turned his focus to championing the Bible in schools and across the public square, including criticizing the increased attention paid to evolution in classrooms. "Why should the Bible, which the centuries have been unable to shake, be discarded for scientific works that have to be corrected and revised every few years?" Bryan demanded.[4] Many evangelical Christians, confronted with an increasingly changing and confusing America, agreed with him. Bryan's fervent opposition to evolution led him to Dayton to defend a state law enacted earlier that year making it "unlawful for any teacher in any of the Universities, Normals and all other public schools of the State which are supported in whole or in part by the public school funds of the State, to teach any theory that denies the Story of the Divine Creation of man as taught in the Bible, and to teach instead that man has descended from a lower order of animals."[5]

Bryan might not have been the handsome political prodigy that he had been three decades earlier, but he continued to make an impression. He had struggled with his weight for years. Now that he was in his midsixties, Bryan had grown increasingly overweight as his appetite remained unchecked, and he battled heart problems and diabetes while his hair grew thinner. Despite all of that, Bryan remained a dynamic speaker, and his Sunday school classes outside Miami—far from his political base in Nebraska—drew thousands of listeners. Bryan might have been an old lion who had seen better days, but he remained relevant on the national stage and commanded the support of millions even as his strength moved from the Great Plains to the South.[6]

Bryan was in Dayton helping the prosecutors against Scopes, aiding McKenzie, Tom Stewart, and Sue Hicks. Bryan had made his reputation on the stump and the campaign trail, whereas Clarence Darrow had spent decades becoming one of the most celebrated lawyers America had ever seen. He was more than an attorney; he was a folk hero. Despite being in his late sixties, Darrow had never stood higher in the public's imagination. Only the year before, Darrow had taken up the cases of admitted murderers Nathan Leopold Jr. and Richard Loeb, two teenage sons from prominent Chicago families, who had killed a fourteen-year-old boy. Everyone knew Leopold and Loeb were guilty; Darrow took their cases anyway and had them plead guilty at the start of the trial. After those pleas were in, Darrow launched a memorable defense, insisting that his clients suffered from a form of mental illness and, therefore, should not face the death penalty. After Darrow's stirring summation, which lasted twelve hours, the judge ruled that Leopold and Loeb would spend the rest of their lives in prison instead of being put to death. Even though Darrow had technically lost the case, he scored one of the most impressive wins in American judicial history.

Jurors and judges looked past Darrow's wrinkled suits and messy hair when he presented a case. Standing six feet tall, he had sharp blue eyes and a quick wit that dominated a courtroom, and his every motion and action before the bar helped with his arguments and efforts. Darrow, like Bryan, saw himself as a champion for the common man. They had once been allies, with Darrow backing Bryan's political efforts, but had split in recent years, dividing over religion in the public square and the nation's future. Darrow, an outspoken agnostic whose father had been a freethinker, had been considering retiring, but he grew interested in Scopes's case after learning that Bryan was helping the prosecution.[7]

But all of Darrow's skills and expertise were not bearing fruit in Dayton. After the judge rejected hearing from all the scientists and experts on evolution whom Darrow had ready to testify, the famed attorney now faced a dilemma. The case was going nowhere, and nobody could deny that Scopes had violated the law by teaching evolution. Darrow was heading for a big loss. Even his supporters were starting to lose interest in the case.

Darrow needed a dramatic development to salvage the case, and as the trial reconvened on Monday afternoon, he rolled the dice with a gutsy legal gamble. He well knew that he faced more than his share of challenges and obstacles from the moment Raulston slammed the gavel down to open the case. With an eye on the next election, Raulston, one of the most prominent Republicans in southeast Tennessee, had brought in a preacher, who opened the trial with a rambling prayer beseeching God to "give the court this morning a sufficient share of the divine spirit as will enable the court to so administer its affairs as that justice may come to all and that God's standard of purity and holiness may be upheld." The minister then reminded the courtroom that everyone there would face God's judgment, before pleading "for the cause of truth and righteousness."[8]

Darrow had been a lawyer for a long time but, looking back at the prayer, admitted that this was a new experience. "I had practiced law for more than forty years, and had never before heard God called in to referee a court trial," he later wrote. "I had likewise been to prize fights and horse races, and these were not opened with prayer." After the first session adjourned, Darrow approached Raulston and told the judge it was not "fair or suitable" to start the trial with a prayer. In the second session, Darrow offered a formal objection, which Raulston quickly overruled.[9]

Things only got worse for Darrow and Scopes. After listening to a prayer expressly calling for his client to lose, Darrow sat through Raulston's reading the entire first chapter of Genesis aloud to the courtroom. When Darrow looked up at Raulston, he noticed the judge was sitting under a sign that read READ YOUR BIBLE DAILY.[10] The famed lawyer could be pardoned if his mind went to another part of the Old Testament, since he was clearly in the lion's den like Daniel.

Things had not gone much better for Darrow as the trial continued. On the first day of the trial, Darrow signaled his intent to have "a considerable number of scientists" serve as expert witnesses.[11] Darrow wanted these expert scientists and even some theologians to explain evolution to the jurors, almost all of whom were unfamiliar with it. Darrow intended to expose a hole in the prosecutors' case by arguing that Scopes certainly taught evolution, but that did not mean he had violated the law by teaching against the Bible. After all, under a strict reading of the statute's double requirement, the teacher had to do both to be guilty. Yet, in the classroom, Scopes never denied "the Story of the Divine Creation of man," as the law demanded.[12] No such evidence was presented against the accused, and none of his pupils testified that their teacher ever theorized that the Bible or passages from Genesis were in error.

Much of Darrow's case hinged on bringing in those experts. Darrow thought "a jury drawn from Dayton, Tenn., would not permit a man to commit such a heinous crime as Scopes had been charged with and allow him to go scot-free." The jurors needed to be educated on what evolution was—and what it wasn't—for Scopes to be found not guilty. Darrow was counting on the jurors hearing from the witnesses he had assembled.[13]

The two sides had sparred over witnesses during the sessions throughout the latter half of the past week. On Wednesday, before the prosecution's witnesses took the stand, Malone took over in much of the proceedings, pummeling Bryan for blurring the lines between his faith and his politics. Keeping Scopes from the stand, Darrow and the defense team brought out their first expert witness, Maynard Metcalf, a rotund and balding middle-aged zoologist who had a PhD from Johns Hopkins University and taught at his alma mater, Oberlin College. Darrow expertly led Metcalf, who presented an excellent—and, more important, understandable—explanation of evolution.[14]

But if Metcalf's testimony went well for Darrow and the defense team, their momentum stalled in the following days. On Thursday, the two sides clashed over the need for expert testimony with fine performances by Malone, Bryan, Stewart, and even William Jennings Bryan Jr., a former federal prosecutor. On Friday morning, in a quick ruling, Raulston refused to allow Darrow's witnesses to testify in front of the jury, insisting they were not relevant to the case.[15]

As Darrow and the defense team left the courthouse on Friday, they sounded defeated.

John Neal, Scopes's principal attorney, talked to the Associated Press after the trial was adjourned until Monday. "This ends our hope for a trial of this case," Neal admitted about Raulston's ruling.[16]

Several other prominent journalists joined the colorful and acerbic columnist H. L. Mencken, one of the most popular writers in the nation, in leaving Dayton, thinking the trial was over. Four decades after the trial, Scopes remembered, "Newspapermen began deserting Dayton like birds in migration" since "they thought the trial might just as well be over."[17]

As the weekend began, Mencken all but called it a game. "All that remains of the great cause of the State of Tennessee against the infidel Scopes is the formal business of bumping off the defendant," he wrote in Saturday's *Baltimore Evening Sun*, and his words circulated across the nation that weekend. "There may be some legal jousting on Monday and some gaudy oratory on Tuesday, but the main battle is over, with Genesis completely triumphant."

Mencken further accused Raulston of "leaping with soft judicial hosannas into the arms of the prosecution."[18]

But Mencken was wrong. The main battle was not over. Darrow still had a chance, albeit a remote one.

Over that muggy weekend, Darrow grappled with what to do after Raulston's ruling. None of the witnesses whom the prosecution had paraded before the court testified that Scopes had mentioned the Bible or Divine Creation when he taught evolution. Despite that, the judge had ruled that the case focused on whether Scopes had lectured on evolution—which he clearly did—instead of on whether he'd taught "any theory that denies the story of the Divine Creation of man as taught in the Bible."

Down in the count, Darrow mulled over his options. Had the jurors—who Darrow could attest from his questioning knew almost nothing about evolution—heard from the experts, they could have learned that evolution did not necessarily conflict with the Bible or the theory of Divine Creation. Despite Bryan's and the prosecution's best efforts to muddy the waters, teaching evolution did not undermine the Bible, which the statute required.

Having failed to convince the judge to accept his experts, Darrow needed a miracle of his own for there to be any chance of winning the case.

And over that weekend, Darrow came up with a daring and risky plan.

2

Champion of the Underdog

While his parents had helped and encouraged him in more ways than he could ever recall, the most celebrated attorney in American history never quite forgave them for giving him his first name.

Born on April 18, 1857, the fifth of eight children, Clarence Seward Darrow grew up in Kinsman, Ohio, a small town just south of Lake Erie on the border with Pennsylvania. While his older brothers were named after famous political and religious figures, Darrow had no idea where his parents came up with his name, an uncommon one in rural Ohio, and never quite got them to answer his questions about it. At least young Clarence knew his middle name was in honor of William Henry Seward, the antislavery senator from New York best known for serving as Abraham Lincoln's secretary of state. "Perhaps my mother read a story where a minor character was called Clarence," Darrow speculated in his autobiography. "I fancy I have not turned out to be anything like him. The one satisfaction I have had in connection with this cross was that the boys never could think up any nickname half so inane as the real one my parents adorned me with."[1]

Happily for his later career, Darrow had at least escaped being named after a preacher or a pastor. Darrow's father, Amirus, had attended a Unitarian seminary, but "when he had finished his studies he found that he lost his faith," thanks to his educational pursuits. He moved to Kinsman, a village of around five hundred residents, where he made furniture and served as the town's undertaker. When Darrow looked back at his life, he painted his father as an agnostic: "Even the mild tenets of Unitarianism he could not accept." By the time Clarence was born, Amirus and his wife, Emily, "had left the Unitarian faith behind and were sailing out on the open sea without a rudder or compass, and with no port in sight."[2] Despite that, Emily would lead the children to church every Sunday while Amirus stayed in his library and studied his books, not wanting to impose his agnosticism on young Clarence and his siblings.[3]

Clarence heeded his father's unspoken lessons. "The end of wisdom is the fear of God; the beginning of wisdom is doubt," Amirus maintained. Clarence learned that lesson well from his father. Despite how most townsfolk considered Amirus a sinner and scorned his company, he reveled in his reputation as the "town infidel," challenging his neighbors' conventional beliefs. Looking back at his parents, Darrow admired their struggle out of poverty, but noted that his father always enjoyed reading more than working, even when he was short on cash. "My father was a visionary and a dreamer," Darrow wrote. "My mother was more efficient and practical. She was the one who saved the family from dire want." All through his life, Darrow would display the traits of both of his parents.[4]

Still, while Amirus and Emily often served as contrasting influences on Clarence and their other children, in some areas they stood united, including rejecting orthodox religious thought and championing unpopular positions. Busy raising eight children—one of whom passed away soon after Clarence was born—Emily stood with her husband on reforming society. "She was an ardent woman's rights advocate, as they called the advanced women seventy years ago," Darrow recalled in the early 1930s. "Both she and my father were friends of all oppressed people, and every new and humane and despised cause and ism." Despite his admiration for Seward and his opposition to slavery, Amirus was one of the few Democrats in the town; most of his neighbors had joined the fledgling Republican Party. The Darrows were also agnostics living in a religious area and, on one of the most divisive issues of nineteenth-century America, supporters of free trade in traditionally protectionist Ohio.

An avid reader who could never find enough books in a little farm town such as Kinsman, Amirus passed on his love of books to his young son. Clarence also inherited his father's passion for justice and opposition to the death penalty. When Clarence was seven or eight, Amirus recounted how he attended a public hanging in his youth— and how ashamed he was of watching it. Still, there were barriers between the father and the son. Thanks mainly to the coffins lined up along the walls in his father's furniture shop, Clarence, already wary of death and the promises of an afterlife, avoided it, which ensured he did not spend much time with Amirus. Many years later, while arguing against capital punishment in the famous Leopold and Loeb case, Darrow's mind wandered back to his father's story and those coffins in the shop as Darrow dwelled on death and duty.[5]

Along with his father's influence, Clarence always acknowledged his close ties to his mother. She passed away from cancer in 1872, when Darrow was only fifteen. Despite insisting that his memory of her was "not very clear," Darrow's love for her never faded. Six decades later, in one of the most moving parts of his autobiography, Darrow related that he had walked by the churchyard where she was buried many times, but only once could he find the strength to enter it to visit her grave. "Somehow it is hard for me to lift the latch or go down the walk or stand at the marble slab which marks the spot where she was laid away," Darrow wrote. "Still I know that in countless ways her work and teaching, her mastering personality, and her infinite kindness and sympathy have done much to shape my life." Darrow's family remained emotionally restrained and undemonstrative despite his admiration for his parents and their strong influences on their children.[6]

While he ranked as one of the most learned students in the region, Darrow did not enjoy school, in retrospect dismissing the grammar, math, and history lessons he received as useless. Staying in school throughout his teens, Darrow grew increasingly annoyed as the teachers often wandered into religious topics. Half a century after attending high school, Darrow dismissed the school where he was taught: "Schools were not established to teach and encourage the pupil to think." However, the school offered some benefits for young Clarence, including letting him spend more time with girls and playing baseball. Throughout his life, Darrow loved baseball, rooting for the Chicago Cubs and often checking the box scores before reading the rest of the paper.[7]

Finishing up at the local academy, Darrow went to Allegheny College in Pennsylvania, where his father had studied. While Darrow enjoyed science, he found the pursuit of Latin and Greek a challenge, with no relevance in the real world. After a year at Allegheny, Darrow returned to Kinsman, deciding not to return to school so as to help his father's financial situation. Working at a local factory, Darrow quickly found that manual labor wasn't to his liking. He ended up teaching in the district school during the winter, generally enjoying sharing his knowledge and opinions with his students despite the wide range of ages. Refusing to discipline his students with corporal punishment, Darrow liked teaching. He also relished interacting with the students, playing baseball with the children and forming strong bonds with them and their families. Over the years when Darrow returned to the area, he always tried to reconnect with his former students and see them as much as possible.[8]

Darrow spent his time in the schoolhouse studying law. Looking back at his decision to pursue a legal career, Darrow could not pinpoint what motivated him to do this, outside of listening to lawyers offer political speeches or patriotic addresses during the holidays. Still, he had enough of his father in him to appreciate the give-and-take of debate. "I enjoyed the way the pettifoggers abused each other, and as I grew toward maturity I developed a desire to be a lawyer," Darrow recounted. After three years of teaching school, Darrow moved to Ann Arbor for a year to study at the University of Michigan law school, which, when Clarence was seven, his father had briefly attended before abandoning his studies to go back to making furniture and coffins. Instead of finishing up the two-year program, Darrow left after a single year to apprentice under a lawyer in Youngstown, Ohio, around thirty miles south of where Darrow had grown up. Right after his twenty-first birthday, in 1878, Darrow passed the bar, much to the surprise and delight of his father. "Like most parents, the success of the son was his success," Darrow wrote about Amirus's pride that Clarence had passed the exam. Feeling he would not make his mark in Youngstown, the new lawyer headed back home to start his new career.[9]

Darrow might rank as one of the most outstanding lawyers in American history, but his first decade in the legal field proved underwhelming. The young lawyer worked in northeastern Ohio, making a good living and marrying Jessie Ohl, a local girl. After three years in Andover, only ten miles from Kinsman, Darrow moved to Ashtabula, a town of five thousand on the shores of Lake Erie, some fifty miles northeast of Cleveland. In 1883, Darrow became a father when Jessie gave birth to a son, whom they named Paul. Darrow dabbled in politics, getting involved with the Democrats and being elected town counsel, but his chief passion was cards. In Ashtabula, Darrow spent his nights playing poker with friends. While he might have been a successful country lawyer, during this part of his life Darrow showed no hints of becoming one of the most legendary attorneys America has ever produced.[10]

As his twenties ended, Darrow grew increasingly restless and discontented with his comfortable, if unexciting, life and career. Thanks largely to his father, Darrow followed politics intently during his youth, supporting Democrats in the 1872 and 1876 presidential contests. When Grover Cleveland first ran for president in 1884, becoming the first Democrat to win since 1856, Darrow helped on the campaign. Almost fifty years later he called the reform-minded Cleveland "one of my idols," praising that president's "courage, independence and honesty." Darrow also expanded his reading, including what he called "radical political doctrines." Reading economists such as Henry George and legal reformers such as John Peter Altgeld, Darrow found a "new political gospel that bade fair to bring about the social equality and opportunity that has always been the dream of the idealist." Like his parents, Darrow felt increasingly compelled to make a difference—and he could not do that in Ashtabula.[11]

Like so many Americans before and since, Darrow decided to roll the dice. In 1888, a decade after passing the bar, Darrow moved to Chicago and left his comfortable life behind. Determined to make a difference in the world—and realizing that he simply could not do that as a country lawyer in northeast Ohio—even with a wife and young child, Darrow took one of the biggest gambles of his life. His decision to move marked the turning point of his life as he became one of the most prominent attorneys in the country.

Darrow quickly made his mark in Chicago. He joined literary and political clubs, stumping on behalf of the Democrats in the 1888 elections and weighing in on Henry George's economic theories. He met George and became good friends with Altgeld, one of the most prominent legal and political reformers of the last two decades of the nineteenth century. In Darrow's first two years in Chicago, he grew increasingly prominent, becoming a popular political speaker and slowly expanding his legal practice across the city. When Mayor DeWitt Clinton Cregier needed a special-assessment attorney to work for the city, Altgeld recommended Darrow, who flourished handling assessments, taxes, and licenses, while offering legal advice to Chicago officials. Three months into that post, Darrow was promoted to assistant corporation counsel for the city, making $5,000 a year, more money than Darrow had ever before earned. Seven months into that assignment, Darrow was promoted again to serve as corporation counsel, representing the city for the Columbian Exposition. Darrow left the city's employment to work for the Chicago and North Western Railway Company. Just five years after leaving Ohio, Darrow was an acclaimed lawyer in Chicago.[12]

Darrow felt out of place working for the railroad company. While his new coworkers treated him well, Darrow knew "my general views of life were not such as fitted me for this kind of career," and it was "hard for me to take the side of the railroad company against one who had been injured in their service or against a passenger." Still, the post let Darrow remain active in politics, and he helped manage Altgeld's successful gubernatorial campaign in 1892. Events would soon ensure Darrow lined up on the side of his principles even as he left the Chicago and North Western Railway Company to focus on defense law.[13] Darrow garnered some attention in 1894 when he defended Patrick Eugene Prendergast. In an echo of the assassination of President James Garfield in 1881, Prendergast decided to murder the man he blamed for not getting him a government job. The nation was shocked when Prendergast shot and killed Chicago mayor Carter Harrison Sr. Despite Darrow's best efforts to argue that his client was insane, Prendergast was found guilty and hanged. This case marked Darrow's first courtroom opposition to the death penalty, a theme that lasted throughout his career. "I tried to prevent all hangings in the State, and occasionally snatch a brand from the burning," Darrow noted. Still, even with his tangled hair and wrinkled suits, Darrow was becoming one of the top lawyers in the region, thanks to his wit, his being quick on his feet, and his building rapport with juries, playing on their emotions when needed and telling stories that they could understand, even relate to.[14]

While Darrow could not save Prendergast from the gallows—the only time one of Darrow's clients received the death penalty—the lawyer had impressed Eugene V. Debs. In 1893, railroad workers led by Debs, a former Indiana state representative, formed the American Railway Union (ARU), which quickly grew into one of the largest unions in the nation. Debs and the ARU burst on the national scene in 1894 after the Pullman Company cut workers' pay. Distressed Pullman workers joined the ARU, which refused to work with trains with Pullman cars. This strike ranked as one of the pivotal moments in American labor history when trains in the western half of the country shut down in the summer of 1894 as 250,000 workers in twenty-seven states boycotted Pullman cars. The Cleveland administration turned to the army to end the strike because it interfered with the U.S. mail. When the troops came to break the strike, they clashed with ARU members and more than thirty of the strikers were killed, including thirteen in Chicago. Despite advising the ARU against the strike, Debs eventually supported it, and the media identified him as the brains behind it. With the federal government issuing an injunction to end the strike and charging Debs with conspiracy to restrict commerce, the union leader needed an excellent attorney—and he turned to Darrow.[15]

Working with other well-known lawyers, including a former president of the American Bar Association, Darrow handled Debs's defense, leading it through a mistrial after a juror took ill. With the government abandoning the conspiracy case to press on with other charges, a federal judge found the labor leader guilty of contempt of court, sentencing him to six months in prison and other leaders of the strike to three months. Working with former U.S. senator Lyman Trumbull of Illinois, the author of the Thirteenth Amendment and an old ally of Abraham Lincoln's, Darrow took the case all the way to the Supreme Court, which unanimously ruled against Debs.[16] Looking back on the case some thirty-five years later, Darrow insisted "there was not one word of evidence" connecting Debs to the violent conflict between the army and the strikers.

Still, even as Debs and ARU leaders served time in prison, Darrow emerged as one of the big winners from the case. Instead of merely defending Debs and his allies, Darrow went on the attack, announcing that he intended to call George Pullman, the owner of the company that bore his name, and other railroad executives as witnesses. When Pullman refused to take the stand, the newspapers, which had been against the strike, began to change sides. Thanks to this publicity, Clarence Darrow emerged from the Pullman Strike as one of the most famous lawyers in America. He took to lecturing, giving him an ideal podium from which to weigh in on public events and continue to advance his legal career.[17]

With his newfound fame, Darrow grew increasingly active in politics. In 1896, with his friend Altgeld running for reelection, Darrow tried to claim a larger spot on the political stage. While hard to believe in this day and age, the debate over monetary policy—

whether to use gold or silver—divided Americans on party and class lines in one of the most frenzied battles in our political history. With the presidential election turning into a referendum on coinage and monetary policy—with the wealthy and the GOP wanting to rely on the gold standard and farmers and the working class pushing the Democrats to embrace silver—Darrow's position was easy.

Darrow stood squarely for silver, taking a position against Cleveland and William McKinley, the Republican nominee for president. "Not only had I been steadily aligned with the Democratic party, but my sympathies were with the common man," Darrow insisted later. "I was for the debtor rather than creditor." He joined Altgeld in the Illinois delegation as the Democrats held their convention in Chicago and met for the first time a young and largely unknown former congressman from Nebraska by the name of William Jennings Bryan, who was three years younger than Darrow.

Taking to the podium to offer one of the most memorable speeches in political history, the handsome and magnetic Bryan, who had not yet lost control of his weight, left an impression on Darrow. Wearing dark coats and burning with religious intensity, Bryan contrasted with the rumpled Darrow. "He had a strong voice," Darrow remembered. "He had complete control of himself and knew just what he wanted to say. . . . Then, and always, he was a master of technique; he knew exactly how to hold an audience in the hollow of his hand, as it were. His voice, his personality, his knowledge of mob psychology, his aptness for forming rhythmical sentences left him without a rival in the field." Bryan's speech stirred the convention, with one longtime politician thrashing his coat against his chair in a burst of near-religious fervor.

Listening to Bryan's celebrated "Cross of Gold" speech, Darrow was swept off his feet by the young politician even as he relied on religious imagery to stir the crowd. When he invoked a "crown of thorns,"

Bryan raised his hands and lowered them as if putting a crown of thorns on his head. When he ended by saying the Republicans and the upper class would not "crucify mankind on a cross of gold," he stretched out his arms—as if being nailed to a cross. The crowd remained silent for a long moment and then burst into cheers. Nothing like it had ever before been seen in American politics.

Darrow was among the crowd caught up in this new political phenomenon. "I have enjoyed a great many addresses, some of which I delivered myself, but I never listened to one that affected and moved an audience as did that," Darrow recalled. "Men and women cheered and laughed and cried." Darrow even called Bryan "a political Messiah who was to lift the burdens that the oppressed had borne so long," and the speech produced the "greatest ovation that I had ever witnessed." Despite the reaction, the Illinois delegation remained a little wary of Bryan, even as he went on to win the nomination. The day after the convention closed, Darrow and Altgeld talked about Bryan's speech and the convention. "It takes more than speeches to win real victories," Altgeld told Darrow. "Applause lasts but a little while. The road to justice is not a path of glory; it is stony and long and lonely, filled with pain and martyrdom." Altgeld paused, then said, "I have been thinking over Bryan's speech. What did he say, anyhow?"[18] Like many members of the crowd, Altgeld was impressed with Bryan's rhetoric but promptly forgot the content of it.

Altgeld's political wisdom must have lingered with Darrow throughout 1896. At Altgeld's urging, Darrow ran for Congress, taking on Republican congressman Hugh Belknap, an undistinguished incumbent. Running in a Democratic district, Darrow "felt sure of my election," especially with Bryan and Altgeld on the top of the ticket. Wanting to help his fellow Democrats, Darrow took to the stump for both Bryan and Altgeld, ignoring his own race even as Republicans began to pour money into Illinois in general and Chicago in particular. Bryan and Altgeld went down to defeat in Illinois, and McKinley won the presidency. Belknap held Darrow off by around one hundred votes thanks to the Democrat's not paying much attention to the district. "Even one day in my district amongst my friends would have assured my election, but I cared too little for the position and felt too sure," Darrow wrote more than three and a half decades later, noting that he opted to campaign for Bryan in battleground states.[19]

Darrow remained politically engaged, but the 1896 defeats loosened his ties with the Democrats, even as Altgeld partnered with him for a few years. While having backed Bryan in 1896, Darrow began to drift away from him in the subsequent years. "On the whole, during most of his career he remained true to the cause of the people, as he understood political and social questions," Darrow later wrote of Bryan. "But his vision was narrow." The Democrats nominated Bryan again for president in 1900. Darrow campaigned for him since the Democrats opposed American imperialism after the Spanish-American War. Once again, McKinley beat Bryan. After the Democrats nominated the colorless Judge Alton B. Parker, who was run over by the colorful Republican Teddy Roosevelt in 1904, Bryan claimed his party's presidential nomination a third time in 1908 as he took on William Howard Taft. In 1908, Bryan came to Chicago and met with Darrow, hoping the lawyer would stump for him again. But Darrow had no interest in Bryan's central issues— the federal government's guaranteeing bank deposits and the direct election of U.S. senators—and turned down the offer. "That year I took a vacation instead of making campaign speeches," Darrow wrote later. "I felt that I had followed Bryan long enough. But it seemed to have been decreed that I was to see him once more, which came about in a rather strange manner." Despite Darrow's bowing off the political stage, he and Bryan would meet again in an unlikely place, a small town in Tennessee.[20]

Things only got worse for Darrow after losing to Belknap. In 1897, he and Jessie divorced on amicable terms, and she gained custody of their son, fourteen-year-old Paul. A year later, Darrow asked for a reconciliation, but she rejected his proposal. Darrow continued to represent some corporations, but he increasingly worked for laborers and unions. Still lecturing on the needs for economic justice and equality, Darrow put his money where his mouth was, representing Amalgamated Woodworkers Union employees in Wisconsin when they went on strike and were replaced with scabs. When almost 150,000 coal miners went on strike in 1902 under the auspices of the United Mine Workers, President Roosevelt turned to Darrow to serve on a commission to arbitrate the dispute, garnering the Chicago lawyer more national exposure. With millions of Americans wondering how they would keep their houses warm during the winter, newspapers covered the arbitration intently. Darrow represented the miners as more than 550 witnesses testified before the commission. The miners did not get everything they wanted, but, on the whole, they did well, seeing their shifts drop from ten hours a day to nine and seeing their pay increase by an average of 10 percent. Thanks in large part to Darrow's work on the commission, the strike ended after five months in October 1902, just in time for Americans to have adequate supplies of coal to keep their houses heated before winter set in.[21]

With a national following thanks to the publicity he received from defending the miners and the railroad workers, Darrow's personal life grew stable when he met and married Ruby Hammerstrom, a journalist and society figure who was a dozen years younger than the famed lawyer. After they married in 1903, as Ruby began to pick out his clothes, Darrow started dressing better. However, his suits somehow always remained wrinkled, and he never quite evolved from being a country boy, even when he moved to one of the most fashionable parts of Chicago. While he thought about leaving the law to focus on writing and lecturing, Darrow continued to practice even as he found time to write an autobiographical novel about growing up in the country. Darrow also continued to flirt with politics, though he ultimately decided against running for mayor of Chicago in 1903.[22]

Darrow continued to enjoy a national reputation as a champion of the underdog. After former Idaho governor Frank Steunenberg, an avowed enemy of organized labor, was killed outside his home by Harry Orchard at the end of 1905, the murderer confessed that the leaders of the Western Federation of Miners, including William "Big Bill" Haywood, had ordered him to kill the politician. With the only evidence being the word of the murderer, Darrow came out to Idaho to represent the union leaders, even as they had already been convicted in the newspapers. Facing a tough prosecutor in William Borah, who later ranked as one of the greatest orators in the U.S. Senate's history, Darrow did what he did best: he flipped the script and turned the trial around, making it about the union leaders' enemies.

"This is not a murder case, and Bill Haywood is not on trial," Darrow insisted, referring to the well-known labor leader. "The mine owners of the state of Colorado have sent these men to Idaho thinking that conditions and the people were different here. That they have sent them here—the mine owners of Colorado—that they might try and hang and execute and kill forever the Western Federation of Miners. And it is that organization, and through them all organizations, and not Haywood, that is on trial in this court."[23]

Amirus Darrow had passed away in 1904, but his passions for justice and standing up for the powerless lived on in his son. The prominent attorney had also inherited his father's love of politics and his pugnaciousness. Looking back at his life, Darrow asked, "Who am I—the man who has lived and retained this special form of personality for so many years? Aside from the strength or weakness of my structure, I am mainly the product of my mother, who helped to shape the wanton instincts of the child, and of the gentle, kindly, loving, human man whose presence was with me for so many years that I could not change, and did not want to change."[24]

Of course, other men besides his father influenced Darrow. While his opponents would not have believed it, the Founding Fathers inspired Darrow—and one, in particular, inspired his fight for free speech and self-expression.

"Ideas have come and gone, but I have always been a champion of the individual as against the majority and the State," Darrow recalled near the end of his life. "I advocate the fullest liberty of self-expression."

Darrow was proud that he "had fought for the right of the individual to choose his own life," which he defined as a person "doing the thing he wants to do." More famously, that could be defined as "the pursuit of happiness," a concept that Darrow always celebrated.

"Of all the political leaders of the past, Thomas Jefferson made the strongest appeal to me," Darrow wrote. He praised the Sage of Monticello's "vigorous intellect" and called Jefferson a "giant figure." Darrow pointed to Jefferson's opposition to the Alien and Sedition Acts as one of the pivotal moments in American history. Jefferson understood that the laws "were despotic and violated all human rights," and he fought to repeal them.

"The statesman knows that laws should be like clothes, made to fit the citizens that make up the State," Darrow insisted. "He knows that when a protest is long and persistent, the law should be repealed."

With all his political and legal knowledge and experience, Darrow upheld Jefferson as the best example of a statesman and drew inspiration from him throughout his life.

As the 1910s started, Darrow was flying high. He was one of the most illustrious lawyers in America, and his personal and financial lives had become stabilized thanks in large part to Ruby. He was celebrated across the nation as a champion of the underdogs and the working class. Nothing, it seemed, could shatter the new life he had created.

"A Passion for Lost Causes"

In Los Angeles on a rainy January night in 1912, Mary Field opened the door to the apartment she and her sister Sara shared to find Clarence Darrow wearing a drenched coat with a bottle of whiskey in one pocket and a pistol in the other.

Mary had met Darrow back in 1908, and they had grown close over the years, even becoming lovers despite his second marriage, though the romantic connection between them had nearly ended by early 1912. Darrow lifted the whiskey bottle and startled her with a simple sentence:

"I'm going to kill myself."

Darrow reached into his pocket for the gun.

A stunned Mary could respond with a single word only: "Why?"

"They're going to indict me for bribing the McNamara jury." Darrow started to cry. "I can't stand the disgrace."

Darrow put the gun on the kitchen table and remained silent for a moment before they began to talk. As they sat at her kitchen table smoking cigarettes and downing the whiskey, Mary comforted Darrow—he was always "Darrow" to her and never "Clarence"—and offered religious arguments against suicide, something the famed attorney quickly rejected. More effectively, she weighed in on his reputation, insisting that the only way to clear his name would be to move forward and fight back against the charges. After a few harrowing hours, Darrow finally agreed with her and put the gun away. He slipped his coat back on and headed out into the rain as the darkness gathered around him.[1]

While now a little-remarked-upon part of his storied life and legendary career, Darrow came extremely close to losing it all. Darrow, usually one of the most irrepressible of men, fell into a deep depression, as that stormy night with Mary clearly illustrated. As he confessed to her, Darrow was deathly afraid that his reputation would be tarnished. For two years, he had to stay in Los Angeles, coming close to bankruptcy thanks to legal costs and his inability to work as he fended off the accusations.

Darrow had originally come to Los Angeles in 1911 on the behalf of the American Federation of Labor (AFL) to represent John and James McNamara. The brothers, both union leaders, had been charged with bombing the building housing the *Los Angeles Times*, a fierce opponent of organized labor, leading to a fire that killed twenty people. The AFL went all out to help the McNamara brothers, calling on unions across the country to donate to their legal defense funds. Eyes across the nation fixated on the case, which was seen as an important battle in the continued war between unions and companies.[2]

As he made preparations for the case, Darrow seemed different, less engaged than before even as he took three months to study the bombing. His discoveries only made his outlook even more bleak. Looking back on the case twenty years later, Darrow admitted, "The situation looked almost hopeless." On a weekend in November 1911, Darrow met with some of his closest allies, saying that he was going to push for the McNamara brothers to make a plea bargain because it was the only way to save them from the death penalty.[3]

But any hopes for a simple plea vanished on November 28 when Darrow was accused of having his investigator Bert Franklin deliver $4,000 to one of the jurors on the case. After observing Franklin give the juror the money, the police arrested him in front of Darrow. Confronting these new accusations, Darrow had the McNamara brothers plead guilty, with James getting sentenced to life and John facing fifteen years.[4]

Promised immunity for his testimony, Franklin flipped on Darrow, serving as the star witness for the prosecutors. Accused of bribing jurors, Darrow hired California attorney Earl Rogers to defend him against the charges. Already worn-out from the McNamara brothers' case, Darrow struggled with mental health issues, as he revealed when he told Field he would kill himself. "The intense strain on my mind and feelings was undermining my health, and I did not feel the strength and enthusiasm necessary for the fight," Darrow admitted years later. Still, as Field knew only too well that he would, Darrow rebounded and attempted to fend off the charges when he realized his reputation was on the line: "I summoned my courage and braced myself for the ordeal."[5]

Biographers and historians continue to argue about Darrow's guilt. Early biographers such as Irving Stone and Arthur Weinberg insisted the government and businesses targeted Darrow by staging the bribe and luring him to the scene. More recently, scholars including Geoffrey Cowan and John Farrell have convincingly shown Darrow's likely guilt.[6] Darrow had to stay in Los Angeles for the trial, even representing himself after Rogers took ill. In one of his finest courtroom performances, Darrow was found not guilty in the first trial. The jurors could not reach a unanimous decision in the second trial on a separate but related charge, leading to a mistrial. Darrow avoided prison, but his reputation took a significant hit with rumors that he had reached an agreement with prosecutors to never return to Los Angeles, a city he largely avoided in the years to come.[7]

Whether or not he authorized the attempt to bribe a juror, the accusations were a turning point for Darrow. Organized labor was furious with Darrow for having the McNamara brothers accept a plea bargain and admit their guilt. The unions never forgave Darrow for letting them down in a prominent case, especially with the added embarrassment of the bribery accusations. After the McNamara brothers' case, Darrow, who had built a national reputation for representing unions and workers, never again handled a major labor case.

Back in Chicago, an exhausted Darrow insisted that he was done with being a lawyer, a common pronouncement that ran throughout his life, though money had become a problem. To make ends meet he resorted to selling many prized first editions from his library. Darrow remained popular as a lecturer, and as the McNamara case faded in the rearview mirror, slowly he began to practice law again. "There was but one thing to do," Darrow recalled. "I must go back to work. So I went to my office without delay. I made no statement, gave no explanations, I offered no excuse or extenuation." Peter Sissman, an old friend whom Darrow had mentored two decades earlier, formed a law partnership with the famed attorney, who was now in his midfifties. By 1915, with unions refusing to work with him, Darrow had turned his attention and talents to criminal law, becoming one of the most celebrated defense lawyers in the nation. Even with his tarnished reputation, Darrow was recognized as one of the best attorneys in the country. Taking high-profile cases in Chicago and across the Great Lakes region, Darrow mounted an impressive comeback, and by 1917, the year he turned sixty, all traces of the bribery scandal had vanished.[8]

While he no longer represented labor unions, Darrow closely followed politics. Despite opposing imperialism and U.S. involvement in the Spanish-American War, when World War I broke out in the summer of 1914, Darrow's passion for the underdog ended his pacifism. "When Germany invaded Belgium I recovered from my pacifism in the twinkling of an eye," Darrow wrote. "When I read of the German army marching through Belgium I had exactly the same reaction that I would experience if a big dog should attack a little one." Darrow hoped President Woodrow Wilson would act tougher with Germany and back England, France, and Russia against that nation. Despite his support of Wilson's policies, Darrow helped ensure some of the opponents of America's entering the war were not arrested. Darrow lectured on the war and even toured the Western Front in France.[9]

Although he supported the Wilson administration and American involvement overseas, Darrow continued to fight for justice, even for some of the most prominent critics of the war effort. Darrow's old friend Eugene Debs, who remained active in politics, including running numerous times for president as the Socialist Party candidate, had given a speech against the war. A federal judge ruled that Debs had violated the Sedition Act and sentenced him to ten years in prison. Despite their differences over the war, Darrow visited his old friend in jail and lobbied the Wilson administration to release him, meeting with Attorney General A. Mitchell Palmer on the matter. Wilson refused to release Debs, but after being elected president in 1920, Warren G. Harding pardoned him. Looking back at this ten years later, Darrow mused over the strangeness of politics. "I had always admired Woodrow Wilson and distrusted Harding," he wrote. "Doubtless my opinions about both in relation to affairs of government were measurably correct; still, Mr. Wilson, a scholar and an idealist, and Mr. Palmer, a Quaker, kept Debs in prison; and Mr. Harding . . . unlocked the door."[10]

His reputation now restored from the bribery accusations, Darrow continued to weigh in on the issues in a rapidly changing America. Generally avoiding political campaigns and elections, Darrow continued his outspoken fight for justice, championing civil rights for African Americans and weighing in against the Eighteenth Amendment, which imposed Prohibition on the nation. Trumpeting his support for liberties and challenging popular public opinions, Darrow steadily served as the country's conscience on legal and moral issues. Nowhere was Darrow more outspoken than in his opposition to the death penalty. He soon had the biggest stage of his career to argue against capital punishment.

=

Almost a century later, the murder of Bobby Franks by Nathan Leopold and Richard Loeb continues to horrify.

Leopold and Loeb came from two of the wealthiest families in Chicago. Despite being only nineteen when he helped murder Franks, Leopold had already graduated from the University of Chicago and spoke more than a dozen languages, five of them fluently. Leopold had plans to study law at Harvard University and was already an accomplished ornithologist. Loeb also displayed his brilliance early, graduating from the University of Michigan when he was only seventeen and starting grad school at the University of Chicago.

But despite their intelligence and wealthy backgrounds, the two young men had shadows in their past. Growing up, both of them spent more time with their governesses than they did with their parents. Loeb's governess spurred his ambitions and also convinced him he was superior to the rest of the human race. Leopold's governess repeatedly sexually molested him. While they had been casual friends during most of their youth, Leopold and Loeb grew closer thanks to their fascination with crime, at first working together stealing a camera and a typewriter, before moving on to arson and vandalism, all while dreaming up the "perfect crime." They also became lovers, though Leopold took their relationship far more seriously than Loeb. Leopold's learning also led the two young men down a dark path. An avid reader of Friedrich Nietzsche, Leopold embraced the German philosopher's theory of the *Übermenschen*, supermen who stood above ordinary human ethics. Leopold explained the concept of the supermen to Loeb, insisting they had "certain superior qualities" and were "exempted from the ordinary laws which govern men." The superman, insisted Leopold, is "not liable for anything he may do." Leopold and Loeb decided to put that theory to the test.

After planning the "perfect crime" for more than half a year, on May 21, 1924, Leopold and Loeb rented a car and offered a ride to fourteen-year-old Bobby Franks, a distant cousin of Loeb's who lived across the street from the Loebs, when he was walking home from school. With Leopold behind the wheel, Loeb sat in the back seat as he stabbed Franks several times with a chisel before gagging the boy as he died. They drove to Wolf Lake in Indiana, pouring acid on Franks's face and dumping the body by some railroad tracks. Leopold called Franks's mother demanding a ransom, and trying to show their superior intelligence, the pair mailed a ransom note after burning most of the evidence.

But despite their intelligence and effort to stage the perfect crime, things quickly fell apart for the murderers. When confronted by the police, Leopold, looking to show off his intelligence, could not keep himself from talking, while Loeb offered a few leads. They had also not done a good enough job hiding the body, which a local worker discovered. Leopold's distinct glasses—he was one of only three men in Chicago with a specific frame—were found by the body. Rounded up by the police, both young men confessed and began to turn on each other. Loeb insisted Leopold planned it all. For his part, Leopold claimed only to have driven the car while Loeb murdered Franks.[11]

Due to the murderers' backgrounds, the case quickly drew national attention, making headlines across the country, especially when their confessions to the police became public.

"The thing that prompted Dick to want to do this thing and prompted me to want to do this thing was a sort of pure love of excitement," Leopold told the police. He said that "the imaginary love of thrills, doing something different" and "the satisfaction and the ego of putting something over" led them to murder Franks. Statements such as this led the press and the general public to demand Leopold and Loeb get the death penalty, and with their confessions on file, almost everyone thought the government would hang them. People across America even volunteered to serve as their executioners.[12]

The entire nation was ready to give Leopold and Loeb the death penalty for their heinous crime. Then Clarence Darrow took their case.

Now sixty-seven, Darrow readied for the most publicized case of his career to that point. Asked by the families of the two murderers to take the case, Darrow realized he would be able to command the spotlight and pound away at the death penalty. Almost ten years after the case, Darrow mulled over why he had taken it: "The act was a shocking and bizarre performance; the public and press were almost solidly against them. In a terrible crisis there is only one element more helpless than the poor, and that is the rich. I knew then, and I know now, that except for the wealth of the families a plea of guilty and a life sentence would have been accepted without a contest. I knew this, and I dreaded the fight."[13]

Darrow had expected some publicity for the trial, but the coverage surprised him. Realizing that the case had garnered so much attention, with most of the general public ready to hang Leopold and Loeb, Darrow thought, "The feeling was so tense and the trial so near that we could not save the boys' lives with a jury." Darrow could not even "find a single man who had not read all about the case and formed a definite opinion." After mulling over his options, Darrow decided the best course was for Leopold and Loeb to offer guilty verdicts on charges of kidnapping Franks and murdering him.[14]

When the case began on July 21, 1924, Darrow caught everyone—the prosecutors, the assembled reporters, even the presiding judge—off guard with the guilty plea. Surprised and outraged responses filled the courtroom while Darrow quietly waited to continue. Once things died down, Darrow tipped a few of his cards: "A court can no more shirk responsibility than attorneys. We shall ask that we may be permitted to offer evidence as to the mental condition of these young men, to show the degree of responsibility they had, and also to offer evidence as to the youth of these defendants and the fact of a plea of guilty as further mitigation of the penalties in this case." Even with the judge noting that a guilty plea could still lead to the death penalty, Leopold and Loeb confirmed their guilt, and Darrow offered to have almost twenty psychiatrists—still called alienists in the mid-1920s—testify on the defendants' mental states.[15]

The prosecutors and Darrow spent the month after the guilty plea preparing to clash on the sentencing. Crowds gathered each time court was in session, people shoving one another to try to hear Darrow speak or to catch a glimpse of the two murderers who had become famous after their faces had been plastered across newspapers and magazines nationwide. With the press playing up Leopold's intelligence and Loeb's good looks, the killers garnered far more attention than anyone, including Darrow, could have expected. Women even reached out to both of the killers with marriage proposals. Darrow had a front-row seat for a new phenomenon in American history: the murderer as a celebrity. Leopold and Loeb would soon be followed by John Dillinger, Bonnie and Clyde, John Wayne Gacy, Ted Bundy, Paul John Knowles, Jeffrey Dahmer, David Berkowitz, Aileen Wuornos, and Charles Manson.[16]

Still, if Darrow was confused over his clients' fame, despite being in his late sixties he remained well-informed about scientific and medical advances. Darrow had taken a considerable risk when he turned to psychiatric experts to evaluate Leopold's and Loeb's mental health as he tried to show they were guilty by reason of insanity. This was an almost unheard-of strategy, but Darrow showed he remained in touch with current trends by employing it. During most of Darrow's life, Americans had generally dismissed mental health issues. But that was changing after World War I. Returning soldiers who had seen too many of their comrades and friends dying in waves during futile attacks against trenches and who had experienced the horrors of being gassed came home with mental traumas, something that Americans had not experienced in more than half a century. Darrow argued that Leopold and Loeb suffered from mental illness instead of simply writing them off as insane—and after seeing so much suffering during World War I, Americans were ready to listen to Darrow.[17]

After the court heard from the psychiatrists, Darrow had his moment in the sun. On August 22, in one of the greatest arguments ever displayed in an American courtroom, Darrow made his case against the death penalty, insisting that the publicity around the case led to more voices calling for Leopold and Loeb to hang: "When the public is interested and demands a punishment, no matter what the offense, great or small, it thinks of only one punishment, and that is death." Darrow reviewed the history of the death penalty and insisted it did not lead to justice. "Your Honor would be merciful if you tied a rope around their necks and let them die; merciful to them, but not merciful to civilization; and not merciful to those who would be left behind." Noting all of the attention the case had received, the old lawyer painted it as a pivotal moment in legal history: "Your Honor stands between the future and the past. I know the future is with me, and what I stand for here. . . . I am pleading for life, understanding, charity, kindness, and the infinite mercy that considers all. I am pleading that we overcome cruelty with kindness and hatred with love. I know the future is on my side."[18]

Darrow beseeched the presiding judge to spare the lives of his two notorious clients. With tears running down his face at the conclusion of an astonishing summation that lasted more than twelve hours over two days, Darrow said, "I am pleading for the future; I am pleading for a time when hatred and cruelty will not control the hearts of men, when we can learn by reason and judgment and understanding and faith that all life is worth saving, and that mercy is the highest attribute of man."[19]

More important for Darrow, the judge was swayed to his side. After hearing Darrow's argument, the judge agreed to save Leopold and Loeb from the death penalty, though he sentenced them to life behind bars for killing Franks and added ninety-nine years for their kidnapping the boy. While parts of the public were outraged, Darrow's words also hit home for many of the Americans who read them in their morning newspapers.

Darrow shed no tears for the killers. He found Loeb to be a "kindly boy," while Leopold had "the most brilliant intellect that I had ever met in a boy." But they also had committed the "most foolish, most motiveless act that was ever conceived in a diseased brain." Talking to them, Darrow found, despite the violent crime they had committed, they had "no malice or hatred" of Franks and called the murder plot "childish and silly," which proved their "abnormal mentality." Darrow insisted that sentencing Leopold and Loeb to death would reflect not justice but only the government bowing to popular pressure. Still, Darrow took no joy as the judge sentenced them to spend the rest of their lives in prison. "The lives of Loeb and Leopold were saved," Darrow, continuing his staunch opposition to the death penalty, wrote later. "But there was nothing before them, to the end, but stark, blank stone walls."[20]

If the case made household names out of Leopold and Loeb, it also elevated Darrow to new heights. Having saved his clients from the gallows, Darrow himself became a celebrity, a precursor to famous lawyers such as F. Lee Bailey, Melvin Belli, Roy Black, Leslie Abramson, Robert Shapiro, Johnnie Cochran, and others. Darrow became one of the prominent figures of the Roaring Twenties. Standing six feet in height, the old man was slowing down, dealing with rheumatism and neuralgia, which led to painful spasms in his face.

Less than a year after Darrow saved Leopold and Loeb from being executed, Russell Owen profiled the attorney in the *New York Times*, praising him as the "champion of the minority" with "a passion for lost causes." Owen put his finger on Darrow's style in the courtroom and when lecturing: "He dominates by sheer intellectual power, and his manner when he is not roused in debate is one of courteous consideration marked by a delightful sense of humor." Owen portrayed Darrow as a "rather awkward figure in baggy trousers upheld by suspenders, without a coat, one shirt sleeve torn half off, and thin hair sticking damply out in all directions." Despite praising Darrow's mastery of the courtroom, Owen also realized that the lawyer enjoyed writing far more than practicing his trade.[21]

Even with his rumpled appearance, Darrow stood alongside icons of the 1920s such as Scott and Zelda Fitzgerald, Charles Lindbergh, and Jack Dempsey. Darrow's iconic status was only reinforced when he visited his former mistress, the now-married Mary Field Parton, for a party on the last night of March 1925. During the party, Mary's nine-year-old daughter, Margaret, told Darrow she had something for him. To his surprise, Margaret offered Darrow a piece of paper autographed by Babe Ruth and asked the old lawyer to sign it. "Fame at last, alongside Babe," Darrow said as he signed *Clarence Darrow, Pinch Hitter.*

Having signed his name next to that of the Sultan of Swat, Darrow grew serious. "America has taken another step back to the Dark Ages," he told the partygoers, and he began talking about a new law in Tennessee, championed by his old political ally William Jennings Bryan, that prohibited the teaching of evolution in public schools. Now at the end of his career, Clarence Darrow was about to take on the most important trial of his life.[22]

"A Town of Hopes and Nightmares"

For most of its history, Dayton, Tennessee, avoided the spotlight. However, there was always something special about the small town in the southeastern part of the Volunteer State.

A look at the Civil War in Tennessee offers no insight into Dayton. Even as the Union and Confederate armies maneuvered through the area during the summer and fall of 1863 in the Tullahoma, Chickamauga, and Chattanooga campaigns, Dayton simply played no part. As historic as it is now, Dayton was not on the maps at that time.

The town was founded early in the nineteenth century as Smith's Crossroads. William Smith, a schoolmaster from New England, had moved to the area in 1812 and, looking to build his fortune, in 1820 opened up a general store in Dayton as more travelers took to the roads in southeastern Tennessee. Thanks to its location in the Tennessee River Valley, easily accessible to Chattanooga and Knoxville, the town slowly grew as the decades went by, though it largely remained off history's stage. Still, significant events flirted with Smith's Crossroads now and then. Exiled Native Americans from all over the Southeast passed through Smith's Crossroads on the Trail of Tears. At the start of the Civil War, Confederate forces held Northern prisoners near Smith's Crossroads. Later in the war, when the Army of the Cumberland came through on the way to take Chattanooga, Smith's Cross-roads served as a headquarters for some of the Union commanders.[1]

Despite these roots, instead of looking away to the past of Dixie, Dayton personified the New South that emerged after Reconstruction. Even the town's new name sounded a note in the national chorus for reconciliation between the North and the South. Dayton was named after the much larger city in Ohio.[2]

With a post office and a few stores, Dayton had around 175 residents when the railroad came to town in 1880. While geography hindered the town for most of the nineteenth century, it also gave it a boost thanks to its location halfway between Knoxville and Chattanooga. The Southern Railway spurred Dayton to new growth even as the company's officers wanted to rename the town yet again to give it a unique feel. The residents of Dayton rejected the railway's plan to name the town Sequatchie even as the city continued to grow, becoming the seat of Rhea County.

Besides the railroad, more opportunities expanded in Dayton, something Sir Titus Salt, a prominent English politician and businessman, quickly realized. Backed by "Glasgow capitalists," Salt, an investor in mines and other industries in Europe and the United States, wanted to turn Dayton into the iron-manufacturing center of the nation, building coal mines and investing heavily in the area through his Dayton Coal and Iron Company. Salt, also a leading politician out of Yorkshire and a religious reformer, relied on friends such as accountant Alfred Allott and John Crossley to help with investments across the ocean in Tennessee. One of Salt's sons crossed the Atlantic to examine the area in the late 1870s and did so again in 1883 as Salt and his colleagues planned "large investments in the manufacture of iron, steel, and cotton." They poured the equivalent of $35 million today into the Dayton area.

The company built around two hundred houses for new employees and created thirty miles of railroad tracks to help transport coal and iron out of the hills surrounding Dayton and to ship them to Chattanooga and beyond. The new investments changed the landscape, with the hills looming over town transformed thanks to the mines. Dayton's churches with their steeples and the courthouse, the town's tallest buildings and some of the most busy, were soon overshadowed by a series of smokestacks, some as high as two hundred feet. The town even garnered something of an international flavor thanks to the engineers and mine employees from Scotland working for the company, crossing the ocean to offer their expertise and experience. Even after Sir Titus Salt Sons and Co. Ltd. sold the company to other investors and pulled out of Dayton in the early 1890s, the area continued to flourish due to the investments pouring in.

The Dayton Coal and Iron Company transformed the town, bringing money and greater stability to the area in the decades that followed. Making coke—a key ingredient from coal used to create iron—the company put Dayton on the map as the nineteenth century ended. By 1890, the town boasted more than 400 percent growth since the decade before, with 926 residents and almost 2,000 people in the immediate area, including some temporary residents working in the mines. As the new century began, the town had nearly 1,200 people. Dayton was set to become one of the chief industrial centers of the South.

The company certainly changed Dayton's appearance. Before the Dayton Coal and Iron Company came to town, there were some striking homes, such as the plantation-style home on East Idaho Avenue that S. D. Broyles, who served in the Confederate cavalry, built in 1861, right before he went to war. Some of the new homes in Dayton followed that example, such as the Magnolia House, which Dr. Walter Fairfield Thomison built on South Market Street. Thomison, the chief doctor for the Dayton Coal and Iron Company, looked to the past, creating a Greek Revival home with slender columns to mirror the old plantation homes. The company even started a Catholic school and day care for its employees, creating a stately Victorian building on Delaware Avenue to educate the miners' children. Just next to it was "the Mansion," an eighteen-room home that the local manager lived in and that hosted Dayton Coal and Iron Company executives and investors during their annual trips to Tennessee. With money pouring into town, an impressive array of late-Victorian and Edwardian homes lined the town's new streets.

But the good times did not last long. Even with the best efforts of the Dayton Coal and Iron Company and local leaders, Dayton failed to launch. The 1800s ended, and despite the growth, the new century began with a series of nightmares.

Dayton experienced a horrendous Christmas in 1895. On December 20, a gas accident at the Nelson Mine outside Dayton devastated the town, leaving twenty-eight miners, some of them merely boys, dead. The gas lingered so long it took days for the mine to be cleared and the bodies recovered.

Just when the town started to recover, disaster struck again. On May 27, 1901, as spring turned to summer in the Tennessee Hills, a quiet Monday afternoon was shattered when an accident with dynamite filled the Dayton Coal and Iron Company's Richland mine, two miles outside town, with coal dust. A terrible explosion rocked the mine, leading to a massive cave-in and burying miners. A three-hundred-foot blast roared out of the mine entrance, killing more than twenty miners and burning their bodies. By the time a rescue team from town arrived, twenty-eight miners were dead, the same number that had been killed at the Nelson Mine five and a half years earlier. "The two undertaking establishments at Dayton were turned into morgues, where the mangled bodies were dressed and prepared for delivery to their families," a journalist reported after the tragedy.[3] A reporter from the *Chattanooga Times* spent the night in Dayton and wrote, "Far into the night the air was pierced with the shrieks and cries of bereaved wives, mothers, and children."[4]

Dayton did not even have time to recover before the next terrible mine accident, as the new century continued to plague the town and the Dayton Coal and Iron Company. Only months after the accident at the Richland mine, in March 1902, the Nelson Mine once again saw a deadly accident, this one leaving twenty-one miners dead, another staggering blow to the small community.

The series of mine accidents—and the bad press they generated—helped sink the Dayton Coal and Iron Company. It struggled through the first decade of the twentieth century, facing challenges with capital, disputes with labor, and a changing economy. Dayton tried to turn to such businesses as a hosiery factory and agriculture—including growing strawberries—to fill the void as jobs left town. When he arrived in the area in the 1920s, John Scopes, a shrewd observer of the region, noted that corn surpassed strawberries. "Corn seemed to be the major crop, most of it apparently going into corn whiskey—one of the normal, if illicit, products of the region," Scopes recalled. "Fires that broke out regularly in the mountains may have been accidents; just the same, they protected still locations by obliterating the telltale smells of cooking corn marsh."[5]

Census numbers reveal the population living within the city limits grew by more than 67 percent between 1900 and 1910 as more farmers and miners moved from outside Dayton to live in the town itself. But even with that growth and farmers continuing to live in the area, Dayton began to stall during the first decade of the twentieth century.

At the center of Dayton stood the embodiment of its ambitions and challenges. In 1891, the Rhea County Courthouse opened in the center of town, capturing many of the hopes and disappointments that Dayton experienced in the last decade of the nineteenth century and the first one of the twentieth century.

Three stories high, the brick building looked better suited for Ravenna or Venice than a small town in southeastern Tennessee. On the eastern side of the courthouse, a clock tower with a belfry stretched toward the heavens. On the western side, a smaller tower jutted out. The courthouse, an odd mix of the Romanesque Revival and the Italianate styles that proved so popular in the latter half of the nineteenth century, continued to inspire Dayton residents and tease what the city might become. Even as the town fathers planned the building, they looked ahead, hoping that an ambitious floor plan would ensure more prominent trials. On the second floor stood the large courtroom, which would be famous for a brief moment in 1925. Designed to be the largest courtroom in the state, the windows that stood above the wooden floor offered commanding views of downtown Dayton and ushered in gentle breezes on hot summer days.

But if the courtroom impressed, the surrounding downtown did not. Two of the sides of the square around the courthouse had been developed with one- and two-story buildings hosting shops and offices, including Robinson's Drug Store, which developed into one of the town's social centers. With thirty-five rooms for rent, the Aqua Hotel, next to Robinson's, served some of the best food in the region. While those blocks offered a hint of what Dayton could be, the two largely empty blocks off the courthouse square served as a grim reminder of the challenges the town continued to face.

Thankfully, there were other signs of hope for the town, including the Rhea County High School, better known as Central High School. Housed in a large, blockish building, opened in 1906, Central was the first public high school in Dayton's history, and it served as a reminder of the town's future. The school would soon garner national attention thanks to a slim, unassuming teacher there by the name of John Scopes.

Even with the new school, the population began to shrink. In 1913, the Dayton Coal and Iron Company finally closed, laying off hundreds of local residents. The demise of the mines only accelerated the number of people leaving town. However, the Cumberland Coal and Iron Company swooped in to buy much of the Dayton Coal and Iron Company's holdings. While it kept the smokestacks puffing and continued to employ around four hundred men, the Cumberland Coal and Iron Company simply did not have the same impact in Dayton as its predecessor. The 1920 census showed the town's population had fallen by 15 percent, but that did not account for all the miners, railroad hands, and other company workers who used to live outside town—and had now packed up their bags and left Dayton for good.

As the nation entered World War I, life went on in fading Dayton, but every now and then events would jolt the sleepy town and waken it to the greater world. Sergeant Alvin York, who won the Medal of Honor for leading attacks against German positions, hailed from nearby Pall Mall in Fentress County and garnered national attention for his heroics. However, he would not be immortalized on the silver screen until Gary Cooper played him in the 1941 film *Sergeant York*. By the time Scopes arrived in Dayton in 1924, the buzz around York's heroics "had died down." Looking back at York's fame in the area, Scopes insisted that many residents of Dayton and the surrounding area saw themselves in the famed soldier. "Most of the mountaineers probably didn't consider Sergeant York's exploits extraordinary," Scopes wrote a half century after York became a household name. "Each one, I'm sure, thought he would have done as well, had he been faced with a similar opportunity." Scopes found the residents of Dayton and the region to be a "self-reliant breed."[6]

After the war ended and the influenza epidemic passed, and even with the Eighteenth Amendment imposing Prohibition, America looked ahead to better days as the Roaring Twenties started. The bulls stamped through the stock market as the nation enjoyed new heights of prosperity. Hollywood brought stars of the silver screen to towns across the country. A different form of music, previously unknown to most Americans, could be heard on their newly bought radios, leading F. Scott Fitzgerald to dub the era the Jazz Age. More Americans drove cars, young women started opting for shorter dresses, and the 1920 federal census showed more people living in cities and towns than in the country for the first time in the nation's history.

But if America was driving full speed ahead on the highways during the 1920s, Dayton was falling back, in danger of being lost in the mountains and hills. The town was becoming irrelevant despite the presence of hardware shops, drugstores, the Aqua Hotel, and even the new movie theater. Even the Southern Railway, which had been instrumental in the town's growth, played less and less of a role in Dayton. By the 1920s, Scopes noted the trains "went through" town, with "most trains whistling without stopping." The greater world impacted Dayton, regardless. After the war, like many other parts of the South, Dayton saw a growth in religious fervor even as the schools remained more focused on sports and basic principles of education. Clarence Darrow weighed in on the town's lack of prestige and recognition, insisting it "had never been heard of very far from home."[7]

Scopes, who knew Dayton far better than the celebrated attorney did, found Dayton's social scene to be limiting, which impacted its commerce and kept the town off the national stage. "Society was divided along several distinct, if unoriginal lines," Scopes remembered about

Dayton. "Many persons found social expression in their churches; others were primarily concerned with the school or with business." With no chamber of commerce, local business leaders usually met at the country club and—as Scopes could famously attest—the drugstores. Even with the country club and the movie theater, Scopes recalled the churches "constituted at least three-fourths of Dayton's social life."[8]

Indeed, the churches helped shape Dayton. All over the small town, especially along Market Street, two blocks south of the courthouse, Dayton's residents had plenty of options when it came to churches. On Market Street stood Cumberland Presbyterian Church, a simple white wooden structure, and parishioners were already getting excited about the possibility of a new building. Also on Market Street, where it had stood since 1888, was the imposing Dayton Methodist Episcopal Church, with a steeple on its left side. Also founded in 1888 was the First Avenue Methodist Episcopal Church, a redbrick building with a white steeple. Even as most of Dayton struggled, the churches at least continued to thrive.

Everyone in town seemed to realize Dayton needed a boost, but nobody seemed to know what to do. Perhaps the Dayton resident who spent the most time thinking about how to promote the town was George Rappleyea, a short, quick-walking engineer. He saw the world and its opportunities through thick eyeglasses. Rappleyea, who had lived in New York and New Orleans, had been brought to Dayton in 1922 by the Cumberland Coal and Iron Company, which wrestled with difficulties even as it ran six factories and employed four hundred people in the area. Within two years, Rappleyea ranked as one of the leading men in town when it came to business and social events, and he clearly liked Dayton. As the Cumberland Coal and Iron Company continued to struggle, Rappleyea began to put his lively mind to work on how to bring Dayton back.

In the meantime, as Dayton moved into the mid-1920s, the town continued to miss out on the growing prosperity. While Florida and other parts of the South boomed during the Roaring Twenties, Dayton only fell further and further behind. Of course, there were some changes over the years. The home S. D. Broyles built right before the Civil War, the oldest home in Dayton, was sold in 1908 to "Red Jim" Darwin, who owned a store on Market Street. Proclaiming his store had "Everything to Wear," Darwin had done well for himself in Dayton, though his family had always been something of achievers. Red Jim could even trace his family all the way back to William Darwin, a distinguished Englishman from the eighteenth century. Of course, other members of William's family had made more of a mark than the Tennessee merchant, including his great-grandson, a biologist and scholar who, like Abraham Lincoln, had been born on February 12, 1809. Soon Charles would be the most famous Darwin in Dayton instead of his distant relation—as the nation turned its eyes to this sleepy town to battle over the divisive issue of evolution.

5

The Crusade against Teaching Evolution

While it's tough to imagine in our age of rapid technological changes, the decade following America's entry into World War I ranks as one of the most transformative times in the nation's history. As America joined the war, nativism surged across the country, while fundamentalist Protestants imposed Prohibition. Americans suffered through the Spanish flu epidemic. As President Woodrow Wilson lingered in the White House recovering from a stroke, Republicans in the U.S. Senate rejected his peace treaty, ensuring America did not join the League of Nations. In large cities and small towns, Americans purchased radios and cars and enjoyed a wave of movies.

During those years, America experienced changes like never before, but the nation looked inward following the war and the pandemic. After the Russian Revolution, in the first Red Scare, spurred by Attorney General A. Mitchell Palmer, Americans began to mistakenly see communists all over the country. Across the South, the Great Plains, and the Midwest, the Ku Klux Klan resurfaced for the first time in the twentieth century. Facing a rapidly changing America, evangelical Christians grew increasingly active in politics and social issues, especially backing Prohibition and standing against evolution.[1]

Charles Darwin had readers in America during the nineteenth century, but they often took his theories on evolution and applied them to other areas, including the economy and society. Through the works of Herbert Spencer and other writers, Americans used Darwin's theories in the social realm. Embraced by many thinkers and businessmen during the Gilded Age and the start of the twentieth century, social Darwinism—basically applying the "survival of the fittest" to running society—applied natural selection to history, politics, economics, and other areas.[2]

While Darwin garnered more than his share of scientific critics, most of the opposition in America to his ideas focused on religious and social matters.[3] After World War I and the influenza epidemic, as Americans became uneasy about the future, fundamentalist pastors took advantage of the new means of communication—national magazines, newsletters, and radio—to take their crusade against evolution to the larger stage. Insisting that evolution was contrary to the biblical account of creation and threatened Christianity, William Bell Riley, the longtime pastor of the First Baptist Church in Minneapolis, formed the World Christian Fundamentals Association (WCFA) and the Anti-Evolution League of America to take the fight against evolution to the national level, often descending into conspiracy theories and anti-Semitism.[4]

If Riley had his followers, the attention-grabbing Aimee Semple McPherson took the battle against evolution to a new audience. Charismatic and entertaining, McPherson used her pulpit at Angelus Temple in Los Angeles to reach a nationwide audience over the radio. She claimed that the very idea of survival of the fittest undermined Christianity and warned that teaching evolution in schools would hurt children's morals and turn them against traditional values. A savvy tactician on media and politics, McPherson had no problem working with politicians, including William Jennings Bryan, to help further her aims.[5]

Riley and McPherson might have been important figures, but they stood in the shadow of baseball's legendary Billy Sunday. With his father dying during the Civil War and abandoned by his mother, Sunday grew up at the Iowa Soldiers' Orphans' Home during the 1860s and 1870s, before his hard work and athleticism paid off as if he were living a Horatio Alger story.

Mentored by John Scott, a colonel in the Civil War who served two years as Iowa's lieutenant governor, Sunday met the fabled baseball player Cap Anson. One of the most popular players of his era, Anson was impressed with the young man's skills. Anson recommended Sunday to A. G. Spalding, the president of the Chicago White Stockings and the founder of the sports equipment company that still bears his name, who signed the young outfielder from Iowa. Sunday played for the White Stockings—today's Cubs—before heading to the Keystone State to play for the Pittsburgh Alleghenys— now the Pirates—before signing with the Philadelphia Phillies. Sunday proved an excellent fielder and a talented base stealer during his eight years in the majors. He proved less effective at the plate, hitting .248 over his eight seasons, though that stat looks far worse today than it did in the dead-ball era. Still, Sunday never showed much power, hitting only twelve home runs over his eight seasons. Despite that, he was a valuable player on some talented teams as the White Stockings claimed two National League pennants during his five years in Chicago from 1883 through 1887.[6]

But Sunday found a greater passion than baseball—the salvation of souls. During the 1880s, Sunday had a conversion experience and grew progressively active in the church as he played baseball in Pennsylvania. In 1891, Sunday turned down a contract to continue his baseball career to work for the YMCA and enter the ministry. Despite never going to seminary, Sunday became one of the leading pastors in America, crossing the nation throughout the 1890s and the first two decades of the twentieth century to preach and weigh in on the issues, from backing Prohibition and American entry into World War I to opposing evolution.[7]

Speaking to hundreds of thousands of Americans across the nation, Sunday railed against evolution with fiery rhetoric. To Sunday, Darwin was "an infidel," and modern education was "chained to the devil's throne" thanks to teachers lecturing on evolution in the classroom.[8] Sunday even proclaimed, "Old Darwin is in hell," as he continued his crusade against evolution.[9]

Sunday and other religious leaders took their anti-evolution message to millions of Americans, and the likes of William Jennings Bryan and other political leaders took the fight into the political arena. Realizing that an increasing number of religiously motivated voters opposed teaching evolution, elected officials, including governors and legislators, quickly took action.

In the early 1920s, with the nation thinking it was on the wrong path after the war and the influenza pandemic, officials in several states across the South debated bills prohibiting teaching evolution in public schools. In 1921, South Carolina considered the issue, but no legislation was passed. The following year, Kentucky mulled a proposed prohibition, but the bill went down to defeat by one vote. Popular University of Kentucky president Frank McVey got much of the credit for stopping the bill through his vocal opposition. While McVey garnered applause for his effort, a young student at the university by the name of John Scopes would be a more prominent champion of teaching evolution in the classroom.[10]

In 1923, opponents of teaching evolution scored their first win in Oklahoma. A bill on textbooks that overwhelmingly cleared both chambers of the legislature included an amendment that stated, "Provided, further, that no copyright shall be purchased, nor textbook adopted that teaches the 'materialistic conception of history' (i.e.) the Darwin theory of creation vs. the Bible account of creation." In March 1923, Governor John Walton signed the first law in the nation opposing teaching evolution in public schools.[11]

Responding to concerned voters and churches, state officials, including governors, found ways to chip away at the teaching of evolution. For example, at the start of 1924, North Carolina governor Cameron Morrison removed two biology textbooks from the public school curriculum because they incorporated discussions of evolution. Morrison did not want to see textbooks with "a picture of a monkey and a man on the same page" and ensured the state government followed suit.

"One of those books teaches that man is descended from a monkey and the other that he is a cousin to the monkey. I don't believe either one of them," Morrison told members of the press.

"You don't think much of evolution?" one of the reporters asked.

"I believe in evolution if you will let me define evolution. Evolution is progress, and I believe in the development of man from a lower form of human life to a higher. I don't believe in any missing links.

"If there were any such thing as a missing link, why don't they keep making them?"[12]

North Carolina was not alone. Throughout the 1920s, every state in the South except Virginia saw legislative efforts to stop the teaching of evolution in public schools. The issue was not limited to the South, despite Clarence Darrow's insistence that the only reason the bill failed in Kentucky was "it seemed to be too far North."[13] The debate spread across the country as the state legislatures of California, Delaware, Minnesota, New Hampshire, and North Dakota voted on bills on teaching evolution.[14]

In 1924, the issue came to Tennessee, thanks to the Reverend W. L. Murray, a Nashville preacher who, once a month, took to the pulpit at the Primitive Baptist Church in Lafayette, a small town just north of Hartsville and right below the Kentucky border. John Washington Butler, a farmer who served as a state representative, heard Murray preach against evolution and read Darwin and some of the arguments against teaching evolution. Taking the stump in fall 1924 as he ran for a second term, Butler promised voters that he "would introduce a bill to stop the teaching of evolution." Once he won reelection, Butler did just that.[15]

When he returned to Nashville, Butler introduced a proposal "prohibiting the teaching of the Evolution Theory in all the Universities, and all other public schools of Tennessee, which are supported in whole or in part by the public school funds of the State, and to provide penalties for the violations thereof." The bill made it "unlawful for any teacher in any of the Universities, Normals and all other public schools of the State which are supported in whole or in part by the public school funds of the State, to teach any theory that denies the Story of the Divine Creation of man as taught in the Bible, and to teach instead that man has descended from a lower order of animals." Butler's bill ensured "any teacher found guilty of the violation of this Act, shall be guilty of a misdemeanor and upon conviction, shall be fined not less than one hundred ($100) dollars, nor more than five hundred ($500) dollars, for each offense."[16]

A reporter from the *New York Times* met Butler in the summer of 1925 and found the state legislator to be quiet and "deeply religious" while insisting "there is nothing of the bigot in his manner." Still, when

Butler defended his bill, he relied on fiery rhetoric: "The Bible is the foundation upon which our American government is built. The evolutionist who denies the biblical story of creation, as well as other biblical accounts, cannot be a Christian." Evolution, claimed Butler, "goes hand in hand with modernism, makes Jesus Christ a fakir, robs the Christian of his hope, and undermines the foundation of our government."[17]

With Butler championing the bill in the state house, state senator John Shelton introduced the companion measure in the upper chamber. Butler had an easy time getting his proposal through the house, moving it through on a 71–5 vote at the end of January 1925. Shelton had a more challenging time getting his proposal through the senate. He reached out to Billy Sunday, William Jennings Bryan, and other national religious and political figures for help. Some of them pitched in, and Sunday kicked off a series of events and meetings in Memphis, where he praised the legislators for taking "action against that godforsaken gang of evolutionary cutthroats." During his two-and-a-half-week campaign in Memphis, around two hundred people came out to hear Sunday and his crusade against evolution. The state senate fell in line, passing Shelton's bill on a 24–6 vote in the middle of March,[18] as Sunday's influence helped push the bill over the finish line.[19]

If the bill garnered little opposition in the legislature, some local editors colorfully expressed their displeasure with it. The *Chattanooga Times* called out Bryan and backers of the Butler Act in a memorable editorial: "Perhaps if there is any other being entitled to share Mr. Bryan's satisfaction at this Tennessee legislature it is the monkey. Surely if the human race is accurately represented by that portion of it in the Tennessee House of Representatives, the monkey has a right to rejoice that the human race is no kin to the monkey race." Other newspapers across Tennessee called for the law to be "booted into a waste basket."[20]

Once the bill cleared both chambers, it was sent to Governor Austin Peay. While best known today for the state university that bears his name, Peay ranks as one of the most prominent governors in Tennessee's history. Elected in 1922, the new governor promised to reform the state, and he followed through. During his two full terms in office, Peay streamlined the state government, lowered residential property taxes while raising them on businesses, and, by implementing a tax on gas and car registrations, vastly expanded the number of paved roads across the Volunteer State. Before Peay was elected, Tennessee had less than 250 miles of paved roads. When he died in office in 1927, Tennessee had more than 4,000 miles of paved roads. He also untangled the knotty problem of the state's debt and had the state operating in the black during his four and a half years as governor.[21]

Peay also left his mark on education. In the same year that he signed the Butler Act into law, Peay also oversaw one of the most substantial education reforms in Tennessee's history. Under Peay, the school year expanded to eight months, and schools throughout the state from rural areas to cities received more funds. Teachers also saw their pay increase and their salaries come to them on a regular schedule, though they, in turn, had to become more professional, including obtaining licenses. Even though he signed the Butler Act, Peay was no mere reactionary beholden to fundamentalist voters.[22]

Despite his progressive credentials, Peay, much like William Jennings Bryan, tried to balance his liberal politics with his faith. The governor always considered himself to be an "old-fashioned Baptist" at heart, and he warned college students about the dangers posed by "scientists and cranks" who spread doubt. "The Christian faith of our people is the bedrock of our institutions," Peay insisted.[23]

With the bill on Peay's desk, prominent figures and organizations lobbied the governor on what to do with it. The Science League of America and other groups across the nation called on him to veto the bill, and some religious and education leaders in Tennessee, including the Episcopal bishop and the president of Fisk University, urged the governor not to sign it. However, Peay heard more from supporters of the Butler Act, while the leadership of the University of Tennessee remained silent about it. Insisting the bill was not "going to be an active statute," Peay signed it into law.[24]

Peay and the legislators drew criticism at the national level, including from Clarence Darrow. After his work on the Scopes Trial, Darrow ripped into the governor for signing the law. Peay "wanted to veto it, but did not have the courage," Darrow insisted. "So he contented himself by saying that he did not believe that it would amount to anything." Darrow attacked the law as "silly and senseless" since Tennessee schools "were teaching that the earth was round instead of flat, and the day and night were due to the revolution of the earth on its axis and not from the sun and moon going around it." Offering his usual jaded take on religion, Darrow insisted all these lessons "are flat contrary to Genesis and, in fact, they refute the Bible account much more clearly than does the doctrine of evolution."[25]

While Peay did not think much of the new law and thought it would not impact Tennessee, attorneys, activists, educators, the media, and organizations from across the nation started examining it. During the spring of 1925, the American Civil Liberties Union (ACLU), which had doubled down on its support of academic freedom the year before, gave the new Tennessee law more and more of its attention. On the other side, Bryan and other critics of evolution celebrated the law and continued to defend it. More than a few experts realized that a high-stakes fight over the law was coming.[26]

Like Governor Peay, John Washington Butler did not think the law would have much of an impact outside Tennessee. "I never had any idea my bill would make a fuss," Butler admitted that summer. "I just thought it would become a law and that everybody would abide by it and that we wouldn't hear any more of evolution in Tennessee."[27]

But despite what Butler thought, Tennessee—and the rest of the country—was about to hear a lot more of evolution as the nation debated the law he'd proposed thanks to a trial in Dayton.

"We've Just Arrested a Man for Teaching Evolution"

G eorge Washington Rappleyea could never seem to sit still. Originally from New York, Rappleyea spoke with an odd accent—John Scopes thought he was a Cajun—and his five-and-a-half-foot frame was always in motion. He walked quickly, always giving the impression that he was consumed with nervous energy. He was in his early thirties when he made his contribution to history.[1]

Rappleyea had reason to be nervous. A mining engineer who managed properties held by the Cumberland Coal and Iron Company, he had a front-row seat to watch Dayton's continued economic decline. While he might always have been in motion, Rappleyea had established something close to roots in southeastern Tennessee. He had met his wife, a nurse, in Chattanooga while he had been her patient, and they often held parties in their home in Dayton.[2]

A Methodist who had no problems accepting both his Christian faith and evolution, on May 4, 1925, Rappleyea read the *Chattanooga Daily Times*—and his lively mind went into overdrive as he came up with a plan to help Dayton's struggling economy.

In that edition of the paper, the American Civil Liberties Union (ACLU) ran a news release about the recent state law prohibiting teaching evolution in public schools. The release could easily have been mistaken for an ad or a post in the classifieds: "We are looking for a Tennessee teacher who is willing to accept our services in testing this law in the courts. Our lawyers think that a friendly test case can be arranged without costing a teacher his or her job. Distinguished counsel have volunteered their services. All we need now is a willing client."

Looking up from his paper, a smile on his face and a gleam in his eye, Rappleyea started putting a plan together to put Dayton back on the map—and end its economic problems.[3]

During World War I, the Wilson administration had cracked down on free speech, including antiwar protesters. Eugene Debs, the labor organizer whom Clarence Darrow had represented in the aftermath of the Pullman Strike, had served more than two years in prison for speaking out against the war. Led by Roger Nash Baldwin and Crystal Eastman, defenders of conscientious objectors during World War 1 and champions of civil rights and the First Amendment formed the National Civil Liberties Bureau (NCLB) in 1917 to advocate for free speech. After the war ended, the organization grew, and in 1920, the NCLB renamed itself the ACLU.[4]

As the ACLU established itself in the 1920s in the aftermath of the war and the Red Scare that followed it, many prominent attorneys were drawn to the group. Arthur Garfield Hays and Clarence Darrow soon found themselves working alongside the organization. With the new law banning the teaching of evolution taking effect in Tennessee, the ACLU quickly decided to take the case. As the ad noted, they just needed to find a teacher willing to challenge the law—and George Rappleyea had one in mind.[5]

Rappleyea had several reasons for wanting to challenge the evolution law in Dayton. He recognized that holding the trial would put Dayton on the map and help local businesses by giving the town some much-needed publicity. With Chattanooga turning down the chance to host a challenge to the Butler Act, Rappleyea wanted to move quickly and bring the national spotlight to Dayton before another town tried to claim it. Rappleyea pitched the idea to F. E. "Doc" Robinson, the owner of a local drugstore and the chairman of the Rhea County School Board. Robinson listened and soon found himself drawn to the idea.

With their plan in place, Rappleyea and Robinson reached out to local attorneys. First, they contacted the town attorneys, a pair of brothers named Herbert and Sue Hicks. (Sue Hicks had been named after his mother, who died in childbirth.) After listening to Rappleyea and Robinson, the Hicks brothers agreed to prosecute the case, provided they could settle on a defendant. Wallace Haggard, a local attorney whose father owned a bank, agreed to help the Hicks brothers. All they needed now was to find a teacher who had lectured on evolution.[6]

Rappleyea had already been thinking about having John Scopes, a young educator who was better known for coaching the football and baseball teams than for his work in the classroom, as the defendant. Scopes had been to Rappleyea's house for a few parties, but they were not close by any means.

"Rappleyea already knew me as an independent thinker, and he knew that I had subbed as a biology teacher during that spring," Scopes noted in the autobiography he wrote four decades later. "He reasoned that, if Doc Robinson asked me, I would agree to become a defendant in a test case. Relying upon this analysis of my character, he convinced the businessmen of the town that the publicity of such a case would put Dayton on the map and benefit business. His was a convincing argument and the businessmen went along with it."[7]

May 5, the day after Rappleyea had read the ACLU's call for teachers in Tennessee to challenge the law, proved warm, though summer, with its scorching heat, had not yet hit Dayton. With the school term already over, John Scopes lingered in town, putting off his plans to visit his parents in Kentucky. Looking back four decades later, Scopes wrote that he stayed in Dayton that summer because two of his students had just been in a car accident and were still recovering. Just as important, as he later confessed, Scopes was getting close with a "beautiful blonde" who had shown some interest in him.[8]

On that Tuesday afternoon, Scopes was playing tennis with a few students when a little boy called out to him, "Mr. Robinson says, if it's convenient, for you to come down to the drugstore." Thinking Robinson wanted to talk about matters related to the school, Scopes, still in his sweaty tennis clothes, walked the three-quarters of a mile to the drugstore. When he got there, he found himself facing some of the leading men in Dayton.[9]

Robinson and Rappleyea sat at a table in front of the soda fountain with the Hicks brothers and Wallace Haggard. Other businessmen also sat around the table, including another drugstore owner and a postman. Scopes recalled only half a dozen men around the table, but at least nine men later claimed to have been there and took part in a photo reenacting the moment.[10]

Robinson urged Scopes to sit down, and Rappleyea started the conversation:

"John, we've been arguing. I said that nobody could teach biology without teaching evolution." A confused Scopes agreed, and Rappleyea pointed to a shelf full of textbooks, including *Civic Biology* by George William Hunter. Rhea County relied on the drugstore to distribute its textbooks.

Scopes got the book down from the shelf and went through it with Rappleyea while the other men peered down on its pages. "You have been teaching 'em this book?" Rappleyea asked.

"Yes." Scopes told the men that he had taught about evolution when he substituted for the regular biology teachers. "Rappleyea's right. You can't teach biology without teaching evolution. This is the text, and it explains evolution."

"Then you've been violating the law," Robinson said.

Scopes froze. While he was familiar with the Butler Act, as he noted in his autobiography, he "never worried about it" and wasn't sure of its technicalities. He insisted that other teachers had also taught evolution from the same book. "There's our text, provided by the state," Scopes pointed out. "I don't see how a teacher can teach biology without teaching evolution."

Robinson handed Scopes the newspaper that Rappleyea had read the day before, and Scopes read the blurb from the ACLU looking for teachers.

"John, would you be willing to stand for a test case?" Robinson asked. "Would you be willing to let your name be used?"

In retrospect, this was the turning point of John Scopes's life. After that moment, he would no longer be an obscure teacher in a small town, coaching mediocre baseball and football teams in this quiet part of Tennessee.

But Scopes showed no hesitation. Looking back at this moment, Scopes insisted he dreamed of a chance to make his mark on the world—and this was his opportunity.

"I realized that the best time to scotch the snake is when it starts to wiggle," Scopes wrote. "The snake already had been wiggling a good long time."

Sitting at the table in the drugstore, sipping the soda Robinson had offered him, Scopes made the decision that changed his life.

"If you can prove that I've taught evolution, and that I can qualify as a defendant, then I'll be willing to stand trial," Scopes finally said.

As the other men asked him what he had taught in the biology class, Scopes said he had reviewed the final exam material for the students. He wasn't sure if he had taught evolution to them or not.

"Robinson and the others apparently weren't concerned about this technicality," Scopes later remembered. "I had expressed willingness to stand trial. That was enough."

With Scopes agreeing to stand trial, Robinson broke the news to the world. He left the table and walked over to the telephone to call a newspaper in Chattanooga: "This is F. E. Robinson in Dayton. I'm chairman of the school board here. We've just arrested a man for teaching evolution."

The arrested man, Scopes, finished up his drink and went back to his tennis match.[11]

———

News quickly spread that Dayton would be the scene of a trial focused on the Butler Act. After calling the paper in Chattanooga, Robinson reached out to the *Nashville Banner*. Rappleyea responded to the ad the ACLU had run in the Chattanooga paper, sending a telegraph to let the organization know that Scopes would be prosecuted for teaching evolution. Sure enough, the next morning, the *Nashville Banner* ran a front-page story on the case, noting that the ACLU would handle the expenses for both the prosecution and the defendant. The *Banner* misidentified Scopes as the "head of the science department of the Rhea County high school," while trumpeting Rappleyea, the "manager of the Cumberland Coal and Iron Co.," as the man who had charged the teacher with breaking the law. The Associated Press and other outlets soon picked up the news, and word of the trial quickly spread across the country.[12]

Scopes wasn't particularly surprised to see the mining engineer garner some publicity in the first accounts of the trial. While he was not sure how Rappleyea would personally benefit from the trial, Scopes suspected that "he hoped to open up the Tennessee coal business or win some new industry as a result." Still, Scopes knew Rappleyea well enough to know "he wouldn't have done the things he did if he hadn't had an angle."[13]

With his lively mind and strong personality, Rappleyea was always full of ideas. Despite his short frame, messy hair, and thick glasses, the engineer had charisma. A born promoter and booster, Rappleyea's angle should have been fairly obvious. Dayton had seen better days and was missing out on the economic boom of the 1920s. With coal companies and mining operations continuing to shut down across the region, Dayton faced challenges. The boom of the 1880s—which had seen the town grow from three hundred residents at the start of the decade to more than twenty-seven hundred in the area by the end of it—had long since passed. When the Dayton Coal and Iron Company (DCIC) went under in 1913, Dayton lost its primary source of income and jobs. Rappleyea and the rest of the leadership of the Cumberland Coal and Iron Company tried to hold on as best they could running the remains of DCIC, but Dayton continued to shrink. By 1920, the town's population had fallen to eighteen hundred.[14]

Rappleyea wanted to boost the town's economy—and he and other business leaders gambled that being in the national spotlight in the debate on evolution would lead to more jobs and opportunities. And John Scopes—an unassuming, university-educated, ordinary young man—was the perfect protagonist to ensure Dayton would not be seen as a backwater town full of hillbillies and fundamentalists.

"An Ordinary Young Man Comes to Dayton"

Overshadowed by larger-than-life figures such as Clarence Darrow and William Jennings Bryan, John T. Scopes was overlooked even at the trial that bore his name.

Scopes's unassuming appearance ensured he didn't stand out in a crowd. Despite being only in his midtwenties, his hairline was already receding, and his closely cropped hair made his already prominent ears stick out more. With eyeglasses perched over his protruding nose, Scopes did not garner much attention. But this ordinary man was, as he noted in the title of his autobiography, the "center of the storm." While much of his existence before the trial mirrored that of many ordinary Americans, some strands of Scopes's life led him to his brief time in history's spotlight in Dayton.

Some four decades after the trial that made him famous, Scopes pondered his connection with Darrow. Cheerfully admitting that, outside of his father, no man influenced him as much as Darrow, Scopes noted that the legendary attorney had taught him "that a man is the sum of his heredity and his environment." All those years later, Scopes found himself agreeing with Darrow but adding another factor into the mix: "My own life is a study in environment, heredity, and chance."[1]

Born in Paducah, Kentucky, in 1900, Scopes was the son of a railroad machinist who was a minor labor leader. Reviewing his father's life, Scopes insisted that he was shaped by the 1894 railroad strike, the same event that helped make Clarence Darrow a household name.[2] Scopes always remembered his father as a consummate reader, whose taste ran from Charles Dickens to scientific books, including the works of Charles Darwin. "My father had read to me from Charles Darwin's *Origin of the Species*, *Descent of Man*, and *The Voyage of the Beagle*, which I had then finished reading for myself," Scopes wrote. "Although not a trained scholar, I thought Darwin was right. It was the only plausible explanation of man's long and tortuous journey to his present physical and mental development."[3]

Whatever his father's lessons, Scopes enjoyed a quiet childhood, spending it in Paducah before moving to Danville, Illinois, when he was thirteen. While not as grand as Chicago, some 140 miles to the north, Danville, located in the central part of the Land of Lincoln near the Indiana border, offered a different world to young John. There he fell in love with movies and watching vaudeville comedians. Perhaps more important, he experienced the world beyond a small town such as Paducah, including integrated schools. While both towns had around twenty-five thousand residents in 1910, Danville was booming—growing 70 percent in the past decade. That offered a very different dynamic from what young Scopes had experienced in Paducah. However, the Black students remained segregated in their own row in the class and, since John and his sister came from the South, they were seated right behind them, a detail that Scopes remembered fifty years later: "Those four seats in the stronghold of the egalitarian North taught me early in life that hypocrisy and prejudice have no Mason-Dixon line but flourish in all locales in all seasons, and that the evils of self-righteousness, in its many guises, go endless on."[4]

Still a teenager, John's family moved again, heading 160 miles to the southwest to Salem, Illinois. In his memoirs, Scopes stressed that Salem was not New Salem, where Abraham Lincoln spent some of his formative years. But another politician hailed from Salem, one who would play a large part in Scopes's life—William Jennings Bryan. John lived in Salem after Bryan's three presidential campaigns and his stint as Woodrow Wilson's secretary of state, but Bryan remained beloved in his hometown. "Salem especially idolized Bryan and he spoke there frequently, giving me an opportunity to study at leisure the man who would later inspire and assist in my prosecution," Scopes wrote. While finishing high school in Salem, young John heard Bryan speak several times.[5]

John flourished in Salem. He and his father both enjoyed the town library's impressive collection of books, especially the works of Dickens, Jack London, and Mark Twain. Despite his small frame, John made the basketball team in his senior year, only to be kicked off it when he was caught at a saloon. Looking back at his youth, Scopes admitted he used to sneak off to have a beer while in high school, the slow start of what became a problem throughout his life. Besides sports, which grew increasingly important to him, during his high school years John also started questioning religion, leaving the Presbyterian Church after a local minister tried to convince the young men in his Sunday school class about the evils of cities, painting all of the inhabitants of them as sexual deviants. Having broken with the church, John kept goading the local faithful. When he graduated from high school in 1919, having been too young to enlist for World War I, John led his friends to make fun of a local minister who lisped through his false teeth when he spoke.

The graduating senior soon had another target when Bryan offered the commencement address. While conceding Bryan was "probably the best orator that America ever produced" and "one of the most perfect speakers I have heard," John and his friends laughed at the great man when he "made a pronounced whistling effect" when speaking. The laughter disrupted the event, upsetting school officials. Bryan was also not amused as he "stared hard at us and after he had his speech flowing evenly again his eyes would dart periodically at us, as if warning us to keep our silence thereafter." John and his gang remained quiet during the rest of the speech, but the moment had left its mark on him and on Bryan.

"The incident was so unusual, and possibly traumatic, that, to my surprise, Bryan remembered it six years later when I next saw him in Dayton," Scopes recalled. He had learned that Bryan, whatever his gifts as a speaker and a political leader, was like a heavyweight prospect with lots of speed and power but saddled with a glass jaw. Bryan simply could not take a punch.[6]

After graduating from high school, Scopes saved money from working for the railroad and other odd jobs to start college that fall at the University of Illinois at Urbana. After a year, following some severe illness, Scopes transferred to the University of Kentucky. While studying at the university, Scopes grew friendly with some of the science faculty and learned more about evolution. With dreams of going to law school, Scopes graduated with a BA in law and minored in geology. However, other illnesses put on hold his ambition of pursuing a graduate education.[7]

Scopes attended the University of Kentucky at an exciting time as the school looked to make significant reforms and become one of the country's leading public universities. Much of the credit for that belongs to Frank McVey, who took over as the university's president after serving a decade as the University of North Dakota's president. Starting at Lexington in 1917, McVey led the university, which had become bogged down in financial problems and was hindered by too much nepotism, in a bold, new direction.[8]

McVey also led the charge in the Bluegrass State to teach evolution in public schools. He grew politically active, and in 1922 he and several of his faculty members went all out to help defeat a bill in the Kentucky legislature to stop the teaching of evolution in public schools. The proposal went down by one vote, thanks largely to McVey's efforts and the help of faculty members such as William Funkhouser, who taught biology, Glanville Terrell, a professor of philosophy, and Arthur Miller, who specialized in geology and evolution.[9]

At least one student at the University of Kentucky was taking notes. Scopes studied under Funkhouser and praised him: "He taught zoology so flawlessly that there was no need to cram for the final examination; at the end of the term there was a thorough, fundamental grasp of the subject in bold relief in the student's mind, where Funkhouser had left it." The young student also studied under both Terrell and Miller, calling them "two of my favorite teachers," but Scopes also called them unflattering nicknames. Miller was dubbed Monks thanks to his teaching evolution, an easy label and one that would garner more fame with the Scopes Monkey Trial.[10]

Still planning to go to law school, Scopes completed the paperwork to participate in the University of Kentucky's teacher-placement program. After losing its coach in the summer of 1924, going through the poll of candidates from both the University of Tennessee and the University of Kentucky, Rhea County reached out to Scopes, offering him $150 a month to teach math and science while also coaching football, basketball, and baseball. Having never played sports in college and having only been on his high school basketball team for a single year, Scopes was surprised by the offer. "They had decided to gamble on me in spite of my lack of a college athletic record," he wrote four decades later. "I had played basketball in high school and had a good background in mathematics, physics, and chemistry, and that apparently satisfied them. It was my best offer and I accepted it." His dreams of going to law school were put on hold for the moment.[11]

So, in the summer of 1924, Scopes began working at Rhea Central High School in Dayton. Founded in 1906, the school had slowly grown over its first two decades. In 1907, only three students graduated in the school's first senior class. But after operating under its founding principal, J. C. Fooshee, for fifteen years, the school started to flourish under W. F. Ferguson, bringing in a new auditorium in 1920 and expanding its athletic programs. Ferguson was still serving as principal when Scopes started working at the school.[12]

At the start, Scopes thought he had made the right decision. As he got to know the area and its citizens better, Scopes "enjoyed the people and my job from the beginning" and found Dayton to be a "tranquil place," but he quickly learned of the various cliques of the residents. With no chamber of commerce, Scopes realized the local businessmen would meet around tables at the country club or, as he would famously discover, at a drugstore. But luckily, through his role as a teacher and a coach, Scopes soon found himself accepted by every social circle in town, becoming friendly with George W. Rappleyea, Ben McKenzie, and other town leaders.[13]

During his time in Dayton, Scopes stayed at a boardinghouse owned by Bill Bailey, who was also the proprietor of the largest hardware store in the area. The house stood at the corner of Fourth Avenue and Market Street, not too far from downtown. From the front porch of the house, Scopes could see the county courthouse, which would soon become famous across the nation.[14] Despite Bailey's being a "quiet man who ruled his family with an iron hand," Scopes liked his landlord, though he was always puzzled why Bailey collected pencil stubs. Scopes ate with the Baileys and appreciated their helping him out during his first months in Dayton.[15]

In his new role, Scopes quickly learned that "coaching was the most important part of my job" and focused on the football team. With his lack of experience and having "claimed no profound insight into the mysteries of football," Scopes often found himself bombarded with unsolicited advice from former players who continued to live in Dayton. Still, the team successfully went 6-4 in his sole season as the coach. In the summer of 1924, right after he graduated from the University of Kentucky and in the first weeks of his new job, a year before Scopes became a household name, the team posed for a photo. Sitting on a staircase, the group of clean-cut young men—all white since they attended a segregated school—do not leave much of an impression on the modern viewer. Even among his players, Scopes largely failed to stand out. Sitting on one side in the back row of the photo, Scopes could easily be overlooked, as so often happened in his life. Only his skinny tie and receding hairline distinguished him from the young men on the team.[16]

Looking back some four decades later, Scopes realized, even with his admitted lack of football experience, he had "a fairly easy time of it" as he coached the team in the fall of 1924. Rhea County almost upset "the team that became runner-up to the state champion" thanks to "one unlucky break." Scopes thought both the football team and the basketball team he also coached "worked hard . . . and took direction as well as any coach could expect." Reflecting on his football coaching career, Scopes found it a "satisfying though sometimes harrowing season" with "pleasant memories" and a "windfall of friendships that have survived the decades."[17]

Despite Dayton's being a small town, with only around seventeen hundred residents in the 1920 census, though more people lived outside the city limits, Scopes enjoyed his life there. He joined other young people at the weekly dances, dating a few local girls who had just graduated from high school. Too far removed in age to be too friendly with his fellow teachers after hours, Scopes often encountered his students in his social efforts. Not surprisingly in a small town, most of his social life in Dayton revolved around the local churches. Despite not having been an avid churchgoer during his time in Kentucky and Illinois, Scopes started attending, especially since, as a teacher, he was expected to, and it was the best way he could see all of his friends. "I had one of the best attendance records of my life that year," Scopes wrote about his experiences at the end of 1924 and the start of 1925. "I went to church every Sunday. Of course, everyone else did too; there was nowhere else to go on that day of rest." Looking back at his church attendance in Dayton, Scopes never wrote about any religious or spiritual reasons why he spent his Sundays in the pews.[18]

At Rhea County High School, Scopes concentrated more on coaching than teaching. He tried to avoid the weekly assemblies where students would hear from local business leaders who talked about their efforts to improve Dayton, at those times even letting some of the students hang out with him in the labs in the school's basement while he smoked cigarettes. As much as he enjoyed the town and its community, Scopes rolled his eyes at these speakers and their efforts to boost Dayton. "Anyone capable of thought could see that no individual had made that much of a dent in Dayton's living pattern," Scopes wrote. "The morning after an assembly Dayton would be exactly the same as it had been the year before and the year before that. The directors did not let that discourage them; each week's program relentlessly followed its predecessor, echoing the same fulsome words and similarly meaningless metaphors."[19] Yet Scopes would end up entangled in the town boosters' efforts to garner publicity for Dayton—and he ended up paying a steep price.

Outside of former football players offering coaching advice, Scopes found that he had a great deal of freedom. "Most of the people in Dayton didn't care what we did," he remembered. "Only a few of the Fundamentalists complained that we should conform to what was expected of us and attend the assembly programs instead of our ungodly, smoke-filled lab periods." Ignoring his religious critics, Scopes kept letting the students hang out in the basement while he continued to smoke.

Fittingly enough, considering he coached baseball, Scopes was the faculty's utility infielder, playing in whichever role he was needed. His duties included monitoring study halls, where the students often grew unruly. Scopes was a disciplinarian, making sure students stayed in line. After one of his football players would not stop throwing things in a study hall, Scopes took an eraser and "clobbered the boy on the head so fiercely the clout echoed throughout the study hall." When reflecting on the incident, Scopes showed no regrets over getting physical with the student. "Order had been restored, unorthodox though my method had been," Scopes wrote. "It was the last time I had any discipline trouble at Central High."[20]

Despite his limited experience, Scopes showed in his first year of teaching at Dayton that he had the makings of a valuable, even excellent, educator. But not much else stood out about the young newcomer to town. Before a fateful May afternoon when he met with Rappleyea and other local businessmen, Scopes lived an ordinary life, no different from those of many of his fellow Americans of his generation emerging after the chaos and changes in the aftermath of both World War I and the influenza epidemic. Beyond annoying Bryan at his high school graduation, Scopes did not stand out from the crowd except in one crucial area—persistence. While he might have drifted during his first three years in college, he finished his degree, showing a good deal of focus and hard work. In his first year teaching and coaching in Dayton,

Scopes found he had a knack for connecting with students, and even with his lack of experience with football, he enjoyed coaching.

In the 1950s, many years after leaving Dayton, while living in Shreveport, Louisiana, Scopes got a call at the office.

"Hello, Coach?" a man with a Southern accent asked.

Scopes was taken aback, since he had not been called Coach in almost thirty years. On the line was Luke Welch, who'd played left guard under Coach Scopes. Welch was passing through Shreveport on his way to Waco, Texas, where his namesake son played at Baylor. Welch's son would be drafted by the Los Angeles Rams in the tenth round in 1952.

Hanging up the phone after talking with the elder Welch, Scopes found himself happy with his connection to the young football player.

"I hadn't produced an all-American, which may have been my fault; at least one of my players, however, had fathered a 'gridder' of some regional note, a fact bringing its own peculiar satisfaction," Scopes wrote. "Luke's call was one of the pleasant reflections that Dayton has cast on my life."[21]

That conversation summoned up fond memories of when Scopes had been a quiet, often-overlooked teacher and coach in a sleepy Tennessee town—before he stepped into the whirlwind of a national controversy.

"The Principles of Our Government and the Principles of Christian Faith"

William Jennings Bryan, like Lord Byron, as in his famed quote about himself, woke up one day and found himself famous—and that day was Thursday, July 9, 1896.

On that muggy day in Chicago, Bryan, who had served two terms as a representative in Congress but lost when he ran for the Senate in 1894, took his first bow on the national stage at the Democratic National Convention with one of the most powerful speeches in American political history—one that almost took him to the White House.

Vaulting out of nowhere, at age thirty-six the youngest man ever nominated by a major party for the presidency, Bryan defeated far-better-known candidates to claim victory at the Democratic convention after five ballots. Despite losing in the general election to William McKinley, Bryan remained a significant force in American politics and culture for the rest of his life, traveling across the globe to meet with famous figures such as the great Russian novelist Leo Tolstoy and shaping American foreign policy as Woodrow Wilson's secretary of state.

But Bryan always remembered his roots and, like his sometime ally and ultimate opponent Clarence Darrow, treasured the legacy left to him by his father. Born in Salem, Illinois, in 1860, more than fifty-five years before young John Scopes lived in the town, Bryan graduated at the top of his class at Illinois College. He studied law at Union Law College in Chicago, where he worked with Lyman Trumbull, one of his era's most powerful and principled senators. While Bryan learned a great deal from his professors and mentors, his father, Silas, had the most influence in shaping his son. A staunch Democrat in the tradition of Andrew Jackson, who championed the people over the powerful, Silas Bryan had a respectable political career, serving in the Illinois state senate and later as a circuit judge. More important, Silas showed young William that a man could rise in politics while embracing his faith. "My father was as much at home with ministers as he was politicians," Bryan later recalled. "He saw no necessary conflict—and I have never been able to see any—between the principles of our government and the principles of Christian faith."[1]

Moving to Nebraska to start his career since there were more opportunities in the Cornhusker State, Bryan followed in his father's footsteps regarding politics and their shared faith. Settling in Lincoln in 1887, Bryan flourished in one of the fastest-growing states in the nation, becoming one of the most prominent attorneys in Nebraska. Bryan remained focused on politics despite his blossoming legal career, stumping for Grover Cleveland and Democrats across Nebraska. He burst on the political scene in 1890 with the nation facing economic turmoil and debating trade and tariffs. Thanks to a series of solid performances in a series of debates, Bryan ran for Congress. He upset the Republican incumbent, becoming only the second Democrat to represent Nebraska in the House in the first quarter century of its statehood. Once on Capitol Hill, Bryan broke with Cleveland and more conservative Democrats, calling for more federal aid to farmers, lower tariffs, and championing the use of more silver instead of gold in the national currency. That last issue cost Bryan in 1894 when he ran for the Senate as the Cleveland administration and conservative Democrats helped sink his campaign.

A congenital optimist who always remained convinced he could sway crowds with his oratory, Bryan relied on his public speaking skills to rebound politically. After his defeat in the Senate race, Bryan crossed the nation on a speaking tour, generating attention as a potential dark horse presidential candidate in the early stages of the 1896 presidential election. But even with the Democrats keeping the two-thirds rule, ensuring that a supermajority of the delegates at the convention backed the presidential candidate, Bryan was not considered one of the top contenders for the nomination. After William McKinley easily wrapped up the Republican nomination, his campaign manager, Mark Hanna, expected Representative Richard Bland, who represented Missouri for a quarter century in Congress, to be the Democrat the Republicans would face in November. When Hanna's aide Charles Dawes—who many years later, as Calvin Coolidge's running mate, would clash with Bryan and his brother Charlie in the 1924 presidential election—suggested Bryan could win the nomination, Hanna dismissed the possibility.[2]

But then came that muggy Thursday in Chicago.

Democrats from the South and the West clashed with supporters of the Cleveland administration over monetary policy as the supporters of "free silver" clashed with the "goldbugs" on the party platform. Convinced that he could win the nomination if the convention heard him speak, Bryan, who was there as a delegate, had been biding his time, letting other supporters of silver stumble before the convention crowd. Bryan confidently told his friends and allies that he would offer the speech of his life and win the nomination—which is exactly what happened.

Speaking on the rather mundane subject of monetary policy, Bryan electrified the crowd with his rhetoric, tying together the strands that would chart his political course for almost thirty years as he defended ordinary Americans and extolled Christianity as an active force in the public square. "If they dare to come out in the open field and defend the gold standard as a good thing, we shall fight them to the uttermost, having behind us the producing masses of the nation and the world," Bryan said in some of the most celebrated political rhetoric in American history. "Having behind us the commercial interests and the laboring interests and all the toiling masses, we shall answer their demands for a gold standard by saying to them, you shall not press down upon the brow of labor this crown of thorns. You shall not crucify mankind upon a cross of gold."

The crowd went wild—and Bryan became a household name. With none of the candidates winning a two-thirds majority on the first four votes at the convention, Bryan won the Democratic nomination on the fifth ballot. While he lost to McKinley in November, Bryan effectively ended the dull, static politics of the Gilded Age, where candidates from both parties praised business interests. Bryan represented the farmers and workers who had been hit hard by the economic downturn. Candidates had traditionally refused to actively campaign for the presidency. But Bryan altered history and stumped the nation, thrilling crowds with his oratory. Most defeated presidential candidates faded from the public scene, but after losing to McKinley, nobody expected Bryan to vanish, especially as he was only thirty-six years old.[3]

Still, when the excitement had died down, more than a few observers recognized the limits of Bryan's oratory, including Clarence Darrow.[4]

═══

Unlike most politicians of his era, Bryan retained his popularity, even being a beloved figure in parts of the country, namely the South, the

West, and the Great Plains. Losing to McKinley again in their 1900 rematch and then getting bested by William Howard Taft in 1908 did nothing to dispel the Bryan magic. Even when he gave up his presidential ambitions, Bryan remained one of the most politically influential men in the country. He helped Woodrow Wilson defeat Tammany Hall and win the Democratic presidential nomination in 1912. After Wilson became the first Democrat since Cleveland to win the presidency, Bryan reaped the rewards, ending up in the cabinet as secretary of state. Even holding high office, though, Bryan placed his religious principles first. Fearing that Wilson was leading the nation into World War I, Bryan, a frequent critic of American imperialism and military actions, resigned his post in June 1915.

While he continued to support Wilson and stumped for him in his successful reelection campaign in 1916, Bryan changed direction after bowing out of the cabinet, growing less politically active and focusing more on other activities, including social issues, religion, and the Florida real estate boom. Despite his stances on evolution, Prohibition, and the need for more faith in politics, Bryan was not a conservative. Someone such as Bryan is almost impossible to comprehend in our polarized political age. He embraced liberal positions thanks mainly to his religious faith and continued commitment to Jeffersonian democracy. Bryan continued to champion average Americans, pushing for establishing a minimum wage, denouncing big business, and calling for an eight-hour workday. He saw both Prohibition and women's suffrage as linked, helping reform the nation and improve the lives of its inhabitants by having them live more moral, godly lives.[5]

Working with Billy Sunday, the former baseball player who became one of the most popular Christian evangelists at the start of the twentieth century, Bryan saw Prohibition and banning the sale of alcoholic beverages as instrumental to improving America's morals. He actively endorsed the Eighteenth Amendment to prohibit "the manufacture, sale, or transportation of intoxicating liquors within, the importation thereof into, or the exportation thereof from the United States and all the territory subject to the jurisdiction thereof for beverage purposes," which was proposed in 1917 and ratified less than two years later.

Even as he grew less active on the political stage, Bryan remained in touch with his supporters. In 1901, he launched the *Commoner*, a weekly newspaper he published out of Lincoln, which soon had tens of thousands of subscribers across the nation. For more than two decades, Bryan reached his backers through the paper, where he wrote about moral topics and the various issues of the day.[6] Bryan was also the star speaker on the Chautauqua circuit for almost twenty years, spending nearly every summer from 1904 until his death touring rural America, hitting the small towns as millions of Americans listened to him speak about ideals and his faith.[7]

Outside of the "Cross of Gold" speech, "The Prince of Peace" was Bryan's most famous oration, and he offered it dozens of times on the Chautauqua circuit. In it, he showcased much of what drove him. "I am interested in the science of government, but I am more interested in religion than in government. I enjoy making a political speech—I have made a good many and shall make more—but I would rather speak on religion than on politics," Bryan said at the start of this speech. "Government affects but a part of the life which we live here and does not deal at all with the life beyond, while religion touches the infinite circle of existence as well as the small arc of that circle which we spend on earth. No greater theme, therefore, can engage our attention. If I discuss questions of government, I must secure the cooperation of a majority before I can put my ideas into practice, but if, in speaking on religion, I can touch one human heart for good, I have not spoken in vain no matter how large the majority may be against me."

Drawing on Tolstoy, Bryan stressed the importance of religion and warned of the increasing number of "young men who think it smart to be skeptical; they talk as if it were an evidence of larger intelligence to scoff at creeds and to refuse to connect themselves with churches." Speaking to these young skeptics, Bryan insisted religion was a positive good and an essential part of human life, including serving as the bedrock of human morality. "Morality is the power of endurance in man; and a religion which teaches personal responsibility to God gives strength to morality. There is a powerful restraining influence in the belief that an all-seeing eye scrutinizes every thought and word and act of the individual."

But Bryan touched on more than morality in this famed address, which he repeated throughout the country every summer for almost twenty years. He also spoke about evolution and creationism, issues that were becoming increasingly more important in schools across America.

Bryan talked about his experiences as an undergrad in college when he "became confused by the different theories of creation," but, after studying them, his faith that God created the universe was only reinforced. "No matter how long you draw out the process of creation, so long as God stands back of it, you cannot shake my faith in Jehovah. In Genesis, it is written that, in the beginning, God created the heavens and the earth, and I can stand on that proposition until I find some theory of creation that goes farther back than 'the beginning.' We must begin with something—we must start somewhere—and the Christian begins with God."

Bryan laid out his opposition to evolution in the speech: "I do not carry the doctrine of evolution as far as some do; I am not yet convinced that man is a lineal descendant of the lower animals. I do not mean to find fault with you if you want to accept the theory; all I mean to say is that while you may trace your ancestry back to the monkey if you find pleasure or pride in doing so, you shall not connect me with your family tree without more evidence than has yet been produced. I object to the theory for several reasons. First, it is a dangerous theory. If a man links himself in generations with the monkey, it then becomes an important question whether he is going toward him or coming from him—and I have seen them going in both directions. I do not know of any argument that can be used to prove that man is an improved monkey that may not be used just as well to prove that the monkey is a degenerate man, and the latter theory is more plausible than the former.

"Go back as far as we may, we cannot escape from the creative act, and it is just as easy for me to believe that God created man as he is as to believe that, millions of years ago, He created a germ of life and endowed it with power to develop into all that we see today. I object to the Darwinian theory, until more conclusive proof is produced, because I fear we shall lose the consciousness of God's presence in our daily life, if we must accept the theory that through all the ages no spiritual force has touched the life of man or shaped the destiny of nations."

But there was more to his opposition to evolution. Bryan, the champion of the underdog, insisted that Darwinism "represents man as reaching his present perfection by the operation of the law of hate—the merciless law by which the strong crowd out and kill off the weak." He also argued that the theory of evolution discounted the possibility of divine action and miracles, which, he claimed, were core parts of the Christian faith. "Eliminate the miracles and Christ becomes merely a human being and His gospel is stripped of divine authority," Bryan insisted. While Bryan went on to talk about Christ, peace, and salvation, in "The Prince of Peace" he had argued against evolution to millions of listeners across the country.[8]

As the 1910s turned into the 1920s, Bryan grew less influential politically, even within the Democratic Party. In the 1920 presidential election, Bryan sat on the sidelines for the first time in decades, refusing to back Democratic nominee James Cox due to his opposition to Prohibition. While Bryan held Cox's running mate in high regard—an up-and-coming politician from New York by the name of Franklin Delano Roosevelt—he simply could not support the Democratic ticket.[9] As his political power waned, Bryan turned his attention more and more to various social and religious causes, including opposing the teaching of evolution in public schools.

Moving to Florida and into the Presbyterian Church's top ranks, including serving on critical committees, Bryan began hosting Bible classes in Miami, where he helped promote the growing real estate craze and offered more religious instructions. Bryan found the warm weather beneficial to his and his wife's health, and he saw the potential in the fast-growing Sunshine State. In the pages of the *Commoner* and in speaking to the Nebraska constitutional convention, Bryan insisted "godlessness" was "the greatest menace to the public school system today." Claiming that "we have allowed the moral influences to be crowded out" in the schools, Bryan said, "We do not ask public school teachers to teach religion in the schools, and teachers, paid by taxation, should not be permitted to attack our Bible in the schools."[10]

At the start of the 1920s, Bryan doubled down on his opposition to evolution, offering lectures that were printed and distributed across the nation in pamphlets titled such as "The Menace of Darwinism," "The Origin of Man," "In His Image," and "Back to God." Bryan also toured colleges as he grew increasingly alarmed about higher education, thinking it led America's future leaders to reject Christianity and religious values. Professors and teachers across the nation, and the National Education Association (NEA), pushed back against Bryan's take on evolution.[11] Bryan even tried to get the Presbyterian Church on the record as opposing teaching evolution. In 1923, while serving as a delegate to the General Assembly of the Presbyterian Church convention in Indianapolis, Bryan attempted to become the organization's moderator. He made the election for that post a contest about teaching evolution. While he led on the first two ballots, Bryan came up short, losing to Wooster College president Dr. Charles Wishart, who supported the teaching of evolution.[12]

Still, Bryan never let up, and his march against evolution saw the zeal that had led him to take on economic injustice and imperialism ignited once again for what was to be his final crusade. Looking back at his last years, Bryan's wife and closest adviser, Mary, noted, "His soul arose in righteous indignation when he found from the many letters he received from parents all over the country that state schools were being used to undermine the religious faith of their children."[13] No longer the handsome and dynamic figure of his youth, Bryan was now in his sixties and facing declining health, including obesity and diabetes. Despite that, he continued his efforts, becoming one of the leading evangelists in America and drawing the scorn of supporters of teaching evolution. The caustic Baltimore journalist H. L. Mencken, a gifted writer with a knack for the jugular, labeled Bryan "the Fundamentalist Pope." Despite speculation that he would run for president again, Bryan insisted he was more focused on religious matters and education. Bryan sensed that he was at the end of his life, and while he could not slow down his activities, he could focus on the faith-based ones instead of his political efforts.[14]

Bryan remained prominent on the public stage. He played an active part in the 1924 Democratic convention in New York, continuing his support for Prohibition and even generating whispers that he could claim the nomination one more time. Bryan didn't, but after the convention went on for more than two weeks and 103 ballots, his brother Charles, who had been one of the editors of the *Commoner* and was elected governor of Nebraska in 1922, ended up as eventual nominee John W. Davis's vice-presidential candidate. The Republican ticket ran over Davis and the younger Bryan in November, as Calvin Coolidge won in a landslide.[15]

Still, if William Bryan was disappointed—even if he was not particularly surprised—by the election results, he enjoyed some success in 1924. Growing more active and prosperous in Florida, he took his fight against teaching evolution to Tallahassee. Bryan wrote a resolution that passed the Florida legislature, which revealed why he so passionately opposed teaching evolution in public schools:

> Whereas, the public schools and colleges of this State, supported in whole or in part by public funds, should be kept free from any teachings designed to set up and promulgate sectarian views, and should also be equally free from teachings designed to attack the religious beliefs of the public. Therefore, it is the sense of the Legislature of the State of Florida that it is improper and subversive to the best interest of the people of this State for any professor, teacher or instructor in the public schools and colleges of this State, supported in whole or in part by public taxation, to teach or permit to be taught atheism or agnosticism or to teach as true Darwinism or any other hypothesis that links man in blood relationship to any other form of life.[16]

While Bryan got that resolution passed in Tallahassee, he and his allies experienced less success in Kentucky, where efforts to ban teaching evolution in the public schools came up short by one vote in the legislature. Bryan also took the fight to his critics in 1925, speaking against teaching evolution at Ivy League schools such as Brown and Harvard before turning his attention to events in Tennessee.

Bryan did not play much of a part as state representative John Washington Butler introduced a bill banning the teaching of evolution. Butler's bill quickly passed the Tennessee House of Representatives, and Bryan got involved as the legislation headed to the state senate. In a letter to his friend Tennessee state senator John Shelton, in February 1925, Bryan cited the success in Florida. He even pointed to the defeat of the similar bill in Kentucky, insisting that the proposal went down to defeat in the Bluegrass State thanks to the proposed monetary fine. Despite Bryan's opposition to the inclusion of the fine, the Tennessee Senate passed the bill and sent it to Governor Austin Peay's desk for his signature.[17]

As part of the city's leaders' efforts to bring national attention to Dayton, Sue Hicks, the brother of acting Rhea County attorney Herbert Hicks and an attorney himself, quickly recognized that having Bryan involved would lead to more publicity. Only twenty-nine, Sue Hicks would play a significant part in the Scopes Trial and also win himself an odd bit of fame. Hicks would be immortalized in Shel Silverstein's poem "A Boy Named Sue," which later became a top music hit for Johnny Cash. Like many who heard of Hicks, Silverstein was struck more by his first name than any other part of him.

With the ACLU ready to defend Scopes, Hicks reached out to Bryan, asking him to join the prosecution team.

"We have been trying to get in touch with you . . . to become associated with us in the prosecution of the case of the State against J. T. Scopes, charged with violation of the anti-evolution law," Hicks wrote Bryan. "We will consider it a great honor to have you with us in this prosecution. We will have no difficulty in obtaining the consent of the attorney general and the circuit judge for you to appear in the case."[18]

Bryan quickly accepted Hicks's offer and prepared to uphold the new law he had supported. Despite his continued poor health, Bryan headed to Dayton in his usual optimistic mood, once again ready to defend his supporters and the role of religion in the public square. He could not imagine that he would never leave Dayton and that his reputation as one of the most beloved political figures in American history would be left in tatters thanks to the Scopes Trial and Clarence Darrow.

9

"I Want Darrow"

Most of the American Civil Liberties Union board did not want Clarence Darrow to defend John Scopes. The ACLU's leadership insisted that Darrow would dominate the headlines. They feared that the essential points about free speech and the role of religion in public schools would be sidelined by his knack for publicizing himself. Even worse, they thought that Darrow would transform the trial into a circus.

But if the ACLU did not want Darrow, Scopes absolutely wanted the most famous lawyer in America on his defense team. Despite their commitment to reform and free speech, many of the ACLU's leaders raised their eyebrows and frowned as Darrow stepped forward to volunteer for the Scopes case.[1]

For his part, Darrow had been on the fence about continuing his legal career after saving Leopold and Loeb from the gas chamber. Now sixty-eight, he had been talking about retirement. But the moment William Jennings Bryan announced he would help the prosecution in Dayton, Darrow could not resist the chance to take on the Great Commoner. All Darrow's retirement talk ended as he grew progressively more interested in the Scopes case.

On May 13 at an appearance in Pittsburgh, Bryan told the world that he would represent the World Christian Fundamentals Association at the trial. Bryan had been working closely with that group since it was founded in 1919, and William Bell Riley, its president, reached out to ensure his friend would help with the prosecution. Once Bryan announced he would help the prosecution, Darrow quickly offered his service to Scopes and his defense team. "My object, and my only object, was to focus the attention of the country on the programme of Mr. Bryan and the other fundamentalists in America," Darrow insisted. "Education was in danger from the source that has always hampered it—religious fanaticism."

Pairing up with high-profile divorce lawyer Dudley Field Malone, Darrow reached out to John Randolph Neal, Scopes's counsel, via telegram. Darrow and Malone came out swinging at Bryan in their message, bashing him over living off his lecture fees and promoting real estate in Florida:

"We are certain you need no assistance in your defense of Professor Scopes, who is to be prosecuted for teaching evolution, but we have read the report that Mr. William Jennings Bryan has volunteered to aid the prosecution. In view of the fact that scientists are so much interested in the pursuit of knowledge that they can not make the money that lecturers and Florida real estate agents command, in case you should need us, we are willing, without fees or expenses, to help the defense of Professor Scopes in any way you may suggest or digest."

When Scopes heard about the offer, he simply could not believe it. Darrow and Malone's offer gave Scopes "my first knowledge that some Class-A sluggers were willing to champion our cause." Looking back at the case some four decades later, Scopes did not doubt that Darrow only took the case to take on Bryan.[2]

For his part, in his autobiography Darrow focused intensely on Bryan's activities against evolution far more than he did on any of creationism's other proponents. Dismissing Bryan as "like the traditional boy passing the graveyard at night" who "was whistling to keep up his courage," Darrow painted his opponent as a coward, out of touch with reality. "His very attitude showed that he was frightened out of his wits lest, after all, the illusions of his life might only be dreams." Darrow even went back to his childhood, contrasting his education and his parents' efforts to guide his reading to include Darwin and other scientists with how Bryan was raised. All of the threads in Darrow's life—his support of the underdog, his passion for justice, his commitment to free speech, and even his parents' unorthodox views—readied him for this moment. Having spared Leopold and Loeb from the death penalty, Darrow was ready to participate in another "trial of the century."[3]

The Scopes case, which Darrow had learned about during the American Psychological Association's meeting in Richmond that spring, drew more and more of his attention. Darrow and journalist H. L. Mencken, an outspoken critic of fundamentalists, the South, and Bryan, talked over the Butler Act prohibiting the teaching of evolution in Tennessee schools and the case in Dayton that resulted from it. Despite Mencken's pleas to take the case, Darrow had shrugged it off, insisting his agnosticism would ensure the ACLU would not want him on the case since it would turn the trial into a battle over religion in the public square.[4]

But now that Bryan was involved, Darrow relished the chance to take him on in a clash that would create controversy and command national attention.

Despite not being religious, Darrow painted the trial in stark, almost biblical, terms even as he realized it was more of a publicity stunt than a traditional legal proceeding. "It was perfectly clear that the proceedings bore little semblance to a court case, but I realized that there was no limit to the mischief that might be accomplished unless the country was roused to the evil at hand," Darrow wrote in his autobiography. "So I volunteered to go."[5]

But the ACLU was not sure it wanted Darrow for the case. It tried to find another attorney instead. When Scopes and Neal headed to New York in early June to confer with the ACLU, they met with some of the most prominent attorneys in the nation. The ACLU tried to find a lawyer who could argue the case at a high intellectual level, and they presented Scopes and Neal with the option of working with some weighty figures. Charles Evans Hughes, a former New York governor who had served as a justice of the Supreme Court and almost toppled Woodrow Wilson in the 1916 presidential election, drew consideration. So did Harvard law professor Felix Frankfurter, who would later serve on the nation's highest court. Also in the mix was Bainbridge Colby, who served as Wilson's secretary of state, just as Bryan had done.[6]

The ACLU wanted Colby to take the case with Hughes waiting in the wings if it got to the Supreme Court. But John Scopes had different plans. Even before they left for New York, Scopes told Neal he wanted Darrow to handle the case. To his credit, Neal agreed with his client and did not attempt to sway his decision. While seeing Colby as a "highly capable lawyer," Scopes did not think he would "make a favorable impression in a Tennessee mountain court or in a rough-and-tumble fight" since he was "too dignified." Going to New York, Scopes expected a "no-holds-barred match" against Bryan and the fundamentalists, which ruled out all of the lawyers—except Darrow. "It was going to be a down-in-the-mud fight and I felt the situation demanded a . . . fighter rather than someone who graduated from the proper military academy," Scopes wrote about why he chose Darrow.[7]

Once in New York, Scopes met with the ACLU board, and Malone went all out to convince Scopes to go with Darrow, who also attended the meeting.[8] While he had already decided to bring Darrow on, Scopes played his cards close to his chest, not revealing that he had already decided. Still, when Malone urged the ACLU's leadership to go with Darrow, he encountered heavy resistance, with many prominent men offering their takes on why Darrow was the wrong choice. "The arguments against Darrow were various," Scopes remembered, "that he was too radical, that he was a headline hunter, that the trial would become a circus, that with Darrow on the case, there would be no getting it into the federal courts." Darrow was seen as too hungry for the headlines and far more experienced in criminal courts than at the federal level. After the ACLU's board clashed over who should handle the case, Chairman Roger Baldwin turned to the defendant. Scopes stressed that the trial was already a circus and said he was preparing for a "gouging, roughhouse battle." Scopes knew whom he wanted to represent him and told the board, "I want Darrow."[9]

Still, despite what Scopes said, the ACLU continued to dither over who should represent the teacher. Refusing to take the case by himself, Malone continued to plead for Darrow, while Neal said he would be glad to have the help even as the board kicked over other names, including that of John W. Davis, who had served as solicitor general and lost to Calvin Coolidge in the 1924 presidential election when Charles Bryan was his running mate on the Democratic ticket. However, despite being one of the best lawyers in the nation, Davis expressed little interest, and other attorneys were considered. The meeting ended as Neal and Scopes had to catch a train to Baltimore.[10]

Just before boarding, Neal announced to the press that the defense team was in place. He would be joined by Darrow, Malone, Colby, and Samuel Rosensohn, an attorney who worked with the ACLU. But there would be some changes. Arthur Garfield Hays, one of the founders of the ACLU, would take over from Rosensohn. In the meantime, with Darrow garnering almost all of the spotlight, Baldwin and some of his staff stepped away and grew less involved, realizing the trial would not be a highbrow discussion of the role of free speech and religion. They realized that Darrow and his showmanship in the courtroom would eclipse all of their learned arguments.[11]

John Scopes, tasting fame for the first time, was not enjoying it. The *New York Times* reported that Scopes had turned down as much as $150,000 for the rights to make a movie based on his story. Scopes had also found himself far out of his depth in New York. Lost in Manhattan, he had arrived almost an hour late to a fundraiser the ACLU was having for his case. Sick of all the attention, Scopes headed home to Dayton, only to hear stories about violent arguments over the trial, including a rumor that someone had brandished a gun. Although Scopes discovered the incident was staged for publicity, the young teacher left Tennessee, heading to Paducah to spend time with his parents and enjoy some time out of the limelight. Little did Scopes know that these problems would plague him for the next four and a half decades.[12]

As Scopes encountered the pitfalls of fame, Dayton's leaders started to realize the trial would put the city on the map—but not necessarily in a good way. By the end of June, George Rappleyea, who had famously gathered the meeting at Robinson's Drug Store to use the trial to garner attention for the town, was drawing criticism for setting Scopes up in order to garner publicity for Dayton. Unable to keep quiet about his role in boosting the town, Rappleyea was forced to defend himself before the national media.

"While I originated the case and served at first as prosecutor in the matter, I did it from no ulterior motive," Rappleyea told the Associated Press. "My only object in the matter was to bring about a test of the evolution law.

Clarence Darrow and William Jennings Bryan, once friends, square off against one another in the Trial of the Century in 1925.

BELOW LEFT: 68-year-old Darrow was seated in the courtroom during the Scopes trial when this photograph was taken. America's most famous trial lawyer could command up to $200,000 in fees per case (more than $3 million in today's dollars). He offered to defend Scopes for free and spent his own money on trial expenses.

BELOW RIGHT: William Jennings Bryan in the courtroom during the Scopes trial, wearing his familiar pince-nez spectacles. He was a gifted orator, three-time Democratic presidential nominee, and Wilson's secretary of state. Beloved by legions of religious followers, he was derided by critics who called him a populist demagogue and relentless self-promoter. Sixty-five years old and in failing health during the trial, he died days later while still in Dayton.

John T. Scopes was an affable twenty-five-year-old high school educator and sports coach who earned $150 per month. He agreed to a request from town leaders to test the new state law that made teaching evolution a crime. This posed photograph of him was taken at the outset of the trial.

Henry Louis "H. L." Mencken was an acerbic but popular journalist for the *Baltimore Evening Sun*. His dispatches from the Scopes trial were read by millions. Wrongly assuming the trial was over, he left Dayton before Darrow's famous questioning of Bryan on the outdoor witness stand.

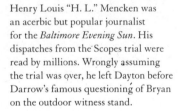

George "Rapp" Rappleyea, an engineer for the local coal mine, instigated the "Trial of the Century" to draw attention to Dayton by challenging the new anti-evolution law. He signed the criminal complaint that triggered Scopes's arrest.

Judge John Tate Raulston, posing here with his wife and two daughters in front of the Hotel Aqua in Dayton, presided over the Scopes trial. An ordained minister and elected judge, he was critical of evolution. His rulings from the bench consistently favored the prosecution, and he held Darrow in criminal contempt for questioning his fairness.

The men who sat around this small table in Robinson's Drug Store on May 5, 1925, devised a plan for a sensational trial that would boost the economic fortunes of Dayton. From left to right: George Rappleyea, school superintendent Walter White, druggist F. E. Robinson, and White's assistant, Clay D. Green, who worked as a teacher with Scopes.

ABOVE: Robinson's Drug Store, where the plan was hatched to legally contest the new state law that forbade the teaching of evolution. It became a favorite place for people to congregate and to see notable participants in the trial.

RIGHT: While a band plays, Bryan steps off the train in Dayton on July 7, 1925, wearing his safari-style Florida sun hat. He received a hero's welcome with hundreds of admirers cheering his arrival at the station. It was already a circuslike atmosphere.

Among the throngs who greeted Bryan at the station were two members of the prosecution team. In a dark suit with his arms folded is Ben McKenzie. Next to him is Herbert Hicks, in a white suit and clutching Bryan's bag.

Darrow's arrival in Dayton was warm but muted. Wearing a hat, he shakes hands with his young client, John Scopes. Between them is co–defense counsel John Randolph Neal. Darrow always courted the goodwill of the press. A journalist stands to his left.

Scopes's main defense trust. From left to right: Dudley Field Malone, John R. Neal, and Clarence Darrow.

Before proceedings ever began, the media dubbed it the "monkey trial," an evolutionary misconception that humans evolved from apes. The festival atmosphere was fueled by carnival acts like the chimpanzee named Joe Mendi, who wore a bow tie and suit to make him appear human-like. People lined up and paid money to have their photos taken with him.

ABOVE: Mendi was trained to play notes on a miniature piano while entertaining children.

RIGHT: The chimpanzee rode astride a pony as young people took turns leading them around a grassy square.

He even drank sodas at Robinson's Drug Store, to the amusement of patrons.

Hucksters and merchants peddled monkey-related souvenirs. This photograph shows women holding monkey dolls, which became a popular item during the trial.

ABOVE: "Read Your Bible" signs like this one were everywhere in Dayton during the trial, including inside the courtroom. Judge Raulston thought there was nothing prejudicial about it. Walking, from left to right: defendant John Scopes, his attorney John Neal, and trial instigator George Rappleyea.

BELOW: Before and during the trial, religious revivals were held and street preachers converged on Dayton, warning of the evils of evolution.

This is what Rhea Central High School looked like in 1924, one year before John Scopes was arrested and charged with teaching the science of evolution to his students in biology class. Tennessee made it a crime to teach from state-approved textbooks that explained Darwin's theory.

The stately Rhea County Courthouse in Dayton was built in 1891 in a Romanesque-Italian style. It was the grandest courthouse in all of Tennessee. Overflow crowds gathered outdoors on the lawns and listened on speakers to the courtroom events, courtesy of Chicago radio station WGMN.

The cavernous courtroom on the second floor was jammed with spectators each day. At the back in front of the double windows stood a newsreel camera that recorded events. The film was flown each day to Chicago. At center-left, Bryan leans over the table to speak with Darrow.

ABOVE: There was seating for five hundred people in the courtroom, with standing room for many more. The large windows provided abundant light and some airflow, but there were no ceiling fans to circulate or displace the stifling summer heat.

BELOW: The Scopes trial was the first to be broadcast live nationwide. Chicago's WGN radio situated microphones throughout the courtroom. In this scene, microphones can be seen in the foreground to the right and center-left.

ABOVE: Judge Raulston and Darrow, far right, shake hands. Bryan, in a bow tie, stands to the left, along with prosecutor Tom Stewart (partly obscured) and co–defense attorney Dudley Malone, standing in front of the radio microphone. Raulston held Darrow in criminal contempt for openly criticizing the judge's bias. When Darrow apologized, Raulston launched into a religiously infused speech, forgiving the lawyer.

RIGHT: As Judge Raulston presided, police deputies tried to maintain order over the sometimes raucous crowd. His rulings consistently favored the prosecution and foreclosed Darrow's ability to present a legitimate defense of Scopes.

Four-year-old Thomas Jefferson "Tommy" Brewer sat atop Judge Raulston's bench and drew the names of jurors out of a hat.

The jury of twelve (absent one) poses on the steps of the courthouse, flanked by the county sheriff (standing far left) and Judge Raulston (standing far right).

ABOVE: The prosecution begins its case against high school biology teacher John T. Scopes, who is charged with the crime of teaching evolution to his students in Dayton, Tennessee.

LEFT: Darrow, without his suit coat, addresses the all-male jury seated in front of him. All but one were devoted church members. Three had read no other book except the Bible. One juror could not read at all. Only a single individual knew anything about evolution.

TOP: This iconic photo shows Darrow holding forth during the trial as he argued for the recognition of science in classrooms and the sanctity of academic freedom.

RIGHT: In the sweltering heat trapped inside the courtroom, Bryan drank profusely from his water glass and fanned himself with his ubiquitous palm leaf fan that was painted with an advertisement for the Robinson Drug Store.

LEFT: Largely silent at the beginning of the trial, Bryan rose to deliver a scathing condemnation of evolution while demonizing his nemesis, Darrow, as a godless agnostic.

BELOW: During the trial, Bryan exploited the platform built outside the Rhea County Courthouse to preach the evils of evolution and its existential threat to Christianity. Days later, on this same outdoor setting, Bryan was unexpectedly called as a witness and was devastated by Darrow's searing examination, in the trial's most dramatic and defining moment.

LEFT: Darrow assembled a team of nationally renowned scientists to explain evolution and how it did not conflict with the Bible's account of the Divine Creation. But Judge Raulston refused to allow them to testify before the jury. Down, but not defeated, Darrow initiated a daring move to call Bryan to the witness stand as an expert on the Bible. Darrow knew that Bryan's ego would not let him resist.

ABOVE: Fearful that the second-floor courtroom might collapse under the weight of the crowd, Judge Raulston moved the trial outdoors to a platform that already existed. This set the stage for the climactic moment in the Scopes trial when Darrow, face-to-face, challenged Bryan's interpretation that everything in the Bible should be accepted literally. The historic confrontation all but destroyed Bryan.

BELOW: Scopes spoke only twice, pleading not guilty at his arraignment and, later, delivering a moving statement at the conclusion of the trial. He vowed to oppose "this unjust statute" because "any other action would be in violation of my ideal of academic freedom."

LEFT: Schoolteacher and defendant John T. Scopes, together with his famed lawyer, Clarence Darrow. They fought for intellectual freedom and the value of science in American education.

BELOW: A broken man, Bryan died in his sleep during an afternoon nap just days after the trial ended. Flanked by an American Legion honor guard, Bryan's casket is placed aboard a special Pullman car to be transported from Dayton to Washington, D.C. People lined the tracks to mourn his passing.

"No person in Dayton thought the matter of any interest when first it was instigated, and even after it was started and the warrant decided upon after the drugstore argument, so little was thought of it that F. E. Robinson, proprietor of the drugstore and correspondent of the *Chattanooga Times*, was undecided whether he should call the paper and tell them of it," Rappleyea added.[13]

As Scopes, the ACLU, and the defense team tried to develop a strategy, Darrow expected to lose the case no matter what happened in Dayton. He hoped to take the case to the federal courts. The ACLU agreed with that and wanted to get the trial out of Dayton. "The American Civil Liberties Union wanted to prevent a fiasco in Dayton, and officials knew the only way to do so was to avoid having the trial there," remembered Scopes. "They believed an irresponsible atmosphere would harm our case and might bury the real issues under a revivalist tent of hoopla and ballyhoo." Darrow, Scopes noted, "felt comfortable in this rowdy atmosphere" and was "pleased to have a crack at Bryan under any circumstances." Darrow assured Scopes that his main objective was to get the case into the federal courts despite his eagerness to take on Bryan.[14]

Scouting the area, Darrow and Colby visited Tennessee at the end of June, a few weeks before the trial in Dayton. That proved enough for Colby, who decided to withdraw from the case, unimpressed with Tennessee and dreaming of a White House bid in 1928. But Darrow, appearing in rumpled clothes as always, enjoyed his introduction to the Volunteer State. "Darrow was a big man, large-boned with a large head and peering blue eyes set deep under an often-frowning forehead," Scopes recalled. "It was easy to like him. He drawled comfortably and hadn't any airs. He gave the impression he might have grown up in Dayton, just an unpolished, casual country lawyer." Characteristically, Darrow went out of his way to observe court cases in east Tennessee as he readied for his show-down against Bryan in Dayton. Darrow also spoke at John Neal's law school in Knoxville before heading back to Chicago.[15]

While Darrow got ready for the case, some of the ACLU's leaders began questioning whether Malone should head to Dayton. Despite calls for Malone to stay in New York to help the defense team, the divorce lawyer insisted on going down to Tennessee. Still, as members of the ACLU recognized, the well-dressed and even better-mannered Malone appeared to personify the upper class in New York. In actuality, Malone was not the stuffy WASP patrician that he came off as. Born in Manhattan in 1882 and educated at Catholic schools, including Fordham, where he earned his law degree, Malone married May O'Gorman, the daughter of powerful U.S. senator James O'Gorman of New York. Although Malone and May were both Catholics, they got a divorce, and Malone married Doris Stevens, a prominent feminist and suffragist, in 1921. Praised "for his charm as a raconteur and for his wit as a speaker and a phrase-maker," Malone took to the political stage, serving as an assistant secretary of state under President Wilson, reporting to Secretary Bryan. An avowed internationalist, Malone clashed with Bryan at the State Department and was glad to see him resign in 1915 over Wilson's response to the Germans' sinking of the *Lusitania*. Despite being friends with Wilson, Malone broke with the president over women's suffrage and the treatment of socialists during the war. Malone ran for New York governor as an independent in 1920, loudly opposed Prohibition, and pushed for the United States to recognize the Soviet Union. Members of the ACLU's board openly wondered if Malone would prove just as controversial in Dayton as Darrow, especially since, during the 1920s, Malone had become the most famous divorce lawyer in America, helping ensure he garnered the distrust, even the hostility, of fundamentalist Christians.[16]

For his part, Darrow welcomed Malone's help, especially after the New York lawyer had promoted him before the ACLU board. Despite his religious upbringing, Malone had never thought much about evolution and certainly did not defend it the way Darrow did. Darrow had never heard his friend "express an opinion as to whether he was convinced of the soundness of evolution" and thought "he was never specially interested in the subject." If science did not interest Malone, Darrow praised him for having "his allegiance on a higher ground," namely freedom. "More than most men one meets, Mr. Malone believes in freedom, in the right of every one to investigate for himself, and he resented the interference of the State in its effort to forbid or control the convictions and mental attitudes of men," Darrow wrote about his friend.[17]

Despite the prominence of Malone and some of the other attorneys, as June passed, just as some of the board members of the ACLU feared, increasingly the trial came down to a clash between Bryan and Darrow, two of the leading figures in American life, who had both captivated the spotlight for decades. While Neal had been Scopes's first attorney on the case, Neal quickly realized that all of the other players would be overshadowed by the two leading actors.

Speaking at an ACLU fundraiser at the Civic Club in Manhattan—the same one where Scopes appeared late—Neal set the stage for a showdown between Bryan and Darrow:

"In the beginning, there were only two clear voices, two individuals, who realized what this case was. One was Mr. Bryan. He saw this law was his child and rushed to its defense. I am glad he did, for there were some people who thought the law would not get properly defended." But, Neal continued, Bryan wasn't the only man who recognized what was at stake in Dayton. "Another man saw immediately what was involved: Clarence Darrow." Turning to his cocounsel, Neal offered a quick look at what drove Darrow. "Despite the despair sometimes in his words, you can see in him a great charity for mankind."[18]

From their brief time together, Scopes felt reassured that he "could look forward to the best defense possible" from his team. Back in Dayton, Scopes regularly drew reporters' attention, even being asked if he was a Christian. Thankfully, most of Dayton's residents treated their schoolteacher as they always had. But inevitably, more reporters and fundamentalist activists flocked to the small town. Having obtained Darrow's services, Scopes realized his life would never again be the same, thanks to the trial—what people were already calling "monkey business."[19]

The Circus Comes to Dayton

Notwithstanding the best efforts of the ACLU, the Scopes Trial did bring a carnival atmosphere to Dayton.

Watching from Dayton and during his trips up and down the East Coast, John Scopes was amazed at the transformation of the sleepy Tennessee town he called home. "Ringling Brothers or Barnum and Bailey would have been pressed hard to produce more acts and side-shows and freaks than Dayton had," Scopes recalled. "A showman like P. T. Barnum would have gloated over the possibilities that Dayton offered and called it *a natural*."[1]

Scopes had his finger on the pulse of how Dayton had transformed in the past few weeks. All over town, street-corner preachers stood on top of cars to denounce evolution and offer their religious insights while men in shirtsleeves grappled with the suffocating heat for a moment before moving on their way, searching for some shade. Salesmen and shops showcased souvenirs of the trial, some of which featured monkeys as a symbol of evolution. A truck equipped with loudspeakers touted William Jennings Bryan's real estate opportunities in South Florida.[2]

In the hills outside town, the fundamentalist Holiness movement held its enthusiastic meetings, which had led to the group's being labeled Holy Rollers. Anti-evolution crusaders sold books to passersby on the streets. Trying to promote the benefits of relocating to Dayton, the town boosters offered up a book of their own. *Why Dayton of All Places?* advertised the town's charms and showcased why businesses should set up shop there. The Dayton Progressive Club helped these efforts, authorizing $5,000 to promote the town while it was in the national spotlight.[3]

Dayton relished the arriving newcomers and the lucrative economic prospects they represented. A reporter for the *Boston Transcript*, W. A. MacDonald, found "something admirable about the way Dayton . . . is approaching its opportunities which arise from the imminent trial of John T. Scopes." MacDonald noted, "Dayton is making the most" of "nationwide interest in the case." To his surprise, he found all his needs taken care of, from the handling of telegraphs to rooms. Even before the trial, MacDonald reported that nightly accommodations were already starting to fill up in Dayton in advance of the July 10 start date. While the reporter from Boston enjoyed the hospitality, he found the service often proved slow.[4]

The cast of characters associated with the trial began to arrive in Dayton. Almost two hundred reporters had already materialized, led by the acerbic and influential columnist H. L. Mencken, a caustic opponent of fundamentalists and the "Bible Belt," a phrase he helped popularize as he dismissed the South on a host of fronts.[5] A brilliant and outspoken wordsmith, Mencken had, from his perch at the *Baltimore Sun*, become one of the most popular writers in the country. In his midforties and still a bachelor, Mencken was at the height of his fame and abilities as the Scopes Trial commenced. A year before heading to Dayton, Mencken had helped launch the *American Mercury*. This lively journal had already garnered attention for its colorful essays attacking American provincialism, often in opposition to religion in general and fundamentalism in particular. Mencken had also won applause for *The American Language*, his effort to pick up the mantle of Noah Webster and showcase the differences in how English was used on the western side of the Atlantic. Mencken's reports from Dayton would help define the trial across the country.[6]

At least five hundred people stayed in Dayton during the trial, with around half of them working for the newspapers and radio. While these visitors offered the local economy a little help, their numbers fell short of what town boosters had hoped and had been prepared for.[7] Always a shrewd observer, Mencken picked up on these fears, reporting to his audience across the nation that "Dayton is full of sickening surges and tremors of doubt" about its effort to garner attention for the town. Mencken dismissed Dayton's hopes that the publicity from the trial would lead to new residents and restart the "fires of the cold and silent blast furnaces down the railroad tracks."

Despite his take, Mencken found Dayton full of surprises. Expecting a "squalid Southern town" with "inhabitants full of hookworm and malaria," he discovered "a country town full of charm and even beauty," which proved more tolerant than the rest of Tennessee. The famed reporter noted that the Ku Klux Klan never found a foothold in Dayton, and he could not find any traces of anti-Catholicism there, either. Despite all of the pleasant surprises he encountered about the town and its inhabitants, Mencken remained convinced Dayton's gamble would not pay off.[8]

As the reporters set up shop in Dayton, the attorneys also surfaced in town. On Independence Day, John Neal arrived and spoke briefly with the press about the possibility of a federal injunction, though that option was nicked a few days later.[9] Bryan turned up on July 7 with much fanfare. He was greeted by a cluster of attorneys from both sides, a deluge of reporters covering the trial, and, as the AP reported, "a host of Dayton citizens." As Bryan stepped off the train, the crowd went wild. He removed his "very wide brimmed hat" and greeted his adoring supporters. A woman pushed her way through the teeming masses to greet the Great Commoner, welcoming him to Dayton, while somebody called out, "Good luck, Bill!"

Moving his way through the throng, shaking hands and bobbing his head, Bryan took a few questions from the crowd.

"Are you ready for the fight?" someone asked.

"It would be better, perhaps, to say that I am ready for the trial."

Bryan removed his coat when the heat got the better of him, and the crowd followed him to the home of Richard Rogers, a pharmacist who worked at Robinson's Drug Store. Paying $25 a week, Bryan stayed at Rogers's house, at the corner of Georgia Avenue and Market Street, during the trial. On the way there, Bryan ran into Neal and they exchanged pleasantries as the flock of spectators eagerly watched.[10]

After settling in and resting at Rogers's house that night, Bryan made his debut in Dayton by throwing down the gauntlet. Speaking to the Dayton Progressive Club in the Aqua Hotel, Bryan painted the looming contest as a "duel to the death" between Christianity and evolution. He said he welcomed the public attention.

"It has been in the past a death grapple in the dark, but from this time on, it will be a death grapple in the light," Bryan proclaimed to the cheering crowd.[11]

Bryan was not the only prominent figure to arrive in Dayton on July 7. With Neal at his side, John Scopes stopped by Dayton on the same day, pausing briefly before heading down to Chattanooga to meet his father. Right before Bryan spoke to the Dayton Progressive Club, Scopes met Bryan in the lobby and they ended up chatting for a few moments, continuing their conversation over dinner.

"John, I know you," Bryan said to Scopes. "I think you're one of those high school students who made a disturbance at that commencement address I delivered in Salem several years ago!"

Scopes blushed over the memory from six years before, but Bryan laughed it off, saying that he hoped they could be friends regardless of being on different sides. While they got along well, Scopes was astonished by how much Bryan ate. The teacher even handed his corn and potatoes to Bryan, who promptly wolfed them down. Bryan walked away with a favorable impression of Scopes, something he noted in his speech to the club.[12]

The two sides engaged in some light, preliminary sparring while taking moments to pose for the cameras. Neal accused Bryan of wanting to add an amendment to the U.S. Constitution banning the teaching of evolution. Bryan enjoyed a strawberry ice cream soda while sitting at the table in Robinson's Drug Store where Dayton's leaders had masterminded the trial.[13]

At least Bryan did not order a "monkey fizz" from Robinson's, which, like other local businesses, tried to capitalize on the publicity generated by the trial. To their surprise, reporters found a sign in front of one store proclaiming DARWIN IS RIGHT—INSIDE. A hand on the sign pointed to J. R. Darwin's Everything to Wear store. Amid all the souvenirs and efforts to cash in, Bryan's presence helped add more weight to the proceedings. Looking back, Scopes conceded that having the prominent politician in town helped ensure Dayton residents "assumed more sedate roles since he remained a respected, even beloved, figure." Bryan's arrival might have gotten much of the attention, but, off center stage, an influx of preachers and their supporters streamed into Dayton. "The monkey signs went down and the religious posters started going up," Scopes recalled. "The theme in Dayton has changed fast, from the monkey business to the God business, and from chuckles and smiles to a semblance of seriousness."[14]

More figures connected to the trial converged on Dayton as the show got under way. Judge John Raulston, balding, with a high forehead and a short tie hanging down on his white shirt, showed up on Wednesday, July 8, telling the media that he was ready to stay all summer in Dayton if needed. He noted that he had received a great deal of unsolicited advice from people all over the country. Scopes returned with his father on the same day that Raulston arrived in Dayton.[15]

That same evening, Darrow left Chicago for Dayton, talking to local reporters and reiterating his opposition to Bryan. While Darrow had hoped that the federal injunction would go through, he told journalists that he welcomed the looming fight in Tennessee.

"Maybe the trial will serve an educational purpose," Darrow said, insisting that civilization itself, and not Scopes, was on trial in Dayton. "If William Jennings Bryan thinks a Tennessee court or jury is going to have any influence on thought and investigations of the world, he's a very gullible man."[16]

Reporters could not help but notice the number of religious signs on windows, businesses, and barns, on telegraph poles, and even attached to trees. All over Dayton, they encountered signs saying READ YOUR BIBLE and asking SHALL WE PAY OUR MONEY TO DAMN OUR CHILDREN? While some of the signs had been erected right before the trial, others had been there for more than a year. Other public displays included some from the town leaders. Robinson's Drug Store featured a sign letting the world know it was WHERE IT STARTED. With the increased attention came fears about crime. With Prohibition in full effect, the local police worked with law enforcement across the state to make sure alcohol was not flowing into Dayton.[17]

While Bryan remained active during the days before the trial, even speaking to the Rhea County School Board on Thursday, Darrow's arrival in Dayton drew far less attention. Accompanied by Dudley Field Malone as he came to town, Darrow met Raymond Clapper, an up-and-coming reporter working for United Press who usually covered politics in Washington. Even Clapper, usually one for understating, found himself caught in the hoopla, insisting the Scopes Trial would be "the greatest battle of the mind since Galileo was imprisoned by the inquisition for teaching that the earth was round."[18] Darrow contrasted his arrival to Bryan's, noting he did not have a crowd waiting for him. That did not surprise or disappoint him, since he was coming to the heart of the Bible Belt. Looking back at his underwhelming entrance to Dayton, he remembered the heat, which almost reached one hundred degrees.[19]

Darrow rented a home from Berry Luther Morgan, whose son "Scrappy" had been one of Scopes's students. While the Morgans vacated the premises during the trial, Ruby Darrow, who came into town after her husband, did not care for the house, especially as they had paid a flat fee of $500 and there was no indoor plumbing.[20] Darrow found some solace in the residence, especially as he found Dayton "so crowded that it became practically impossible to get accommodations of any sort." Things proved so insufficient that Darrow scrambled for ice, butter, and milk. However, he found his new neighbors and almost everyone in the town to be helpful and attentive to his needs.[21]

Since Dayton welcomed Bryan with a dinner, community business leaders, wanting to appear fair to both sides, did the same for Darrow. The famed attorney played up his humble roots, telling his listeners that he came from a small town in Ohio and laughing about his start in the law. Most of all, his sense of humor and goodwill captivated the crowd. "I was playing poker on the side and practicing law, and I almost starved," Darrow said. "But then I started playing poker and practicing law on the side, and I made enough money to go to Chicago and open an office!"[22]

Four decades later, Scopes insisted that Darrow played well in Dayton even if his cause was not as popular as Bryan's. Darrow, Scopes wrote, came off "as a product of a small town" instead of a renowned attorney. "He was the country boy who had gone to the big city and had made good and had not let it hurt him any. He was as plain as Mrs. Bailey's flapjacks. Overnight he became a hit in Dayton."[23]

But Darrow arrived to lousy news. Judge Raulston, a rare Republican in southeast Tennessee, who made no secret of his political aspirations, couldn't resist offering his thoughts to the press before the trial:

"I approach my duties in the trial of the Scopes case with a deep consciousness that the issues are profound. I am concerned that those connected with this investigation shall divest themselves of all ambition to establish any particular theory for personal gratification and that we constantly inquire for the eternal truth."

Raulston left little room for doubt on whose side he thought the eternal truth lay: "If man without inspiration attempts to delve in the mysterious workings of God, he finds himself overwhelmed in perplexities. Therefore, I am much interested that the unerring hand of Him who is the author of all truth shall direct every official act of mine."

Reviewing what the judge had said, Clapper informed readers all across the country that the judge had "definite sympathies for Bryan and the fundamentalists."[24]

Darrow did his best to ignore reporters, but he could not avoid the growing hostility he saw across the town, even if most of it came from visitors instead of residents of Dayton. Convinced that he would lose the case—one of the reasons he did not want to talk to the newspapermen—Darrow knew he was taking up an unpopular cause. Walking through the streets of Dayton, he found himself confronted by hosts of banners such as THE LORD WILL PROVIDE, COME TO JESUS, PREPARE TO MEET THY MAKER, PUT YOUR TRUST IN HIM, and JESUS LOVES YOU. Looking back at his first days in Dayton, Darrow returned to those signs and the heat and dryly noted, "Tennessee can never be blamed if our souls were not saved that hot summer. That torrid land . . . might have inspired one to beware of ever going to a hotter climate." There were some more positive surprises, including the size of the courtroom, which impressed the famed attorney.[25]

While Darrow got accustomed to the town, his client wandered through the streets he knew well, trying to process all the changes. Having never encountered many fundamentalists in his life, Scopes did not know what to make of them. Going to see the Holy Rollers in their church, Scopes watched them shake and moan. As church members started proclaiming their faith, a large woman who was one of their leaders spit chewing tobacco at Scopes and other onlookers, who tried to scramble out of the way.[26]

Despite the help of his friends and his legal team, Scopes found himself overwhelmed by all of this attention. Almost every member of the army of two hundred reporters gathered in Dayton interviewed Scopes. Even the various dances and parties held every night failed to improve Scopes's mood. With every step he took as he walked around Dayton, the young teacher encountered more preachers and other speakers, many of whom were damning him and insisting he was going to hell. "There was never anything like this," Scopes recalled. "It was a carnival from start to finish. Every Bible-shouting, psalm-singing pulpit hero in the state poured out of the hills and brought his soapbox with him." Scopes could only shake his head and try to ignore the preachers, but "the air was filled with shouting from early morning until late in the night." As the trial loomed, Scopes learned about the downsides of being famous.[27]

All around Dayton, the visual religious manifestations proved ubiquitous. Darrow, Scopes, and all the reporters and visitors could not escape them. The READ YOUR BIBLE signs appeared all over town, even on the temporary outhouses set up outside the courthouse to accommodate the expected crowds.[28]

The Scopes Trial quickly became universally known as the Monkey Trial, and the insulting, belittling phrase would haunt Dayton in the years to come. Helping propel that image was a circus owner who brought Joe Mendi—a chimpanzee—to town. Joe was billed as the "$100,000 chimpanzee with the intelligence of a five-year-old." Dressed up in suits and posing for photos, the chimp soon became one of the most popular attractions in town. People even paid twenty-five cents to shake Joe's hand. Joe helped ensure Dayton's gamble of putting the city on the national stage and boosting the local economy by hosting the trial failed miserably. Joe's owner insisted the chimpanzee had been asked to appear at the trial, but he would not testify, a line that produced chuckles and smiles from the crowds.[29]

But behind the laughs, Joe highlighted a growing problem that the town fathers of Dayton could not ignore. The trial was becoming something of a joke, and Dayton risked becoming the "monkey town" instead of a charming place to raise families and set up businesses. The gamble that George Rappleyea and other business leaders had made around the table at Robinson's Drug Store showed signs of not paying off. As Scopes walked through the streets of the town he lived and worked in, he grew uncomfortable as he received more attention from preachers, the media, and the crowds. Just like Dayton, Scopes was starting to face the downside of all the attention the trial was receiving—and Judge Raulston had not even pounded the gavel yet.

Darrow in the Lion's Den

Judge John Raulston opened the trial of the *State v. John Thomas Scopes* on July 10, 1925.

With an extensive collection of prospective jurors taking up many of the chairs in the largest courtroom in Tennessee, His Honor's first order of business was to call on the Reverend Lemuel Cartwright, a prominent fundamentalist Methodist minister, to deliver a fire-and-brimstone prayer. Cartwright praised the prosecution's unabashed support of man's Divine Creation as taught in the Bible and, by implication, demonized the accused for daring to teach a widely accepted scientific theory that might call into question God's "supreme majesty." It was a scolding disguised as a prayer. Cartwright demanded that the judge and jury "transact the business of this court" in a way that "honored and glorified" the Creator of man. "We beseech Thee, our Father, that Thou will give to the court this morning a sufficient share of the divine spirit as will enable the court to so administer its affairs as that justice may come to all and that God's standard of purity and holiness may be upheld."

Upheld was the key word. In other words, Cartwright insisted the word of God as passed down to man in the form of the Bible must be accepted literally. Evolution should be banished, and Scopes—the infidel—convicted. If anyone on the jury voted otherwise, the juror would go to hell, or, as Cartwright put it, be reckoned with on Judgment Day for any deeds not "amenable to God."[1] Clarence Darrow knew exactly what was going on. The aging attorney in the rumpled summer suit, his pants held up by his familiar suspenders ("galluses," as he called them fondly), knew that he was sitting all alone in the lion's den. Besides Darrow, no one else in the courtroom seemed to think it was wrong or prejudicial for a preacher to condemn the accused in this thundering benediction during a trial. So, with the judge's blessing, a highly respected clergyman preordained the outcome of Scopes's guilt before the jury was even sworn in. The stern message could not have been more transparent—the mere idea of evolution was evil, and teaching it in a high school classroom was blasphemous.

As he listened to Cartwright's prayer, Scopes wondered if the minister would ever end. Even worse, Scopes could hear audience members offering "amens, a common reaction in the hills," as the prayer dragged on.[2]

To drive home the unmistakable point, Raulston then read verbatim the first chapter of Genesis from the Bible, reciting how God made everything that exists in six miraculous days. When Raulston came to the part about how man was created, he paused and then elevated his words with a stentorian tone: "And God said, 'Let us make man in our image, after our likeness: and let them have dominion over the fish of the sea and over the fowl of the air, and over the cattle, and over all the earth, and over every creeping thing that creepeth upon the earth.' So God created man in His own image, in the image of God, created He him; male and female created He them."[3]

Raulston's recitation of Genesis lent the biblical account of creation the weight and credibility of his lofty stature. No doubt this was by design. The judge did so under the pretext that any evolutionary assault by Scopes on the teachings of the Bible necessitated an understanding of what the book states. Raulston's take was preposterous, and Darrow saw it for what it was—a devious ploy by the judge to offer his ponderous endorsement that the Bible should be interpreted literally. Darrow kept his eyes on Raulston, noting that the judge tended to show up late since he strode through the courthouse square to pose for photos while "hugging the Bible."[4]

Raulston next did something both curious and suspicious. After reading aloud the first chapter of Genesis, he stopped. Raulston did not explain why he conspicuously omitted the chapters that followed on Adam and Eve, man being made from dust, woman from the rib, a beguiling (and talking) serpent, the Garden of Eden, and so on. Raulston did not read, "The Lord God formed the man of dust from the ground and breathed into his nostrils the breath of life, and the man became a living creature." He did not quote, "For Adam there was not found a helper fit for him. So the Lord God caused a deep sleep to fall upon the man and, while he slept, took one of his ribs and closed up its place with flesh. And the rib that the Lord God had taken from the man he made into a woman and brought her to the man."

Did Raulston deliberately ignore the specifics of how man was supposedly created because he didn't fully believe that it was true? Did he fear that the jury would agree when they heard it repeated in open court from his own lips? More likely, the judge was wary of Darrow's legendary skills and the kind of mockery that might ensue if he ventured further into the mystic details of creationism.

Raulston was well aware that William Jennings Bryan was sitting at the prosecution table and fanning himself to fend off the summer heat. The judge knew that Bryan and his devout fundamentalist followers believed that everything written in the Bible should be taken literally. The judge knew that biblical scholars had long debated whether the story of the founding of humanity should be viewed as an allegory, as inspirational imagery that seeks to convey God's purpose but not necessarily based on actual events or people. Even in 1925, a growing body of theologians regarded Genesis as more mythological in nature and not strictly historical. These scholars viewed Genesis as a literary narrative of loose-knit episodic stories and figurative language passed along for generations but packaged as truth. These same historians and theologians recognized that a written record of the past doesn't always recover actual events, only what was handed down in stories and legends. History—especially ancient history—can blur the lines between fact and fiction. Myths can take on a reality all their own, especially by those such as Bryant who were convinced of biblical inerrancy.

Inside that courtroom in Dayton, Raulston did not want to preside over the great existential spectacle that both Darrow and Bryan envisioned and that the throng of media that had converged from all over the world hoped to cover. From the outset, the judge showed he intended to confine the trial to a simple question: Did Scopes break the law as it was defined?

In reality, the reading of Genesis by Raulston was probative of nothing. Its prejudicial effect was evident and severe. The judge decided early on that he would try the prosecutors' case for them, usurping their role at the outset as he commandeered control of the state's case. Draped in a black robe and physically positioned above Scopes and the attorneys, who were seated before him, Raulston embraced the indelible image of a magisterial figure wrapped in supreme authority. If the judge read aloud that God created the world and man in six days, it must be so.

In the first hour of the trial, Raulston assumed the posture of judge, prosecutor, and jury. No effort was made by him to be equitable or fair by reading a comparable passage from Darwin's *On the Origin of Species* or even the subchapter titled "The Doctrine of Evolution" in Hunter's *Civic Biology*, the high school textbook from which Scopes had taught.

On the contrary, as he read the loaded indictment in open court, Raulston described to the jury the "evil example of the teacher" (Scopes) who "disregarded constituted authority" (the state legislature) "in the very presence of the undeveloped mind" (students). It didn't matter that Scopes was a simple schoolteacher who taught from a biology textbook approved by the State of Tennessee that explained the biologically sourced concept known as evolution. Presumably, students had been reading this scientifically supported hypothesis of man's origin for eleven years, since the textbook was first published in 1914. Now, suddenly, any teacher who dared to use the book in class was not only "evil" but a criminal.[5]

Darrow was incensed at how the trial was, in his view, being corrupted by a biased judge who appeared determined to engineer a cursory conviction. The legendary lawyer raised numerous objections and repeatedly complained about the overt prejudice that infected the proceedings. He accused the court of attempting to "influence the deliberation and consideration of the jury of the facts in this case." Darrow's frustration finally boiled over as he clashed openly with Raulston over the judge's decision to commence each session with spiritual invocations that blatantly reinforced how God was on the side of the pious prosecutors.

As the trial continued, Darrow even accused Raulston of exploiting preachers inside the courtroom to incite an atmosphere of hostility toward his client. Darrow labeled the judge's actions "especially obnoxious."

Darrow told the judge, "I do not object to the jury or anyone else praying in private, but I do object to your turning of this courtroom into a [religious] meetinghouse in the trial of this case. You have no right to do it!"

Despite the provocation of Darrow's caustic rhetoric, Raulston kept his cool and chose to feign innocence in the face of his glaring bias. He absurdly pretended that the words employed by the Bible-thumping preachers were neither a sonorous endorsement of creationism nor a condemnation of evolution.

"I have instructed the ministers to make no reference to the issues involved in this case. I see nothing that might influence the court or jury as to the issues. Therefore, I am pleased to overrule the objection," Raulston decreed, before inviting yet another fundamentalist minister to offer a prayer.

Defeated in his objection and with a menacing stare from the judge, Darrow reluctantly sat down. The minister promptly stepped forward and reinforced the biblical account of how man spontaneously appeared on earth one day because "the Great Creator of the world" commanded it. The minister could have dispensed with his ecclesiastic pretense and seated himself at the prosecution's table.[6]

It was pure sophistry for Raulston to claim that these court-sanctioned prayers could not possibly influence the jury. Even the prosecutors knew that was untrue. Instead, they argued that prayers in court were appropriate because "we are a God-fearing country." They also asserted disingenuously that religion had nothing to do with the criminal proceedings. This prompted Darrow to reply—with all the contempt he could muster—that religion had everything to do with the trial. He was right.

Seeking a fair trial, Darrow directly challenged the judge on principle, not on practicality. He sought only fairness. Besides, the jury didn't need any religious prompting, which Darrow noticed as the trial moved from prayers and Genesis to finding jurors.

During jury selection, Darrow recognized that the deck had been stacked against him. Nearly every panel member proudly proclaimed himself a devout Christian and strict adherent to the Bible. At moments the jury selection bordered on the comical.

The prosecution tried to place a "stealth asset" on the panel. J. P. Massingill was a practicing minister, well known in the community and to the prosecutors for his strident fundamentalist views. Instead of referring to him by his title of "Reverend" or disclosing his profession, the lead prosecutor addressed him as "Mr. Massingill," a deception that did not fool Darrow, who suspected there was a hidden motive. Sensing that his adversaries were far too eager to accept the man for the jury after only eight quick questions, Darrow wasted little time as he unraveled the truth through a skilled cross-examination.

"What is your business?" a wary Darrow asked.

"I am a minister."

"Ever preach on evolution?"

"I don't think so, definitely; that is, on evolution alone."

"Now, you wouldn't want to sit on this jury unless you were fair, would you?" a bemused Darrow continued.

"Certainly, I would want to be fair; yes, sir."

"Did you ever preach on evolution?"

"Yes. I haven't as a subject; just take that up, in connection with other subjects. I have referred to it in discussing it."

"Against it or for it?"

"I am strictly for the Bible."

Darrow rolled his eyes at that answer. "I am talking about evolution; I am not talking about the Bible. Did you preach for or against evolution?"

The prosecution insisted that was not a fair question. Raulston allowed it and Massingill answered, "Well, I preached against it, of course!"

Darrow smirked as the minister confessed his position on evolution. The answer produced so much applause in the courtroom that Raulston admonished the audience and, after being pressed by Darrow, threatened to evict them.[7]

Although Darrow managed to prevent the minister from serving on the jury, those who were eventually selected were deeply religious people. They harbored like-minded opinions that evolution was nothing more than a scurrilous affront to the Bible and should never be taught in schools. Nevertheless, each of the jurors insisted he could be fair and impartial to Scopes.

To his credit, Darrow knew exactly what he was up against. "We realized that a jury drawn from Dayton, Tenn., would not permit a man to commit such a heinous crime as Scopes had been guilty of and allow him to go scot-free," Darrow recalled. "However, there were questions to be argued concerning the meaning of the statutes, and what power the legislature had to make the teaching of science a criminal offense."[8]

During the selection of the jury, Scopes was relieved that Massingill had not been chosen. The defendant realized that he was familiar with every member selected, all of whom wanted "ringside seats" to the trial. Looking back on the jury, Scopes counted six Baptists, four Methodists, a member of the Disciples of Christ, and one member who did not go to church. Reviewing the men who made up the jury—at the time women didn't serve on juries in Tennessee—the young teacher quickly realized, "I had an excellent chance of being convicted, which, after all, was what we expected, so that we could appeal the verdict and get into the Federal courts."[9]

H. L. Mencken observed how the locals treated Scopes, finding they thought "he permitted himself to be used as a cat's paw by scoundrels eager to destroy the anti-evolution law for their own dark and hellish ends." While they might think "Scopes . . . is an agent of Beelzebub once removed," they also believed the teacher "is young and full of folly." The journalist from Baltimore did not think much of the jury selection, thinking the best "Darrow could hope for was to sneak in a few men bold enough to declare publicly that they would have to hear the evidence against Scopes before condemning him."[10]

With the jury selected, the culture warriors of their day were poised for battle as Darrow faced overwhelming odds. A gifted orator with a facile mind, Darrow's ability to persuade a jury arose from an uncommon mastery of language. An eloquent speaker, he effortlessly employed elegant words. Unlike his nemesis Bryan, Darrow never lectured with the arrogance of absolute certainty. He was passionate, to be sure, but he never allowed his convictions to overwhelm his sense of compassion and empathy. As a defense attorney, he would remind jurors of the human frailties that afflict all men and the benevolence of forgiveness.

Darrow's rhetorical artistry in Dayton was on full display once the jury was sworn in. His first maneuver was to openly challenge the charge against Scopes on the grounds that criminalizing the act of "teaching a theory that denies the Story of the Divine Creation of man as taught in the Bible" was manifestly unconstitutional. Darrow was undoubtedly correct in his assessment.

Over the next three days, the defense team, led by Darrow, sought to dismiss the case against Scopes by arguing that every aspect of the anti-evolution statute was a flagrant attack on constitutional rights designed to protect freedom of thought. Religion was being forced down the throats of students in public schools by outlawing any scientific lessons that might cast doubt on the creation of man as stated in the book of Genesis.

The Butler Act had been passed by the Tennessee legislature four months earlier. It had the intended effect of endorsing religion in violation of the Establishment Clause of the First Amendment to the U.S. Constitution. The new law undermined the constitutional principle that church must be separated from state. Looking back at the trial seven years later, mocking how the word was pronounced in Tennessee, Darrow insisted that the teaching of "eevolution" was seen as "treason against religion"—and that was on trial in Dayton.[11]

The Founding Fathers feared religious abuse of government and the flip side of the coin—politicians controlling religion. The Founders expressly prohibited government from promoting any form of theocracy. In a compelling disputation, Darrow pointed this out to the judge, but then abruptly changed course and abandoned any argument based on the federal Constitution, realizing that the federal courts could take up the constitutionality down the road. Understanding why Darrow shifted his strategy requires understanding the legal climate he faced. In 1925, it was not settled law that every protection identified in the Bill of Rights was binding on the states.

The U.S. Constitution reads, "Congress shall make no law respecting an establishment of religion." The Fourteenth Amendment, enacted in 1868, was designed to impose the same duty on states and their legislatures, preventing them from establishing or sponsoring religion, as well.

Unfortunately for Darrow, the U.S. Supreme Court had not yet ruled that the religious prohibitions in the Establishment Clause were binding on the states through the Due Process Clause of the Fourteenth Amendment. The high court would not do so until the seminal case of *Everson v. Board of Education* in 1947. Regrettably, this was too late for Darrow and Scopes.

As a result, Darrow chose to focus his attention on Tennessee's constitution, which essentially replicated the language in the federal document: "No preference shall ever be given, by law, to any religious establishment or mode of worship." In citing Tennessee's Establishment Clause, Darrow patiently explained to the judge how the Butler Act elevated the teachings in the Bible to the exclusion of a well-recognized scientific theory such as evolution. This, Darrow argued, amounted to an establishment of religion and a corresponding penalty on science, thereby violating the state's constitution.

Today it would take a judge—any judge—no more than a few minutes to dispense with the legal arguments and dismiss the indictment against a teacher similarly charged. The law would be stricken from the books as brazenly unconstitutional on both state and federal grounds. Remarkably, not until 1968 was a similar anti-evolution law finally granted review by the U.S. Supreme Court and struck down. The high court validated the same argument that Darrow had made in Dayton forty-three years earlier.

Darrow wasn't just prescient; he was a brilliant student of the law and the Constitution. He understood the Framers' desire to create a religiously neutral society that would allow free expression of faith unimpeded by government dictates advancing a particular sectarian doctrine and suppressing any secular opinions.

However, in 1925 the political and religious environment was dramatically different. In Tennessee and elsewhere, Christian fundamentalists led by Bryan were a powerful force—even in a court of law. Immense pressure was brought to bear on politicians, jurists, and the general citizenry to ignore constitutional principles in favor of feverish religious beliefs. The doctrine of separation of church and state was regarded by the legions of churchgoers in the Bible Belt as anathema to the word of God. The notion that Scopes might be afforded a fair trial by a jury of his peers seemed fanciful at best.

Against the odds, Darrow waged his war against the fundamentalists in court to get the charges against his client dismissed on what's called a "motion to quash" the indictment. In his arsenal of weapons was another provision in Tennessee's constitution that legislators had overlooked when crafting their anti-evolution dictum. Darrow pointed to a part of it that read, "It shall be the duty of the general assembly in all future periods of this government, to cherish literature and science."

By citing this clause, Darrow and his cocounsel John Neal mounted a penetrating argument that was notable for its simplicity. They reasoned that it would be impossible for lawmakers to fulfill their constitutional duty if they stripped the science of evolution from the classroom.

"We can show that not only can the legislature not cherish science, but in no possible way can science be taught or science be studied without bringing in the doctrine of evolution, which this particular act attempts to make a crime. Whether it is true or not, all the important matters of science are expressed in the evolution nomenclature," Neal told the court.[12]

Darrow promised the court that—if given latitude by the judge to do so—he could show that evolution was science based and supported by provable biological facts well established and widely accepted in the scientific community. Observable evidence developed by biologists, early geneticists, anatomists, archaeologists, paleontologists, and many others had independently corroborated much of Charles Darwin's theory of human evolution through natural selection formulated in his book *On the Origin of Species*. Classroom instruction was premised upon this scientifically endorsed treatise. To banish it from education was to ignore the legislature's constitutional obligation to "cherish literature and science," a point over which the prosecutors and defense team clashed during the early stages of the trial.[13]

The lucidity of Darrow's opening argument put Raulston in a tough spot. The judge had wanted a speedy trial and an easy conviction devoid of any larger—and polarizing—debate over evolution versus creationism. At the outset of the trial, he scoffed at Darrow's overtures that roughly a dozen distinguished scientists from around the country were poised to take the witness stand on behalf of the defense to explain the confirmed principles of evolution to the jury. Suddenly, the esteemed lawyer from Chicago had maneuvered the small-town judge into an impossible predicament. Raulston strained to create the appearance of being an objective jurist. Still, any ruling against Darrow's inexorable logic might be viewed by both the jury and the public at large as unjustified, illegitimate, and unfair.

Raulston excused the jury from the courtroom. From his vantage point, the jurors had already heard too much. Perhaps they were now wondering whether they might want to hear from these prominent scientists about the validity of evolution, upon which their decision would be predicated. Darrow was offering sound reasons why the jury should learn more about how species gradually evolved. This was the last thing Raulston wanted in his court.

With the jury exiting the courtroom, Darrow and his cocounsel quickly rose to object. They demanded that the jurors stay for the remainder of their arguments, leading to a tense exchange between Neal and Tom Stewart of the prosecution.

"The jury is the judge of the law and the facts," Neal insisted.

Stewart scoffed at this well-established legal principle by falsely stating, "Oh, that is all foolishness."

Unsurprisingly, the judge overruled Darrow and the jury panel departed. Raulston, it seemed, was determined to choreograph the trial to the prosecution's benefit. He didn't want the jury to witness it.[14]

Darrow and his team read aloud another provision in the state's constitution that reinforced the right of citizens—including teachers—to express ideas and information freely. Twice during the trial, the defense quoted the state constitution's clause that "the free communication of thoughts and opinions is one of the invaluable rights of man, and every citizen may freely speak, write and print on any subject."[15]

The defense argued that any discourse over evolution was protected speech, whether the expression occurred on the street or inside a store or the confines of a public schoolhouse. Scopes, they said, was being punished for exercising his educational freedom to teach a recognized scientific concept—whether opinion or fact—printed in a textbook approved years earlier by the legislature itself. It made no sense.

How could a teacher be prosecuted for doing his job? How could science be criminalized when taught by a person but not outlawed in the accepted text from which he taught? It should be left up to students, the defense argued, to decide what to believe and what not to believe. Anything else was an attempt to suffocate their freedom to think and reason. In a clever analogy, Darrow and his colleagues posed the issue in a different way. What if the legislature were to criminalize "any theory that denies the story that the earth is the center of the universe, as taught in the Bible, and to teach instead that the earth and planets move around the sun?" An act such as that would be "clearly unconstitutional" because it infringed on the liberties of the individual.

The heliocentric theory, first advanced by Copernicus, was well fixed in science and a matter of common knowledge. It could be seen and measured through the study of celestial objects in astronomy. Its accuracy was unquestioned, even though it stood in stark contradiction to the Bible. "Evolution," argued the defense, "is as much scientific fact as the Copernican theory, but the Copernican theory has been fully accepted, as this must be accepted."[16]

Once again, Darrow and his team urged the judge to allow prominent scientists to take the witness stand to help educate the jury. Arthur Garfield Hays told Raulston that he and the jurors needed to be educated on evolution: "Your Honor, and you gentlemen of the jury, would have to know what evolution is in order to pass upon it." This was a polite way of describing the judge and jury as largely ignorant of science.[17]

The prosecution was equally obtuse and didn't have the ability to counter Darrow's brilliance. Outgunned by Darrow, the prosecution simply distilled its objection to a single argument that Ben McKenzie, a wizened old man who thought anyone who believed in evolution was an atheist, made: "We cannot teach any religion in the schools, therefore you cannot teach any evolution, or any doctrine that conflicts with the Bible."[18]

This was dishonest. Schools were already teaching many scientific theories that ran afoul of the Bible, including the Copernican theory of the universe. The point was that students should enjoy the freedom to absorb information and decide for themselves what to think and believe.

The prosecution simply did not impress. Taking off his jacket as the crowded courtroom made the heat even more unbearable, Tom Stewart noted that the Butler Act fell under the state's police powers. McKenzie tried to play to the jury through small-town pride, noting that the defense team came from out of town, namely from big cities such as New York and Chicago.[19]

Raulston seemed to be at an impasse, although his decision to disallow Darrow's scientists from taking the stand was predetermined. He demanded briefs from both sides and informed Darrow that he would give him free rein to summarize his arguments. The jury would be sent home for the day so that they would never hear Darrow's persuasive speech on the legitimacy of evolution and the necessity of scientific testimony in court to prove it.

Darrow took center stage when the court reconvened the following morning and offered a broadside against Bryan, knowing that the press would focus on the longtime politician. Darrow insisted that, thanks to Bryan's efforts at the national level and his political prominence, he "is responsible for this foolish, mischievous, and wicked act" that outlawed the teaching of Darwin's theory. Darrow described the battle between evolution and creationism as something akin to "a death struggle between two civilizations," the enlightened one he championed and the deeply religious, rural one represented by Bryan.

For more than two hours, Darrow held forth on the danger of simple minds and timid men. Despite what many observers had expected, he never once criticized or condemned religion. On the contrary, the well-known agnostic emphasized the importance of "religious freedom in its broadest terms." Darrow argued that educational freedom must enjoy the same privilege: "If religion must go, or learning must go, why let learning go?" Darrow reminded the court that constitutions are designed to preserve freedoms, especially freedom of thought.

"There is not a single line of any constitution that can withstand bigotry and ignorance when it seeks to destroy the right of the individual; and bigotry and ignorance are ever active. Here, we find today as brazen and as bold an attempt to destroy learning as was ever made in the Middle Ages, and the only difference is we have not provided that they shall be burned at the stake. But there is time for that, Your Honor; we have to approach these things gradually."

Darrow called it "absurd" to think that Tennessee's law banishing evolution was legal. The pursuit of knowledge in the world demanded an open mind that kept pace with scientific advances.

More important, Darrow pointed out that the statute never used the word *evolution* in its stated prohibition. There was no mention of it whatsoever. Instead, the law made it a crime "to teach any theory that denies the Story of the Divine Creation of man as taught in the Bible." Darrow correctly observed that evolutionary theory did not necessarily stand in conflict with biblical doctrine. He noted, correctly, that "intelligent scholarly Christians by the millions in the United States find no inconsistencies between evolution and religion."

As for the book of Genesis, Darrow observed that it was "written when everyone thought the world was flat." The Bible is a good book, he reasoned, but not the only book. "The state of Tennessee has no more right to teach the Bible as the divine book than that the Koran is one, or the book of Mormons, or the book of Confucius, or the Buddha, or the essays of Emerson, or any one of the ten thousand books to which human souls have gone for consolation and aid in their troubles. Are they going to cut them out?"

But Darrow didn't stop there. He attacked the language of Tennessee's new statute as vague and ambiguous for failing to specifically state that someone could go to jail for teaching evolution. A man must know clearly what he has done wrong before his freedom is taken from him.

"It should be plain, simple, and easy. Does this statute state what you shall teach and what you shall not? Oh, no? Oh, no? Not at all. Does it say you cannot teach the earth is round? Because Genesis says it is flat? No. Does it say you cannot teach that the earth is millions of ages old because the account in Genesis makes it less than six thousand years old? Oh, no? It doesn't state that. If it did, you could understand it. It says you shan't teach any theory of the origin of man that is contrary to the Divine theory contained in the Bible."

Tennessee's command that no one can teach anything that is antithetical to the Bible would require that "every man must be sure that he has read everything in the Bible and not only read it but understand it, or he might violate the criminal code."

Darrow then turned his attention to the Bible itself, calling it "a book primarily of religion and morals." He added, "It is not a book of science. Never was and was never meant to be." It is not a text on construction or chemistry or mathematics or geology or biology or astronomy. "Man yearns to know more and supplements his knowledge with hope and faith." In this way, science complements the Bible but does not seek to supplant it. Darrow's knowledge of the Bible and religion was on full display. He had read the Bible many times over and knew it better than most. He recognized, for example, that the book offered a myriad of contradictions.

"Can Your Honor tell us what is given as the origin of man in the Bible? Is there any human being who can tell us?" Darrow said, playing with his suspenders and acting as if he were talking to neighbors around the front porch, engaged in a friendly argument. "There are two conflicting accounts in the first two chapters. There are in America at least five hundred different sects or churches, all of which quarrel with each other on the importance and non-importance of certain passages. They do not agree among themselves. There is a great division among Catholics and Protestants.

"Now my client must be familiar with the whole book and must know all about all these warring sects of Christians and know which of them is right and which wrong, in order that he will not commit a crime. This statute, I say, Your Honor, is indefinite and uncertain.

No man could obey it, and no court could enforce it. If this is a good indictment, I never saw a bad one."

Bryan and his fundamentalist followers had accused Scopes of defiling a senseless law, asserted Darrow, "because they are after everybody that dares to think." His client was on trial and threatened with jail "because ignorance and bigotry are rampant, and it is a mighty strong combination." He concluded that prosecutors might just as well indict a man for being no good.

Darrow made the case that freedom of religion is a precious right protected by our Constitution. But religious liberty also means freedom from religion. The free expression of ideas is equally cherished, even—and especially—when they stand in contrast to popular religious thought. Darrow ridiculed the notion that the government is equipped to tell its people what to believe and what not to believe. Individuals have an indefeasible right to decide for themselves.

When the state constitution provided that no preference should be given by law to any religious establishment, that meant freedom from fundamentalist propaganda, said Darrow. But Tennessee lawmakers ignored this sacred promise.

Darrow ended his powerful summation with a dire warning about the future:

"They passed a law making the Bible the yardstick to measure every man's intellect, and to measure every man's learning. Every bit of knowledge that the mind has, must now be submitted to a religious test. I do not pretend to be a prophet, but I do not need to be a prophet to know what will happen. If men are not tolerant, if men cannot respect each other's opinions, if men cannot live and let live, then no man's life is safe. Your Honor knows the fires that have been lighted in America to kindle religious bigotry and hate. If today you can take a thing like evolution and make it a crime to teach it in the public school . . . tomorrow you may ban books and magazines and the newspapers. Ignorance and fanaticism is ever busy and needs feeding. Always it is feeding and gloating for more."[20]

Darrow made a strong impression, including on his client. "Darrow's manner was easygoing and relaxed, almost casual," Scopes recalled. He praised the attorney's "first-class mind," which was "always working at top speed and efficiency." Darrow kept his hands on his suspenders for most of his talk. Unlike many attorneys, he expressed himself through his head movements and expressions instead of speaking with his hands. "It was a central characteristic of Darrow that he engaged his listeners' minds, not their eyes," Scopes remembered forty years later.[21]

Reporting to readers across the nation, Mencken praised "Darrow's great speech," though he insisted it would have no impact even as some of the "morons in the audience . . . hissed at it." Mencken, who had covered Bryan in depth over the years, watched him over at the prosecutor's table, where he "sat tight-lipped and unmoved." Watching Bryan, Mencken realized that the Great Commoner felt confident about the results of the trial no matter what Darrow did. Bryan "has those hillbillies locked up in his pen and he knows it," fumed Mencken. Pondering Tennessee's future, Mencken could not imagine it without Bryan. "He may last five years, ten years or even longer."[22]

Mencken also noted the judge began to grow restless at the end of Darrow's speech. Raulston, who was impatiently checking the clock, had had enough. He adjourned for the day and promised to render his ruling the following morning about whether the scientists and experts could testify. As he packed up his briefcase, Darrow knew the case against Scopes would never be dismissed outright. But he hoped that his arguments had at least pried open the door for his scientists to take the witness stand to explain the verifiable science behind evolution—that it was not some crackpot theory designed to undermine the Bible. But Raulston had to rule on whether the trial would continue and whether he would let witnesses speak before the jury. The prosecutors, from local attorneys to Bryan, would do their best to make sure the judge ruled against Darrow.

12

The Prosecution Makes Its Case

The following day, Judge John Raulston took the bench and announced his decision on whether to let the trial continue with dispatch.

Raulston couldn't possibly counter Clarence Darrow's constitutional arguments on their merits; they were too sound and well reasoned. Instead, the judge simply glossed over them by stating that he "failed to see" how an anti-evolution statute promoted religion. Raulston failed to see because he was being deliberately myopic. He concluded that the state legislature could do as it pleased. It was not the job of his court to question the "motive or wisdom" of Tennessee lawmakers, especially in matters of "popular feeling," which was a nod to William Jennings Bryan and his fundamentalist followers.

With that decision in place, the trial of John Scopes continued.

After a brief opening statement by the prosecution, the defense shrewdly conceded that Scopes had, indeed, taught the theory of evolution. Defense counsel Dudley Malone took the lead and cautioned that his client had not taught evolution in opposition to the Bible. Malone insisted, "The defense contends that to convict Scopes, the prosecution must prove that Scopes not only taught the theory of evolution, but that he also, and at the same time, denied the theory of creation as set forth in the Bible. The defense contends that the prosecution must prove that the defendant, Scopes, did these two things and that what he taught was a violation of the statute."[1]

Malone was correct—not that the prosecution team cared about the elements of proof. They knew the judge did not. Malone, Darrow, and the defense team counted on the jury's ability to comprehend a fine but vital distinction in the law.

Continuing his argument, Malone then tackled an even finer point. He argued that while the story of creation recited in the Bible was not scientifically correct, there was no conflict between evolution and Christianity. To build on this, Malone said the defense intended to call highly educated and accomplished experts to the witness stand.

"We shall show by the testimony of men learned in science and theology that there are millions of people who believe in evolution and in the stories of creation as set forth in the Bible and who find no conflict between the two. The defense maintains that this is a matter of faith and interpretation, which each individual must determine for himself," Malone said.[2]

This brilliant argument was developed by Malone, Darrow, and the other members of the defense team. They sought to portray Scopes as an earnest teacher who merely followed what was written in the state-approved school textbook but never actively taught his students that the story of Divine Creation was wrong. His pupils were allowed to draw their own conclusions freely and endeavor to resolve any inconsistencies on their own.

But Malone also pointed out, "Science and religion embrace two separate and distinct fields of thought and learning." Just as people should be permitted to exercise religion freely, they should be allowed to learn science freely. This was all the more vital because scientific theories had grown exponentially in the nearly two thousand years since the Bible was written by men who believed the earth was flat.

"There is no branch of science which can be taught today without teaching the theory of evolution. It applies to geology, biology, botany, astronomy, medicine, chemistry, bacteriology, embryology, zoology, sanitation, forestry, and agriculture," Malone said.[3]

In meticulous detail, Malone explained the innumerable applications of evolution in a myriad of fields. If science was to be excluded by law, where was man to gain his wealth of knowledge? It cannot be found in the Bible because it "is a work of religious aspiration and rules of conduct which must be kept in the field of theology." More than anything else, it was a book of morals that might guide man's behavior in society.

The defense also attempted to defuse the widespread assumption that "man descended from monkeys," which the prosecution had repeatedly misrepresented during the trial to inflame the emotions of the jury. No scientist of any preeminent standing held such a view. Man evolved in a different direction from monkeys, said Malone.

Watching Malone in action as he started to target Bryan, Scopes found himself impressed. He recognized that Malone presented a very different style from Darrow's even as "they complemented each other perfectly." Scopes thought Darrow was a "kindly, homespun, conversational teacher." Malone was a "flamboyant, emotional orator."[4]

An old foe going back to their time serving in the State Department under President Woodrow Wilson, Malone even quoted large passages of Bryan's writings, contrasting his previous views with his current ones on a host of fronts, including the role of religion in a democratic society.

Scopes knew of Bryan and Malone's often tense relationship over the years, especially from their time at the State Department together, and realized that it was helping his lawyer make his case.

"Malone's peculiar former relationship with Bryan contained the finite ingredients for potential drama and he was least of all the man to ignore the irony of those circumstances," Scopes recalled. "He knew Bryan's character well enough to deal with him on equal footing in an adversary situation, a pleasure he never before enjoyed, and by getting to the heart of their conflict he scored one of the trial's greatest coups."[5]

As Scopes wrote some forty years later, Malone had laid the groundwork for the dramatic showdown between Bryan and Darrow that would eclipse the rest of the trial.

"We believe there is no conflict between evolution and Christianity. There may be a conflict between evolution and the peculiar ideas of Christianity which are held by Mr. Bryan as the evangelical leader of the prosecution, but we deny that he is an authorized spokesman for the Christians of the United States. There is a clear distinction between God, the church, the Bible, Christianity, and Mr. Bryan," Malone said.[6]

Malone, Darrow, and their colleagues were openly baiting Bryan—and the Great Commoner stepped right into the trap.

Bryan rose to object to the characterization. He promised the jury that he would personally explain to them his vast knowledge of the Bible and its unquestioned veracity.

"I ask no protection from the court," Bryan told Raulston. "When the proper time comes, I shall be able to show the gentlemen that I stand today just where I did."[7]

A loud wave of applause thundered throughout the courtroom, but it obscured the real drama of the moment. With his words, Bryan had swallowed the bait. The stage was set for the great debate between Bryan and Darrow.

If Bryan hadn't realized he had agreed to a showdown with Darrow, his cocounsel on the prosecution certainly did. Tom Stewart instantaneously rose to object to any expert witnesses being called, presumably including Bryan himself. Raulston deferred his ruling and ordered the prosecution to begin calling its witnesses.[8]

After that, a series of individuals took the stand as part of the prosecution's burden of proof. The first witness was Rhea County superintendent of public schools Walter White.

Now in his midforties, White's bulky frame, with multiple chins bulging over his tight collar, concealed a first-rate political mind. Despite being a Republican in Tennessee, part of the Democrats' Solid South, White enjoyed a successful political career, becoming one of the most prominent GOP leaders in the state legislature. Like his fellow Republican Raulston, White hoped to use the publicity over the Scopes Trial to advance his political interests. Already, he was looking at 1926, when Governor Austin Peay, who had signed the Butler Act into law, had to run for a third term.

White faced Stewart first, and the superintendent told the jury that Scopes had readily confessed to him that he taught Darwin's theory of evolution to his students straight out of the textbook.

"What did he say?" Stewart asked.

"He admitted that he taught evolution. He said that he couldn't teach the book without teaching evolution and said he couldn't teach biology without violating this law."

"Did he say that it was unconstitutional?"

"He defended his course by saying that the statute was unconstitutional."

On cross-examination, Darrow emphasized that Scopes was following the textbook approved by the state—the same state that criminalized the contents of the book it distributed to its teachers.

"This was the official book adopted by the board, was it not?" Darrow asked White.

"That was the official book adopted by the commission in 1919."

"So, he taught this, which was the official book at that time?"

"Yes, sir."

"You never said anything to him about it or to any other teacher about not teaching it?"

"No, sir. I did not for these reasons—"

An annoyed Darrow interrupted White. "I don't care anything about the reason. . . . Nobody ever said anything to you about it, did they?"

"No, sir."

"Do you know how long this book has been used?"

"It has been used since 1909, the school year of 1909."

"That is all," Darrow concluded, and White stepped down.[9]

Watching from across the courtroom, Scopes was not impressed with White. Faced with the most famous trial lawyer in America, the superintendent was more soft-spoken than usual thanks to stage fright. Darrow had to urge him "to speak loudly, in order for the reporters to hear him in the packed, noisy courtroom."[10]

The superintendent would return to the spotlight in 1926 when he was the Republican candidate to challenge Peay in November. White's role in the Scopes Trial had not helped him. While Republicans broke 40 percent of the vote against Peay in 1922 and 1924, White took only 35 percent.

Darrow's point was obvious. In its zeal to conform to fundamentalists' demands, the State of Tennessee had passed a law that contradicted itself. It encouraged the use of a biology textbook for classroom study but made it a crime for a teacher to actually repeat in class what the pages of the book stated about evolution. Thus, it was perfectly okay for a student to read about evolution. That wasn't a crime. Yet he or she could not listen to the exact same material read aloud by the teacher of the class. That was a crime. The law was inconsistent, hypocritical, and self-defeating. If ever there was an arbitrary and capricious statute, this was it.

The law was worse than that. Years earlier, Tennessee had passed a law requiring teachers to use only books prescribed by the state. The book that Scopes taught from, Hunter's *Civic Biology*, was so approved. Hence, the defendant was compelled to use the very textbook that it was a crime for him to use.

Arthur Garfield Hays made just that argument to the court as he joined Darrow and Malone in defending Scopes:

"The state here prosecutes Scopes—it is a crime as I understand it not to use schoolbooks prescribed by the state, and to use a schoolbook as Professor Scopes used it is also a crime. I assume that the State of Tennessee did not intend to make it a crime if the teacher used it and likewise make it a crime if the teacher didn't use it. I cannot imagine two laws, one of which compels a man to do a thing and another which makes it a misdemeanor for him to do it."[11]

This apparent paradox did not seem to bother either the prosecution or the judge. If it did, they chose to ignore it.

Looking to showcase more testimony against Scopes, the prosecution called two of Scopes's former students to the stand in succession.

Fourteen-year-old Howard "Scrappy" Morgan, the son of local banker Luther Morgan, confirmed that his teacher reviewed with students the subchapter on evolution and how all animals, including man, evolved slowly from simple-cell organisms.

"Did you study anything under Professor Scopes?" Stewart asked. "Did he undertake to teach you anything about evolution?"

"He said that the earth was once a hot molten mass, too hot for plant or animal life to exist upon it. In the sea, the earth cooled off; there was a little germ of one-cell organism formed, and this organism kept evolving until it got to be a pretty good-sized animal, and then come on to be a land animal, and it kept on evolving, and from this was man."

Stewart kept on with his questions: "How did he classify man with references to other animals; what did he say about them?"

"Well, the book and he both classified man along with cats and dogs, cows, horses, monkeys, lions, horses, and all that."

Satisfied that a fourteen-year-old boy had offered a tenuous connection between monkeys and man, the prosecutor sat down. Now, it was Darrow's turn. With the textbook in his hands as a guide, Darrow's cross-examination was both simple and potent:

"Now, he said the earth was once a molten mass of liquid, didn't he?"

"Yes, sir."

"Running molten mass of liquid, and that it slowly cooled until a crust was formed on it?"

"Yes, sir."

"After that, after it got cooled enough, and the soil came, that plants grew; is that right?"

"Yes, sir; yes, sir."

"And that the first life was in the sea. And that it developed into life on the land?"

"Yes, sir."

"And finally into the highest organism, which is known as man?"

"Yes, sir."

A smile on his face, Darrow asked his final question: "Now, that is about what he taught you. It has not hurt you any, has it?"

"No, sir."

The courtroom burst into laughter.

"That is all," Darrow concluded.[12]

Scopes thought Darrow handled the pupil well. Darrow, Scopes remembered, questioned Howard by "approaching casually, talking with him easily, good-naturedly, as though they were sitting together in a classroom." As Scopes noted when he contrasted his attorneys, Darrow always remained something of the teacher he had been all those years ago, even in the courtroom. Still, Scopes thought Howard remained tense, despite Darrow's best efforts.[13]

Next up was seventeen-year-old Harry Shelton, and Stewart offered a familiar line of questioning.

"Did Professor Scopes teach you anything about evolution?" Stewart asked, giving Scopes a sarcastic title.

"He taught that all forms of life begin with the cell."

"Begin with the cell?"

"Yes, sir."

Stewart pointed to pages in the textbook covering evolution. "Did he teach you these pages, 194 and 195? Did you review this?"

"Yes, sir; reviewed the whole book."

Darrow's cross-examination of young Harry was quite brief but artful.

"Are you a church member?"

"Yes, sir."

Darrow tilted his head and raised his eyebrows. "Do you still belong?"

"Yes, sir."

"You didn't leave church when he told you all forms of life began with a single cell?" Darrow asked with a smile as the whispers from the audience grew louder.

"No, sir."

"That is all," Darrow said as Raulston called for no talking in the audience.[14]

Looking back at the prosecution's calling students to the witness stand, Darrow wrote, "The state brought in a number of bright little boys who were pupils" of Scopes's. "They told how Mr. Scopes had tried to poison their young minds and imperil their souls by telling them that life began in the sea from a single cell that gradually developed into the different structures that are now scattered over the earth." Still, the boys "did not see how this had done them any harm."

After the students left the stand, Darrow even overheard one of them asking the other, "Don't you think Mr. Bryan is a little narrow-minded?" Darrow dryly observed, "Both of these boys had already been corrupted by Scopes," and Darrow was "afraid their souls will be lost."[15]

Four decades later, Scopes insisted the boys, who had been in the classroom that day, weren't fully honest in their testimony:

"If the boys had got their review of evolution from me, I was unaware of it. I didn't remember teaching it. I wouldn't claim credit for the boys' knowledge, and I doubt that they had remembered so much from the regular classes. Yet I am sure they had not perjured themselves. Possibly they had read of the process of evolution and thought that I taught it to them."[16]

The prosecution's last witness was F. E. Robinson, the owner of Robinson's Drug Store, where the idea of prosecuting Scopes to garner publicity for Dayton had originated. Robinson also chaired the Rhea County School Board.

Stewart asked Robinson if Scopes had told him that he taught about evolution and was familiar with the new law.

"Scopes told you that he knew of the law?" Stewart asked.

"Yes, sir."

"And you discussed it with him?"

"Yes, sir."

Days after the school term ended, Scopes openly admitted to Robinson and other Dayton residents that he had violated the law by teaching directly from Hunter's *Civic Biology*. This alleged confession was immaterial. The defense had conceded that Scopes taught evolution.

But Darrow was quick to point out that Robinson, in his role with the school board, sold the textbook from which Scopes taught and under which the young teacher was being criminally prosecuted. Robinson wasn't being prosecuted, but Scopes was. The irony was lost on no one, and the courtroom erupted in brief laughter.

Darrow read at length the lesson on evolution printed in the book.

"How many of these did you have for sale?" Darrow asked, indicating the textbook.

"Oh, I have been selling that book for six or seven years."

"Have you noticed any mental or moral deterioration growing out of the thing?"

Stewart jumped in, offering an objection. "Exception."

"I sustain the exception," Raulston said.

Darrow ended by forcing Robinson to admit that he purchased boxes of the textbook from the state board of education, which had approved its contents. Yet the state legislature had decided that teaching from that textbook constituted a crime. Selling it or reading it was no crime at all.[17]

Noting that the prosecutors wanted to have other students testify, Darrow told Stewart just to offer the names of these children since they would all testify that Scopes taught evolution in April. Hays offered a procedural motion to dismiss the case, which Raulston quickly ruled against.

With that, the prosecution rested its case against John Thomas Scopes.[18]

But something was missing. Outside of his quick response to Malone, Bryan had remained silent as the prosecution offered witnesses. Fanning himself in his shirtsleeves, Bryan sat at the prosecutors' table with his son, William Jr., Stewart, and McKenzie, offering little to the prosecutors' case. "The formidable dynamo within the silver-tongued hero, merely slumbered, waiting, waiting, as everyone knew; no one doubted Bryan's Day was nearing," Scopes recalled. "But the people were mistaken. It was not to be. Again, as in his long political career, fate conspired against Bryan."[19]

While he may have been largely silent in the courtroom, Bryan spoke to the reporters gathered in Dayton and got his message out through them.

"The evolutionists have not been honest with the public," Bryan insisted. "Even ministers who believe in evolution have assured their congregations that there is no inconsistency between Darwinism and Christianity. The ministers should tell their congregations that evolution leads logically to agnosticism."

Ignoring Malone, Bryan kept his fire focused squarely at Darrow. "The presence of Mr. Darrow here, an avowed agnostic both as to God and immortality—he has so stated in court before the judge—represents the most militant anti-Christian sentiment in the country," Bryan said, pointing to his opponent's objections to prayers in the courtroom.

"Mr. Darrow's hostility to Christianity, proclaimed for a generation, and his conduct in this case are now known to the world and will arouse the devout Christians of the nation whose prayers ascend in gratitude for the courage of the state of Tennessee," Bryan added, as he readied for a showdown with his old ally turned opponent.[20]

13

"Are We Entitled to Show What Evolution Is?"

Starting their defense effort, Clarence Darrow and his team knew there was no point in disputing the evidence that John Scopes taught evolution to high school students.

Scopes most certainly taught evolution and readily admitted it. Darrow was not opposed to conceding this fundamental claim of the prosecution's. It was an integral part of his trial strategy. Darrow planned to argue that his client never disparaged religion in the classroom and had not taught his students that evolution "denies the Story of the Divine Creation of man as taught in the Bible," as the new Tennessee law expressly prohibited.

Instead, Darrow hoped to convince the jury that evolution and creationism could coexist in harmony. One theory did not necessarily disprove the other. The two theories did not conflict unless a student chose to view them as antagonistic. Scopes played no role in that active decision, Darrow would argue. In other words, every person should be free to draw his or her own conclusions.

As the defense commenced its case, the prosecution was anxious to cross-examine Scopes. Stewart invoked a procedural rule unique to Tennessee that required the defendant to testify first or be excluded from testifying. But following Darrow's counsel, Scopes elected to exercise his Fifth Amendment right against self-incrimination and to remain silent. Darrow had no intention of putting the accused on the witness stand and expose him to a cross-examination that might only underscore his guilt even though the defense had already admitted that Scopes had taught evolution.

"Your Honor, every single word that was said against this defendant, everything was true," Darrow said, talking about the legal proceedings and not the insults hurled Scopes's way.

"So he does not care to go on the stand?" Judge Raulston asked.

"No, what is the use?"[1]

Having deflated the prosecution's ambition to make Scopes the centerpiece of the trial testimony, Darrow shifted the focus toward science. His first witness was Dr. Maynard M. Metcalf, an esteemed zoologist who taught at Oberlin and Johns Hopkins and who had studied evolution extensively.

Raulston had yet to rule on whether any of Darrow's experts would be allowed to testify in front of the jury. So, the twelve members of the panel were asked to depart from the courtroom just moments before Metcalf stepped into the witness box. This testimony would be a trial run of sorts—a chance for the judge to hear precisely what one of Darrow's scientists would have to say in advance of His Honor's ruling.

Metcalf, who had a PhD from Johns Hopkins University, held forth on evolution as a well-accepted scientific principle supported by decades of research and evidence. Looking back on the trial, Darrow praised him as a "man whose attainments were everywhere recognized."[2]

Metcalf attempted to live up to that reputation by educating the courtroom about evolution: "The fact of evolution is a thing that is perfectly and absolutely clear." He described its general characteristics: "Evolution, I think, means . . . change. It means the change of an organism from one character into a different character, and by character

I mean its structure, or its behavior, or its function, or its method of development from the egg of anything else. . . . The term in general means the whole series of such changes which have taken place during hundreds of millions of years which have produced from lowly beginnings . . . to organisms of much more complex character."

Metcalf left no room for doubt over whether he believed evolution was a theory or a fact: "I think it would be entirely impossible for any normal human being who was conversant with the phenomena to have even for a moment the least doubt even for the fact of evolution."[3]

Sitting in the audience, H. L. Mencken found himself impressed with how Darrow led Metcalf, a "somewhat chubby man," through the questions. Still, the journalist from Baltimore grew increasingly distracted as the prosecutors left their table to stand in front of Metcalf as they listened to him. It was a desperate act of intimidation, perhaps. First came William Jennings Bryan, who stood "not ten feet away" from Metcalf. The rest of the prosecutors followed Bryan, but Mencken reported that Metcalf did not lose focus even as they drew near.[4]

Right on cue after Metcalf wrapped up his testimony, the prosecution objected to his testifying before the jury. Scopes, they contended, had admitted he taught evolution. Any testimony from experts was wholly irrelevant and an intrusion on the province of the jury.

Darrow countered by arguing that evolution was a mystery to many laypeople, including members of the jury. He pointed out that only one juror had ever read something on the subject. "We expect to show that it isn't in conflict with the theory of evolution," Darrow said about creationism. "We insist that a jury cannot decide this important question . . . without knowing both what evolution is and the interpretation of the story of creation."[5]

Darrow's cocounsel, Arthur Garfield Hays, then offered a different argument in favor of Metcalf's testimony. The law that Scopes had allegedly violated prohibited him from teaching "that man has descended from a lower order of animals." The prosecution, said Hays, had falsely represented that Scopes had taught his students that man descended from a monkey.

But no evidence of that was ever presented during the state's case. Why? Because the defendant never said such a thing at school. It was an invention of the media and conveniently adopted by the prosecution to inflame public passion. Even if Scopes *had* uttered it in class, it would still not have violated the letter of the law as written.

"In the first order—the primate order—was man, monkeys, apes, and lemurs," Hays noted. "To prove that man was descended from a monkey would not prove that man was descended from a lower order of animals because they are all in the same order of animals—the first order—and that is the use of the term 'order of animals' by zoologists. . . . They might say that man came from a different genus but not a lower order of animals.

"Are we entitled to show what evolution is? Are we entitled to show that the development of man from a cell does not make him a lower order of animals?"

In addition to Bryan, there were half a dozen members of the prosecution's team. Ben McKenzie, flamboyant when arguing a case and often sullen when sidelined, voiced an obstreperous objection to science in general and scientists in particular. McKenzie accused Darrow of attempting to undermine the sound teachings of the Bible.

Judge Raulston interjected, "Let me ask you a question. Is this your position, that the story of the Divine Creation is so clearly set forth in the Bible, in Genesis, that no reasonable minds could differ as to the method of creation, that is, that man was created complete by God?"

McKenzie quickly responded, "Yes."

"And in one act, and not by a method of growth or development. Is that your position?"

"From lower animals—yes, that is exactly right."

"That God created Adam first as a complete man, did not create a single cell of life?" When McKenzie answered yes, the judge continued. "The cell of life did not develop in time?"

"That is right, and man did not descend from a lower order of animals that originated in the sea and then turned from one animal to another, and finally man's head shot up."

"You think the divine story is so clearly told, it is not ambiguous and should be accepted by anyone of reasonable fairness?"

"I do." McKenzie didn't stop there. As if testifying himself as an expert on the Bible, he began reciting from the pages of Genesis and then averred that Darrow's heathen scientists would have the jury believe that man evolved from "some sort of protoplasm" or a "soft dishrag . . . in the ocean"—a reference to the animal species known as the sponge contained in the textbook from which Scopes taught.[6]

Darrow couldn't resist jumping in. He rose and began peppering McKenzie with questions. Judge Raulston did not intervene as the renowned Chicago lawyer commandeered the courtroom.

"Let me ask a question." Darrow turned his attention to the Bible's account of creation. "When it said, 'in His own image,' did you think that meant the physical man?"

"I am taking the Divine account—'He is like unto me,'" McKenzie answered.

"Do you think it is so?"

"I say that, although I know it is awfully hard on our Maker to look like a lot of fellows who are profusely ugly, to say he favored the Master," McKenzie replied, trying gamely to lend a rare bit of humor to the proceedings.

Ignoring McKenzie's attempts at humor, Darrow pressed on. "You think then that you do?"

"You are all right. I don't mind your favoring Him, but when one commits acts against the law, there ought to be some remedy for it."

"Wait a minute. You do think the physical man is like God?"

"Why, yes, I do, and I will give you my reason," said McKenzie.

"I think God knows better. You think men must believe that to believe the Bible that the physical man as we see him looks like God?"

"Yes, sir, and I will give you my reasons as soon as you want them."

"And when you see man, you see a picture of God?"

"Like unto Him and made in His image; and the reason why I believe that firmly is because the Bible teaches it." McKenzie then added that he also believed in the virgin birth of Christ.

"You said there was the first day, the second day, the third day, the fourth day, the fifth day, the sixth day, and so on. Do you think they were literal days?"

"We didn't have any sun until the fourth day. I believe the biblical account."

The discussion wound down as McKenzie lamented that Darrow's scientists were trying to "put words into the mouth of God and substitute another story, entirely different to God's word." The word of God, said the prosecutor, was absolute and unquestioned.

This was not at all what the defense was contending, and Darrow took a moment to correct McKenzie politely. "I think you misunderstand our position. What we claim is that there is no question among intelligent men about the fact of evolution. As to how it came about, there is a great deal of difference."[7]

Watching this exchange, Scopes thought it was one of the few times McKenzie showed any signs of life during the trial. "Mc-

Kenzie was lethargic and drowsy only when he wasn't doing the talking himself," Scopes recalled.[8]

As William Jennings Bryan sat idly listening to this caustic exchange with his longtime nemesis, Darrow, the fundamentalist leader may have felt overshadowed by his colleagues in the prosecution. Mencken watched Bryan throughout the morning, noting he "sat silent throughout the whole scene, his gaze fixed immovably on" Metcalf before listening to the legal exchanges. "Now and then, his face darkened, and his eyes flashed, but he never uttered a sound."[9]

Scopes also noted that, until this point in the trial, Bryan "had not said a word." Instead, "he sat in court, fanning himself with a palm-leaf fan, expressionless, completely deadpan."[10] However, now, after being silent throughout the trial, Bryan rose to interject, but Raulston insisted on adjourning for lunch and bringing more fans as the heat made the courtroom intolerable.

When court resumed in the afternoon session, Bryan offered a lengthy diatribe against science in general, scientists in particular, and any heathen educator who had the temerity to teach the "dangers" of evolution. Addressing the gallery in the packed courtroom, Bryan accused Darrow of trying to "force Darwinism and evolution on your children." Bryan also sought to denigrate Darrow, Malone, and Hays as outsiders, painting a striking contrast between New York and Tennessee, a message that played well in the Volunteer State, with its concerns about urban culture, the evils of alcohol, and a growing cultural divide.

In a mocking tone, Bryan called Darwin's ideas of natural selection ludicrous and a laughingstock, looking to show the differences between traditional Christian belief and what scientists held to be true. "The Christian believes man came from above, but the evolutionist believes he must have come from below." This garnered laughter from the audience before Bryan implored Raulston not to bring in expert witnesses. "We have evidence enough here, we do not need any experts to come in here and tell us about this thing."

Bryan insisted that parents should be able to control what their children are taught in the classroom. "Tell me that parents have not any right to declare that children are not to be taught this doctrine? Shall not be taken down from the high plane upon which God put man? Shall be detached from the throne of God and be compelled to link their ancestors with the jungle? Tell that to these children?

"Parents have a right to say that no teacher paid by their money shall rob their children of faith in God and send them back to their homes skeptical, infidels, or agnostics, or atheists. This doctrine that they want, this doctrine that they would force upon the schools, where they will not let the Bible be read!"[11]

Cheers from the faithful notwithstanding, Bryan's scold was not remotely credulous. Even in 1925, as the trial unfolded in Dayton, Darwin's proposition that all species descended from common ancestors was widely accepted worldwide. Among academics in many fields, it formed a fundamental concept in basic science. Many Christians also accepted the notion, seeing no contrast with evolution and their takes on the Bible's account of creation.

But in this small religious town in Tennessee, Bryan was so consumed by his biblical passions that he was determined to ridicule Darwin. Bending over the prosecution table, Bryan's thick hands fingered through a copy of *The Descent of Man*, penned by Darwin in 1871. Bryan read a complicated passage—wholly without context—about the evolution of mammals and wildly misinterpreted what was written.

To his rapt audience, Bryan, generally an isolationist who had opposed American intervention in World War I, thundered that, according to Darwinism, man developed "not even from American monkeys, but from Old World monkeys!" Laughter consumed the courtroom as Darrow and the defense team sat pensively nearby.

Despite some questions from Malone and Hays, Bryan found his groove and continued his argument. "Evolution is not a theory, but a hypothesis." Bryan insisted that scientists had never been able to connect all the dots. "There had never been found a single species the origin of which could be traced to another species."

Bryan continued this line of attack and tried to show the sharp differences between scientists and God-fearing Christians, such as those who lived in Dayton. "Today there is not a scientist in all the world who can trace one single species to any other. And yet, they call us ignoramuses and bigots because we do not throw away our Bible and accept it as proved that out of two or three million species not a one is traceable to another . . . yet they demand we allow them to teach this stuff to our children, that they may come home with their imaginary family tree and scoff at their mother's and father's Bible."[12]

Bryan's attack on evolution was abstruse, at best. At its worst, it was pure demagoguery designed to obscure Darrow's effort to convince Raulston to permit expert scientists to explain to the jury the biological rationale behind evolution and that it did not necessarily conflict with the Bible. Bryan would have none of it. Evolution, he said, was a deadly scourge intended to kill Christianity.

"The Bible is the Word of God; the Bible is the only expression of man's hope of salvation," Bryan insisted. "That Bible is not going to be driven out of this court by experts who come hundreds of miles to testify that they can reconcile evolution with its ancestor in the jungle. . . . We ought to confine ourselves to the law and to the evidence that can be admitted in accordance with the law."[13]

Watching from the defense table, Scopes recognized that most of the crowd was ready to hear Bryan. "They thrilled as Bryan approached the bench," he recalled. "On his feet, the heavy, big-stomached, colorless man with the fan vanished. He was suddenly the fighting antagonist, and as he spoke, his mood changed from the fighter to the pleader, and he ran through the whole gamut of emotions." Still, Scopes recognized that Bryan was not as skilled a speaker as he used to be. "His mind was not as sharp as I remembered it; still, most of the old fire was there."[14]

After a short recess, Darrow's cocounsel Dudley Malone, the only attorney whose jacket remained on so far despite the wilting heat during the trial, stood up and walked around to the front of the defense table and took a deep breath. Malone began methodically dismantling Bryan's screed, point by point, over the next half hour.

Malone had asked Darrow for the opportunity to rebut Bryan, and the defense team agreed to let him have a chance against his old chief at the State Department. As Scopes had foreseen, the personal tensions with Bryan helped fuel Malone's passion. Malone even slipped off his coat to get the crowd's attention, generating some notice as he changed his usual overly stiff demeanor.[15]

Praising Bryan as "my old chief and friend," Malone said he did not understand Bryan's role with the prosecution. Was Bryan in Dayton as an attorney or a religious missionary or a politician? Malone characterized his adversary as an inveterate "propagandist" who advocated that everything in the Bible, including the Divine Creation of man some six thousand years ago, should be interpreted literally. Biology, anthropology, and archaeology had proven otherwise, the attorney said.

"I don't know Mr. Bryan as well as Mr. Bryan knows Mr. Bryan, but I know this—that he does believe," Malone said. "And Mr. Bryan, Your Honor, is not the only one who believes in the Bible."

Malone then looked to other disciplines besides science, including history and archaeology. He implored the court to allow expert witnesses to educate the jury on the nature and value of evolution-ary evidence—not to undermine religion but to prevent students in classrooms from being deprived of scientific knowledge. Theo-logical and scientific minds might differ, said Malone, but "it is a conflict of ideas." The noble goal of education is to expose the young mind to a variety of theoretical and factual concepts. In one form or another, evolution had been a steady presence in textbooks and classrooms for more than half a century, even in Tennessee. The prosecution had failed to prove that a single person's morals had been corrupted by teaching this theory.[16]

Bryan and his fundamentalist followers were closed-minded and absolutists, argued the defense. They had misappropriated the Bible to exclude all other knowledge and pursuits in the world. If Bryan and his acolytes were left to their own devices, science would be dis-carded as a "poison" that perverts the mind and degrades the soul. Only the Bible would remain.

Getting into his stride, his voice becoming louder as he continued to speak, Malone attempted to sketch the "difference between the theological mind and the scientific mind" as he offered an emotional response that matched Bryan's earlier address.

"The theological mind is closed because that is what is revealed and is settled. But the scientist says, no, the Bible is the book of re-vealed religion with rules of conduct and with aspirations—that is the Bible. The scientist says take the Bible as a guide, as an inspiration, as a set of philosophies and preachments in the world of theology."

Malone painted the trial as a "religious question" and swatted back at Bryan's claims that the defense attorneys had no business in Dayton.

"Mr. Bryan brought all of the foreigners into this case." The nor-mally buttoned-up lawyer won attention as he showed some emotion, even anger, at his old boss at the State Department. "Mr. Bryan had offered his services from Miami, Florida; he does not belong in Tennessee. If it be wrong for American citizens from other parts of this country to come to Tennessee to discuss that which we believe, then Mr. Bryan has no right here, either."

Malone also said Bryan was wrong to argue that the trial was a contest between Christians and nonbelievers.

"Mr. Bryan is not the only one who has spoken for the Bible; Judge McKenzie is not the only defender of the word of God," Malone said, his loud voice roaring through the crowded courtroom and using an honorific title for McKenzie. "There are other people in this country who have given their whole lives to God. Mr. Bryan, to my knowledge, with a very passionate spirit and enthusiasm, has given most of his life to politics."

Raulston was about to interject when, to the surprise of most of the participants, the audience erupted in applause. The crowd, which had been behind Bryan for most of the trial, cheered Malone for his passionate speech—and the blow he had landed on his old rival.[17]

Once again, the defense attorneys focused on the statute and its double requirements. They admitted that Scopes had taught from a textbook the theory that man had descended from a lower order of animal life. But they denied vigorously that their client ever instructed his students that the story of Divine Creation outlined in the Bible was wrong. Under the law, Scopes needed to have done both to be guilty. There was no evidence at all that Scopes had mentioned the Bible, even in a passing reference.[18]

Perhaps fatigued by the arguments and wanting to sharpen the issue, Judge Raulston interrupted Malone. "Let me ask you a question. Is it your opinion that the theory of evolution is reconcilable with the story of the Divine Creation as taught in the Bible?"

"Yes."

"In other words, you believe—when it says—when the Bible says that God created man, you believe that God created the life cells and that then, out of that one single life cell . . . God created man by a process of growth or development—is that your theory?"

"Yes. We have the right, it seems to us, to submit evidence to the court of men who are God-fearing and believe in the Bible and who are students of the Bible and authorities on the Bible and authorities in the scientific world—they have a right to testify in support of our view that the Bible is not to be taken literally as an authority in a court of science."

Malone insisted Bryan was wrong when he portrayed this trial as a duel for the future of America's children. "We have no fears about the young people of America. They are a pretty smart generation."

Malone continued with a plea for offering America's children more options to learn. "For God's sake, let the children have their minds kept open. Close no doors to their knowledge; shut no door from them. Make the distinction between theology and science. Let them have both. Let them both be taught. Let them both live. Let them be reverent, but we come here to say that the defendant is not guilty of violating this law. We have a defendant whom we contend could not violate this law. We have a defendant whom we can prove by witnesses whom we have brought here, to prove, we say that there is no conflict between the Bible and whatever he taught."

Malone finished with an impassioned plea and a final jab at Bryan. "There is never a duel with truth. The truth always wins and we are not afraid of it. The truth is no coward. The truth does not need the law. The truth does not need the forces of government. The truth does not need Mr. Bryan. . . . We are ready. We feel we stand with progress. We feel we stand with science. We feel we stand with intelligence. We feel we stand with fundamental freedom in America. . . . We ask Your Honor to admit the evidence as a matter of correct law, as a matter of sound procedure, and as a matter of justice to the defense in this case."

Once again, Malone had won the crowd. On the top floor of the Rhea County Courthouse, where Bryan and his allies had the home-field advantage, Malone garnered lengthy applause.[19]

Malone had carried the day against Bryan. While Bryan sat down and fanned himself, looking sullen despite his best attempts to look impassive, Scopes enjoyed the reaction from the crowd. "The court-room went wild when Malone finished," Scopes recalled. Even a policeman brought in from Chattanooga to monitor the proceedings was caught up in cheering for Malone. A policeman even pounded his nightstick on a table to express his approval for Malone's speech— and promptly broke the table. "I'm not trying to restore order," he cried. "I'm cheering." Mencken spotted Malone and said, "Dudley, that was the loudest speech I ever heard."[20]

Mencken soon relayed that take to the nation, quickly declaring Malone the victor over Bryan in the "great battle of rhetoricians." Watching from the audience, Mencken found himself impressed with Malone's efforts, even as Mencken admitted it would not affect Raulston. "I doubt that any louder speech has ever been heard in a court of law since the days of Gog and Magog," he reported to readers across the country. "It roared out of the open windows like the sound of artillery practice." While Bryan sat with the prosecutors, Mencken looked over to him and thought Malone had utterly destroyed him: "Malone not only out-yelled Bryan, he also plainly out-generaled and out-argued him. His speech, indeed, was one of the best presentations of the case against the fundamentalist rubbish that I have ever heard." Mencken insisted Bryan "grows more and more pathetic" and was looking "elderly and enfeebled." Dismissing Bryan's speech as a "grotesque performance and downright touching in its imbecility," Mencken claimed that even Bryan's fellow prosecutors seemed put off by it. Mencken cheerfully informed his readers that Malone had easily handled Bryan in Dayton.[21]

Other journalists also said Malone had bested Bryan in Dayton, including Raymond Clapper, who was reporting for the United Press: "The Goliath of the fundamentalists ventured forth to stop the introduction of scientific testimony in the Scopes evolution trial today, but he was met by a missile of unexpected force from the sling of Dudley Field Malone of New York, who stirred even those loyal partisans of the idol Bryan to applause." Clapper added that Malone made a "brilliant plea which was the sensation of the day."[22]

=====

As the bailiff tried to restore order in the courtroom, Darrow was already on his feet and tugging anxiously at his worn suspenders when Judge Raulston invited him to speak.

"Your question, as I understood it, was whether the doctrine of evolution was consistent with the story of Genesis that God created man out of the dust of the earth," Darrow said. "We say that 'God created man out of the dust of the earth' is simply a figure of speech. The same language is used in reference many times in the Scriptures, and it doesn't mean necessarily that he created him as a boy would roll up a spitball out of dust—out of hand. But Genesis, or the Bible, says nothing whatever about the method of creation."

"The processes?" asked Raulston.

"It might have been by any other process, that is all."

"So . . . your opinion . . . is that God might have created him by a process of growth?"

"Yes."

"Or development?" the judge asked.

"Yes."

"The fact that he created him, did not manufacture him, like a carpenter would a table?"

"Yes, that is all. That is what we claim."

A puzzled Raulston couldn't help but press one of America's most celebrated opponents of religion on the matter. "You recognize God behind the first spark of life?"

"You are asking me whether I do?"

Raulston quickly moved back to the case, instead of the views of the celebrated attorney and freethinker before him. "Your theory—no, not you."

"We expect most of our witnesses to take that view. As to me, I don't pretend to have any opinion on it," Darrow shrewdly answered.

This quote was a familiar line often repeated by Darrow. He refused to "pretend" to know that which he did not. The steadfast agnostic was not about to commit to a theological debate on his own opinion, because he had none. He was not a doubter or a skeptic in the conventional sense. He simply adhered to the practical principle that he could not know something beyond material phenomena. Publicly, he offered neither belief nor disbelief in God.

To Darrow, the ultimate spiritual question resided in the realm of the unknown and unknowable. Whether he ever held a sense of inner faith is a different question—one that he never answered. However, he maintained immense respect for the multitude of moral teachings in the Bible, and he harbored no ill regard for those who believed in something he could not.

Raulston pressed Darrow to explain more precisely the theory of evolution that his scientists, if allowed, would convey to the jury.

Darrow complied by offering a rough sketch of the development of life over a long time:

"The theory of evolution as I understand it, and which I believe . . . life commenced probably with very low forms, most likely one-celled animals and probably in the sea. . . . Out of that one form grew another . . . until we reach the apex in man, where he stands alone, but connects his whole history with the primal origins of life. We say that is entirely consistent. It is a process we are interested in and the Bible story is not inconsistent with that."

Raulston followed up with more questions for Darrow. "What I want to be clear on—do you say that man developed directly from that one cell into man or did he develop from that one cell into a lower animal, and so on from one form of animal life to another until the apex man was reached and he was man?"

"One form of animal life grew out of another. All life varies and we are creating those new variations every day. . . . There would be a variation in animal structures on up to man. That is surely consistent with the story that man was created out of the dust of the earth."

But man has something, said Darrow, that other forms of life do not have—a much greater ability to think and reason. It makes human beings the most sophisticated of all animals on earth. It is what separates and distinguishes them as a unique form of life.

By his questions from the bench and the length of time he granted for Darrow's skilled answers, Raulston seemed to be warming to the idea of permitting defense experts to take the witness stand.[23]

Prosecutors must have sensed this, as well. They saw it as a calamity, for they became quite animated as they voiced their adamant opposition. As Tom Stewart argued, in a move better suited for the political arena than the courthouse, he began pounding his fist on the table of the shorthand reporter who was struggling to record the proceedings. "I do not undertake to say that I am right and everybody else is wrong." Then Stewart proceeded to do just that.

Stewart's argument against Darrow was shrewd, if dishonest. The prosecutor misconstrued the law by claiming that *any* effort to teach that man descended from a lower order of animals "necessarily 'denies the Story of the Divine Creation of man as taught in the Bible.'"

But that's not at all what the statute said or how it was crafted. The law had two components, not one. They were joined by the conjunction *and*. The teaching of either would not be a crime. The state had to prove both violations to prevail, and it had not. Scopes had never uttered a word about the Bible or its story of Divine Creation.

Proving one part of the statutory offense, Darrow had argued, did not prove the whole offense. He was right.

Undeterred by Darrow's implacable logic and the evidence in support of it, Stewart simply ignored it. He blindly insisted that legislators had spoken and their word was sacrosanct. The defendant was guilty—period. No experts should be allowed to testify. Allowing them to do so would be transferring lawmaking authority to unelected scientists. They would be substituting their own judgments by contradicting the duly elected legislators.

Darrow must have been fuming at such a blatant misconstruction of the law. The experts had not traveled great distances to Dayton to contravene the legislature but to educate the jury on what evolution was and how it did not attempt to repudiate anything in the Bible. In unison, he and his colleagues stood to object to Stewart's outrageous canard, but the prosecutor kept going, and Raulston did nothing to stop him.

Only when a screaming whistle from a locomotive outdoors interrupted his train of thought did Stewart pause to take a breath. The defense interjected, asking him whether words and phrases in a stat-ute should be given their plain meaning. "No, sir!" shouted Stewart. "The court has a right to leave out the words that do not express the intention of the legislature." It was a preposterous response.

Tennessee had its own peculiar ways of conducting trials and inter-preting laws. An exasperated Darrow, who was accustomed to trying cases in the more "enlightened" venues of major metropolitan cities, had to acclimate himself to the insular ways of a Dayton courtroom. The rules there, as best he could tell, were strange and archaic. The methods of construing laws seemed subjective.

The frustration borne by Darrow and his colleagues can be gleaned from their many objections repeatedly thwarted by prose-cutors and overruled by the court. The State of Tennessee had the home-field advantage. Stewart quipped with confidence, "I am just as sure you are wrong as I am sure I am right!" Laughter and ap-plause filled the courtroom. Darrow was waging an uphill battle against an intractable foe—religious zealotry.

The battlefield was defined as God's word versus science. It was the difference between good and evil. The prosecution said so in court, employing precisely those warped terms. Stewart also reminded the court that Darrow had arrogantly slurred the good name and reputation of Tennessee lawmakers who had penned the anti-evolutionary law, disparaging them as "religious bigots and ig-noramuses." Science and the fancy lawyer from Chicago were the real enemies, spreading the contagion of anti-religion via the foul stench of evolution.

Stewart continued to make his case, trying to derail some of the momentum that Malone and Darrow had garnered with their strong appeals.

"Why have we not the right to interpret our Bible as we see fit? Why have we not the right to bar the door to science when it comes within the four walls of God's church upon this earth? Have we not the right? Who says that we have not?" Stewart glared at Darrow. "Show me the man who will challenge it. When science strikes at that upon which man's eternal hope is founded, then I say the foundation of man's civilization is about to crumble. They say this is a battle between religion and science. If it is, I want to serve notice now, in the name of the great God, that I am on the side of religion! I say bar the door and do not allow science to enter!"

Taking blunt aim at Darrow, Stewart blamed "agnosticism" for driving children from the Bible and breeding "infidelity and atheism." He then scolded his adversary to his face, calling it "a shame that a mentality like his has strayed so far from the natural goal that it should follow—a great God."

Like a preacher castigating a sinner in his flock, the prosecutor lamented "all the good that a man of his ability could have done if he had aligned himself with the forces of right instead of aligning himself with that which strikes its fangs at the very bosom of Christianity." This exaggerated and intemperate broadside fell well beyond the ethical bounds of a prosecutor. But Stewart was determined to stoke the passions of resentment and rage toward his adversary.

Regrettably, Darrow was given no chance to respond to these highly personal attacks. Raulston promptly banged his gavel and adjourned the trial for the day. In the morning, he would render his critical decision on whether Darrow's experts would be allowed to testify.[24]

Even Mencken was surprised by the ferocity of Stewart's efforts as he seemed more focused on appealing to the crowd, as if he were asking for their votes, than on making his case. Reporting to readers throughout the nation, Mencken noted Stewart "is supposed to have some secret doubts about fundamentalism." However, the prosecutor "has shown such pugnacity that it has already brought him to forced apologies."[25]

It would be a restless night of sleep for the defense as they looked ahead to the next day. Darrow and his cocounselors knew the fate of the trial would be determined in the morning when Raulston ruled on their expert witnesses.

The Ruling on Expert Witnesses

The sixth day of trial, July 17, 1925, opened, as usual, with a devout prayer.

The Reverend C. G. Eastwood asked God to bless the court and the jury, granting them "divine guidance in the decisions that shall be made." It was not lost on the defense that the word *divine* was emphasized since the question of Divine Creation was on trial. The clergy in Dayton were making it abundantly clear each day how God preferred the outcome of the case should be rendered.

Given how extensive and labored the arguments had been over the issue of expert witnesses—the better part of five days—Judge Raulston's ruling was stunningly brief. He recited the fundamental arguments from both sides. The judge announced that the prosecution need not prove that Scopes taught "a theory that denies the story of the Divine Creation as taught in the Bible," despite what the statute demanded.

Instead, said the judge, it was sufficient for the state to merely show that the defendant taught "that man has descended from a lower order of animals." Raulston's pronouncement was conspicuously bereft of any legal analysis. It was a declaration, not a reasoned explanation. He summarily accepted without reservation the weak and deficient arguments presented by the prosecution.

From his perch as the presiding judge, Raulston reprimanded scientists for what he regarded as demeaning language. "I believe evolutionists should at least show man the consideration to substitute the word *ascend* for the word *descend* in their theory." This gratuitous swipe revealed the judge's underlying disdain and enmity for evolutionary thought.[1]

Darrow was beyond incensed; he was seething. He had tolerated overt expressions of bias against his client, John Scopes, throughout the court proceedings for a week. Raulston had dared to read Genesis from the bench to open the trial. Each day, the judge had beckoned a preacher to reinforce the defendant's guilt under the guise of prayer. The court had rejected nearly every request by the defense. Almost every motion by the prosecution had been granted.

In Darrow's view, it wasn't a trial but a charade. The outcome felt foreordained. Raulston was acting in partnership with the prosecution and doing the state's bidding by railroading a conviction. Darrow was convinced that any fair standards of justice had been supplanted by a thinly veiled conspiracy to undermine the rights of the accused and corrupt the established law's principles. Scopes had been deprived of any presumption of innocence. He was presumed guilty by a judge who denied him the right to present a defense of his own choosing by calling the many expert witnesses who had traveled from far distances to Dayton.

Looking back on the trial, Darrow simply dismissed Raulston as taken with Bryan. "The judge was much impressed with Mr. Bryan as a leader of the faith," Darrow wrote in his autobiography. On almost every point, Darrow thought Raulston would "automatically decide in favor of the mouthpiece of the fundamentalists."[2]

Darrow was fed up and lashed out at Raulston, sarcastically challenging the judge's fairness and integrity: "Counsel well knows what the judgment and verdict in this case will be."

Darrow also laid his cards on the table, letting Raulston know that all Darrow wanted was for the trial to wrap up: "We have a right to present our case to another court and that is all we are after."

"Isn't this an effort to ascertain the truth?" Raulston asked.

"No, it's an effort to show prejudice," Darrow said sarcastically, generating laughter from the crowd. "Nothing else. Has there been any effort to ascertain the truth in this case? Why not bring in the jury and let us prove it?"

Raulston tried to make out what Darrow was saying. "Courts are a mockery—"

Darrow quickly interrupted, "They are often that, Your Honor."

That line generated some laughter in the courtroom.

Raulston urged Darrow to have his witnesses produce their testimony in affidavits before lecturing the famed lawyer on the power of judges. "Always expect the court to rule correctly," Raulston sniffed.

"No, sir, we do not," Darrow fired back, prompting more laughter from the crowd before he continued with the insults. "We want to make statements here of what we expect to prove. I do not understand why every request of the state and every suggestion of the prosecution should meet with an endless waste of time, and a bare suggestion of anything that is perfectly competent on our part should be immediately overruled."

Now Raulston was livid, and he sharply asked, "I hope you do not mean to reflect upon this court?"

Darrow turned away from Raulston, smirking. "Well, Your Honor has the right to 'hope.'"

"I have a right to do something else, perhaps," Raulston intoned ominously, in a way that every lawyer would understand to mean being held in contempt of court.

Darrow backed down. "All right, all right."

Fed up with Darrow, Raulston struck the gavel, adjourning early for the day. The trial would resume after the weekend.[3]

Sitting with his lawyers, Scopes was not surprised by Raulston's ruling, thinking it the latest "in a long line of frustrating setbacks that had hobbled the defense from the outset." While Darrow cooled off his anger and left it in the courtroom, a worried Scopes could tell the lawyer was disappointed, especially as he thought he would not have a showdown with Bryan.[4]

Scopes noticed that most of the reporters were starting to leave Dayton, among them H. L. Mencken. While he had been cheering for Darrow, Mencken assumed the trial was all but over after Raulston's ruling, accusing the judge of "leaping with soft judicial hosannas into the arms of the prosecution" and showing no respect for the Chicago attorney's points.

"All that remains of the great cause of the State of Tennessee against the infidel Scopes is the formal business of bumping off the defendant," Mencken wrote. "There may be some legal jousting on Monday and some gaudy oratory on Tuesday, but the main battle is over with Genesis completely triumphant."[5]

With the trial paused for the weekend, other journalists also declared the trial over. The Associated Press assured readers that Scopes would be found guilty after Raulston's decision and some dull days in the courtroom next week. William Jennings Bryan acted as if the trial were over, telling journalists that he would lead a pilgrimage to the Holy Land for Easter in 1926. Mark Sullivan, one of the most distinguished journalists in America, who was working on *Our Times*, his masterful six volumes on the first quarter of twentieth-century U.S. history, offered a profile on Bryan, sketching the longtime politician as the big winner in Dayton.[6]

On the seventh day of the trial, on Monday morning, the now-typical God-fearing prayer reverberated off the courtroom walls. The Reverend James Standerfer, a local minister, propounded the wisdom of the Almighty as handed down in the Bible. He chastised some (the defense, no doubt) who "have been stupid enough to match our human minds with revelations of the infinite and eternal." Once again, God weighed in for the betterment of all twelve jurors.[7]

After a cacophony of *amen*s, Raulston immediately announced that he was citing Darrow for criminal contempt under penalty of jail for the previous day's "insults and offenses." The judge ordered Darrow to post a $5,000 bond to secure his appearance at a forth-coming hearing where he would be granted an opportunity to de-fend himself. In today's dollars, that figure would amount to a bond of more than $75,000. Now, both Scopes *and* his famed attorney were facing incarceration. Scopes accused Tom Stewart of bringing the language from the day before to Raulston's attention. "Other-wise, he might have ignored it," Scopes wrote about the judge.[8]

There never was a contempt hearing. Hours after the citation, Darrow apologized to Raulston by stating that he had not real-ized that his words were so offensive until he read a transcript of his exchange with the court. While this ranks as one of the most overlooked parts of the trial, Darrow's apology to Raulston revealed much of what drove him during his legendary legal career.

"I have been practicing law for forty-seven years and I have been pretty busy, and most of the time in court I have had many a case where I have had to do what I have been doing here—fighting the public opinion of the people, in the community where I was trying the case," Darrow said. "I have tried to treat the courts fairly and a little more than fairly because, when I recognize the odds against me, I try to lean the other way as best I can.

"I went further than I should have gone. I don't know that I was ever in a community in my life where my religious ideas differed as widely from the great mass as I have found them since I have been in Tennessee. Yet I came here a perfect stranger, and I can say . . . that I have not found upon anybody's part—any citizen here in this town or outside— the slightest discourtesy. I have been treated better, kindlier, and more hospitably than I fancied would have been the case in the North.

"Some lawyers will overstep the bounds. I am quite certain that I did. . . . I don't think it constitutes a contempt, but I am quite certain that the remark should not have been made, and the court could not help taking notice of it, and I am sorry that I made it ever since I got time to read it, and I want to apologize to the court for it."

Darrow's words led the audience to applaud, both for his apology and his kind words for Dayton.[9]

This mea culpa was grudgingly offered and had quietly been brokered by the prosecution during a courtroom recess. Having accused Stewart of manipulating Raulston on the matter, Scopes also noted that Stewart helped quash the contempt fine. Stewart and other prosecutors feared that holding Darrow in criminal contempt would arouse sympathy for the defense and might have the unintended effect of rallying public opinion against both the prosecution and the judge.[10]

Judge Raulston was likely tipped off by Stewart, who always had a solid grasp on public opinion, that he should take the high road and forgive Darrow. Raulston did—at least superficially.

Of course, Raulston could not help but offer a sermon about his own fidelity to the great state of Tennessee and its laws. From the bench, Raulston read a poem-cum-prayer about "sin and sinners," the glory of heaven, and the fires of hell. In pardoning Darrow, he invoked the forgiveness of Christ:

"The Savior died on the cross pleading with God for the men who crucified Him. I believe in that Christ. I believe in these principles. I accept Colonel Darrow's apology." Quoting the signs all over Dayton, Raulston even urged Darrow to go home and read his Bible, quoting the Gospel according to John: "We commend him to go back home and learn in his heart the words of the Man who said, 'If you thirst, come unto Me and I will give thee life.'"

The audience applauded Raulston for forgiving Darrow as the two shook hands.[11]

One can only imagine what was going through Darrow's mind as the judge preached to the well-known agnostic about the nature of salvation. If there was any ambiguity about Raulston's bias against the defense and in favor of the prosecution, his homily about the righteousness of God's word as spoken in the Bible removed all doubt. His adjudications had been infused with the same religious fervor that had motivated Tennessee lawmakers to pass the anti-evolution statute. It had prejudiced the trial against Scopes and Darrow. Raulston was neither impartial nor neutral—and Darrow knew it.

Watching the apology from the defense table, Scopes again found himself impressed by Darrow and wrote four decades later, "Like everything Darrow did in a court, it was a piece of superior dramatics and a speech that even his enemies couldn't help appreciating."[12]

═══

The heat proved too much even for Raulston, who relied on an electric fan to keep cool. With rumors starting to grow louder that the courtroom was so crowded that the floor was about to cave in, no-body objected when the judge adjourned the trial, announcing he would reconvene outside in the square. While the move was unusual, with so many peopled pressed against one another and sweating in the courtroom, nobody objected.[13]

Of the twelve experts whom Darrow had marshaled for the defense, eight were scientists and four were theologians. Darrow knew the jury needed to hear the experts on the Bible. They were each prepared to explain, said the defense, "that the Bible is both a literal and figurative document that God speaks by parables, al-legories, sometimes literally and sometimes spiritually." The theo-logians would furnish scores of excerpts from the Bible to support their collective conclusion. Indeed, some biblical passages com-prised distinct statements that the human body was created by an extended process now known as evolution.

But these experts would never see the inside of the Dayton court-room with the jury present. As a minor concession, Raulston reluc-tantly consented to have their respective statements—in summary form only—added into the record to preserve Scopes's right on appeal.

Had these immensely respected and eminently accomplished reli-gious figures been permitted to take the witness stand, Darrow would have had a chance to convince the jury that his client had not violated the law. What Scopes taught his students about man's evolution "from a lower order of animals" did not "deny the story of Divine Creation as taught in the Bible," as the Tennessee statute prohibited.

Even more convincing was the statement Tennessee governor Austin Peay had made on March 21, 1925, when he signed the Butler Act into law. Peay had taken the time to read the relevant subchapter on evolution in Hunter's *Civic Biology*—the textbook approved by state law for use in classrooms. He accompanied his signature with a written message to the legislators in Nashville:

"After careful examination, I can find nothing of consequence in the books now being taught in our schools with which this bill will interfere in the slightest manner. Therefore, it will not put our teachers in any jeopardy. Probably, the law will never be applied. It may not be sufficiently definite to permit of any specific application."

Over at the defense table, Arthur Garfield Hays pounced on that statement. "I believe that that statement is important on the question of the public policy of the state and had a bearing upon the question of whether this statute is reasonable or within the police powers of the state," Hays told Raulston.[14]

This stunning statement by Governor Peay should have helped exonerate Scopes. He had taught from that same textbook. State law required Scopes to teach from that book. Here was the governor declaring that, under the new anti-evolutionary statute that he had signed into law, no teacher could be criminally charged for doing his duty. Yet Scopes found himself on trial.

Darrow and his team wanted the jury to read what Peay had written or, as an alternative, force him to testify under a lawfully issued subpoena. But Raulston would entertain none of it. He not only rebuffed calling Peay as a witness, but he refused to permit the jury even to read the governor's statement. It was another in a long series of defeats for Darrow, who was growing accustomed to being stymied by the court at every turn. For the legendary criminal litigator, it wasn't a trial at all—it was a carefully choreographed farce.[15]

The scientists, who were equally compelling witnesses, would have meshed well with the testimony of the theologians. However, they, too, were banished from the courtroom. Their written statements were filed with the court, but the jury was never permitted to read them.

Had it been allowed, their testimony would have been a fantastic tutorial on synthesizing evolution and biblical interpretation. Unlike William Jennings Bryan, these learned men did not believe that the idea of evolution displaces God. On the contrary, they felt that each complemented the other.

All of Darrow's experts were in agreement that intelligent teaching of biology and most everything else in science would be impossible if the established facts of evolution were omitted. A teacher such as John Scopes could no more discard the truth of evolution than he could deprive students of the accepted evidence that the earth revolves around the sun. These same experts also concurred that teaching evolution does not inexorably undermine the Bible, except in the minds of dogmatic fundamentalists, such as Bryan, who convinced themselves that a literalist interpretation of the book is its only correct reading. These experts insisted Bryan's and his allies' views on the Bible were misguided and irresponsible.

Evolution had become a dirty word to religious zealots, argued Darrow. In reality, the term meant nothing more than the historical change process. It is the gradual development and growth of life over countless centuries. Just as man-made products such as automobiles and social institutions such as democratic governments evolve, so do animals, including human beings. We are not now what we once were. In the past, organisms changed; they are changing still. To survive and advance, they must adapt and transform as conditions in their environment change. Life is dynamic, not static, because our universe is that way. To argue otherwise is to elevate ignorance over truth.

Evolution could be proved, contended Darrow and his experts, by a vast body of evidence, gathered meticulously by scientists.

Such evidence of progression can be found in comparative anatomy, embryology, homology, paleontology, vestigial structures in man, geographic distribution of species, genetics, and even blood tests. The proof rendered in each field is consistent with that in others. All of these separate lines of evidence, both individually and collectively, point strongly to the principles of organic evolution. It is a great unifying and integrating scientific conception that explains how the most primitive organisms grew over time into highly complex beings. Evolution provides a better and more accurate understanding of nature.

Accepted and confirmed physical evidence shows that the earth's surface evolved from a molten mass to its present form over millions of years. Dr. Winterton C. Curtis, a renowned zoologist from the University of Missouri, would have explained to the jury how all organic, including human, evolution resembles this cosmic and geologic evolution. Living bodies did not always exist as they are today. They have undergone a remarkable process of biological and anatomical metamorphosis. They did so to endure and progress. That, in its most basic form, is evolution. It does not mean that God did not play any instrumental role in it. Science does not claim to know, one way or the other.

This is precisely what Darrow's experts would have conveyed to the jury if only Raulston had given them a chance; that he did not was a regrettable misjudgment born of his prejudices and those of the community where he lived and presided. Raulston was not about to let a humble teacher and his fancy legal counsel from Chicago insult the word of God by granting sustenance and meaning to the facts of evolution. To Raulston, this kind of illumination was a blasphemous threat to the Bible. He forbade every defense expert from testifying before the jury.[16]

Darrow knew he was losing this case—and losing it badly. He needed a brilliant legal maneuver to have any chance of pulling a rabbit out of his hat.

But for Darrow, now headed downstairs as the trial reconvened outside, not all was lost. In this rigged game he had one more card, hidden up his rumpled sleeve, to play. He would call an expert witness to the stand—namely, William Jennings Bryan, a self-proclaimed expert on the Bible.

15

"I Haven't Gotten Through with Him Yet"

Having rattled Bryan on the witness stand on Jonah and the fish, Darrow knew he was in the national spotlight—and went all out to demolish his adversary.

Darrow quickly switched subjects to a different biblical tale, the one of a great global flood described in the book of Genesis. In a reversal of creation, the narrative has God remaking man amid an earthly deluge. Thanks to his scientific experts, Darrow knew that there was no physical evidence of such a watery torrent in geology, paleontology, and natural history.

"You believe the story of the flood to be a literal interpretation?" Darrow asked. After Bryan said he did, Darrow wanted to know when the flood occurred. The two sparred over the date of the flood as Darrow pressed Bryan on it.

"But what do you think that the Bible itself says? Don't you know how it was arrived at?"

"I never made a calculation," Bryan insisted.

"A calculation from what?"

"I could not say," a confused Bryan responded.

Darrow smiled as he pressed on. "From the generations of man?"

"I would not want to say that."

"What do you think?" Darrow asked, setting Bryan up to offer a self-defeating answer.

"I do not think about things I don't think about."

"Do you think about things you do think about?"

This provoked laughter even though Bryan had more supporters in the crowd than Darrow did.

"Well, sometimes," Bryan answered lamely as the amusement continued.

To Bryan, it sounded derisive. He was not accustomed to people laughing at his expense. It unnerved him. He sensed that his adversary was mocking him. Even worse, the vast outdoor crowd seemed to have joined in. These were his people, his religiously devoted followers. Had they somehow turned against him? Had Darrow twisted Bryan's words to make him appear the fool? Had he made a fool of himself with inarticulate and clumsy answers? Maybe the sweltering heat was taking its toll. Using his handkerchief, Bryan wiped his face. He began fanning himself furiously in the summer broil.

The bailiffs tried to have some order, and the prosecutors attempted to stop the questioning again. Bryan's cocounsel knew Bryan was in trouble. Prosecutor Tom Stewart, a politician at heart who understood public opinion well, stood to interrupt. He complained that Darrow was cross-examining his own witness. It was a frivolous objection since so-called hostile or adverse witnesses are always subject to cross-examination. But Stewart was trying to buy time. He hoped that the pause might help his colleague recoup his balance. Yet Bryan stubbornly rejected the lifeline. His ego was on the line, and he boasted to the judge that his opponent could ask any question he pleased.

"I am objecting to his cross-examining his own witness," Stewart said, realizing this testimony was hurting his case, only for the judge to let Bryan continue.

Even more upset after being laughed at—by a crowd that had been very much in his corner over the past week—Bryan went on the attack, insisting that Darrow and his team knew they were going to lose the case. The now-incensed Bryan falsely accused Darrow of coming to Dayton for the express purpose of attacking religion.

"These gentlemen have not had much chance—they did not come here to try this case. They came here to try revealed religion. I am here to defend it, and they can ask me any question they please," Bryan said, garnering applause from the crowd.

"Great applause from the bleachers," Darwin said dryly, realizing that the crowd was swaying to his side.

Bryan continued on the attack, clashing with Darwin over who was the real champion of the common man. Noticing the applause, Bryan said it came "from those whom you call 'yokels.'"

"I have never called them yokels," Darrow said, a rare moment for him to be on the defensive.

"That is the ignorance of Tennessee, the bigotry," Bryan said, implying that Darrow looked down on Dayton's residents.

"You mean who are applauding you?" Darrow asked crossly.

Pointing to the gathered throng, Bryan shouted, "Those are the people whom you insult!"

Now provoked, Darrow in turn lost his composure and launched a personal attack against Bryan: "You insult every man of science and learning in the world because he does not believe in your fool religion."

"I will not stand for that," Raulston interjected.

"For what he is doing?" an exasperated Darrow asked.

"I am talking to both of you," Raulston said.

"Wait until you get to me," Darrow, expecting to be grilled on the witness stand by Bryan, told Raulston before returning to Bryan and digging in. Darrow boxed Bryan into a corner, forcing him to concede that, according to his belief in the Bible, no human beings were on the earth other than Noah and the people on his ark in the estimated year of 2350 BC.

"Do you know anything about how many people there were in Egypt thirty-five hundred years ago, or how many people there were in China five thousand years ago?" Darrow asked. "Have you ever tried to find out?"

"No, sir. You are the first man I ever heard of who has been interested in it," Bryan replied, generating laughter.

"Mr. Bryan, am I the first man you ever heard of who has been interested in the age of human societies and primitive man?"

"You are the first man I ever heard speak of the number of people at those different periods."

"Where have you lived all your life?"

"Not near you," Bryan answered, to the laughter and the applause of the crowd.

"Nor near anybody of learning?"

"Oh, don't assume you know it all." Bryan's face was growing red, his anger about to boil.

Once again, Stewart tried to stop the proceedings, while Darrow objected to Bryan's giving speeches instead of answering his questions. Despite Stewart's continued efforts, Raulston allowed Darrow to continue.

Bryan seemed determined to showcase his faith and not back down despite Stewart's latest attempts to stop the examination: "I want the Christian world to know that any atheist, agnostic, unbeliever, can question me anytime as to my belief in God, and I will answer him."

"I want to take an exception to this conduct of this witness," Darrow said. "He may be popular down here in the hills. I do need to have his explanation for the answer."

The two sides clashed more over whether Bryan should be on the stand, with Hays and Stewart also debating the matter. Darrow insisted Bryan was an expert witness since he was "one of the most foremost Bible students," but as sarcastic as the famed lawyer might have been, his adversary knew the Bible well and taught classes on it.

Malone jumped in and tried to split the difference. "Your Honor, on this very subject, I would like to say that I would have asked Mr. Bryan—and I consider myself as good a Christian as he is—every question that Mr. Darrow has asked him for the purpose of bringing out whether or not there is to be taken in this court a literal interpretation of the Bible, or whether, obviously, as these questions indicate, if a general and literal construction cannot be put upon the parts of the Bible which have been covered by Mr. Darrow's questions. I hope for the last time no further attempt will be made by counsel on the other side of the case, or Mr. Bryan, to say the defense is concerned at all with Mr. Darrow's particular religious views or lack of religious views. We are here as lawyers with the same right to our views. I have the same right to mine as a Christian as Mr. Bryan has to his, and we do not intend to have this case charged by Mr. Darrow's agnosticism or Mr. Bryan's brand of Christianity."

Malone's speech prompted great applause before Darrow questioned Bryan about Genesis and creation:

"Don't you know there are any number of civilizations that are traced back to more than five thousand years?"

Bryan did not offer much of an answer. "I know we have people who trace things back according to the number of ciphers they have. But I am not satisfied they are accurate."

Darrow pressed on, not content with Bryan's response. "You do not believe that there were any civilizations on this earth that reach back beyond five thousand years?"

"I am not satisfied by any evidence that I have seen."

"Don't you know that the ancient civilizations of China are six thousand or seven thousand years old, at the very least?"

"No; but they would not run back beyond the creation, according to the Bible."

"Have you ever tried to find out?"

"No, sir," Bryan sharply replied, sarcasm breaking through his usual courtesy.

"Do you know there are thousands of books in our libraries on all those subjects I've been asking you about?"

"I couldn't say, but I will take your word for it."

"You have never in all your life made any attempt to find out about the other peoples on the earth—how old their civilizations are—how long they had existed on earth, have you?"

"No, sir."

Having cast doubt on Bryan as an informed authority on the established age of man and how it differs dramatically from accounts in the Bible, Darrow turned his interrogation to the age of the earth. "Mr. Bryan, could you tell me how old the earth is?"

"No, sir, I couldn't."

"The book you have introduced in evidence tells you, doesn't it?"

"I don't think it does, Mr. Darrow."

Darrow handed his rival a Bible. "Let's see whether it does. Is this the one?"

Bryan looked down at the book. "That is the one, I think."

"It says BC 4004? That is printed in the Bible you introduced?"

"Yes, sir."

"And numerous other Bibles?"

"Yes, sir."

"Would you say that the earth was only four thousand years old?"

"Oh, no. I think it is much older than that."

Almost immediately, Bryan realized his mistake. He had conceded under the rapid-fire questioning of Darrow that what was printed in the Bible was wrong. The world was not merely six thousand years old. It did not start in 4004 BC, but long before that date. Indeed, by the time of the Scopes Trial in 1925, scientists had established through geological and other evidence that the age of the earth was between 24 million and 400 million years old.

Yet fundamentalists such as Bryan had clung to a strict reading of the Bible based almost entirely on the word of a seventeenth-century Irish archbishop named James Ussher. At the time, he was a highly respected scholar. Ussher had performed a complex set of calculations based on genealogies identified in Genesis. He computed, mistakenly, that the earth was created in 4004 BC and that the great flood happened in about 2350 BC. Ussher's calculations were deeply flawed, and his conclusions ignored countervailing evidence. Nevertheless, his pronouncements had enthusiastically been embraced by many of the most devout Christians throughout the world as reliable. So much so, these "traditional" dates were printed in tens of millions of Bibles everywhere, including the book that Bryan had introduced into evidence at the outset of the trial.

With this foundation laid, Darrow began questioning a confused and impatient Bryan about how he believed the earth was actually created. "Do you think the earth was made in six days?"

Bryan was sweating, and his normally clear and commanding voice revealed his increasing worries and frustrations. "Not six days of twenty-four hours," Bryan answered, wondering where Darrow was taking this.

"Doesn't it say so?"

"No, sir."

Bryan's fellow prosecutor Tom Stewart didn't like where Darrow was going. Stewart knew that the veteran lawyer from Chicago was both brilliant and clever, armed with cross-examination skills that were unmatched by any other attorney in America. Stewart suspected a trap and feared that Bryan, blinded by his egotism and bluster, would walk right into it. Stewart tried to stop it, but his colleague brushed it aside. Bryan was determined to leap headlong into the abyss.

"I want to interpose another objection. What is the purpose of this examination?" Stewart asked.

"The purpose is to cast ridicule on everybody who believes in the Bible, and I am perfectly willing that the world shall know that these gentlemen have no other purpose than ridiculing every Christian who believes in the Bible," Bryan insisted.

"We have the purpose of preventing bigots and ignoramuses from controlling the education of the United States and you know it!" Darrow fired back.

Bryan only made matters worse for himself when he launched into a heady harangue asserting that he was not afraid of agnostics, atheists, and "unbelievers." He all but dared Darrow to attack him personally for his views on religion, demanding that "this agnostic be given the chance to criticize a believer in the word of God." If the judge was disposed to bring the rancor to an end, Bryan foreclosed it by insisting that Darrow be extended free rein to ask anything he cared.

What unfolded next was a titanic clash between two legendary figures in their battle over the most divisive issue of their time, creationism versus evolution.

"Mr. Bryan, do you believe that the first woman was Eve?" Darrow asked.

"Yes."

"Do you believe she was literally made out of Adam's rib?"

"I do."

"Did you ever discover where Cain got his wife?"

"No, sir; I leave the agnostics to hunt for her."

"You never found out?"

"I have never tried to find out."

"The Bible says he got one, doesn't it? Were there other people on the earth at that time?"

"I cannot say."

"You cannot say. Did that ever enter your consideration?"

"Never bothered me," Bryan admitted.

"There were no other people recorded, but Cain got a wife."

"That is what the Bible says."

"Where she came from, you do not know. All right. Does the statement 'the morning and the evening were the first day' and 'the morning and the evening were the second day' mean anything to you?"

"I do not think it necessarily means a twenty-four-hour day."

"Do you think it does or does not?"

Bryan answered, "I know a great many think so."

"What do you think?"

"I do not think it does."

"You think those were not literal days?"

"I do not think they were twenty-four-hour days."

"You do not think that?"

"No. But I think it would be just as easy for the kind of God we believe in to make the earth in six days as in six years or in six million years or in six hundred million years."

"The creation might have been going on for a very long time?"

"It might have continued for millions of years," Bryan answered.

The crowd, many of whom did not have much formal education but knew their Bibles like the back of their hands, something even Darrow admitted, began to stir and murmur. They realized that Bryan had just admitted that the account of creation in the Bible—the stars, earth, and man—might actually have taken place over millions of years. Therefore, it might be entirely compatible with the theory of evolution. Life emerged, developed, and changed as the earth evolved from a molten mass to its present form. Bryan's confession belied the fundamentalist conviction that the world was merely six thousand years old, as printed in everyone's Bible. What else in the sacred book was mistaken or misinterpreted?

Bryan had started out by telling Darrow, "Everything in the Bible should be accepted as given there." Yet now he seemed to be allowing that not all of the words should be accepted as literal. The more he spoke, the testier he became.

Darrow was tenacious. As he paced in front of and around the witness, his rapid-fire and trenchant questions began to erode Bryan's imperious resolve. As he shifted uncomfortably in his seat on the witness stand, Bryan's confident demeanor seemed to evaporate in the searing summer heat. He paused repeatedly to swallow large gulps of water and to wipe his brow.

Darrow quickly pivoted to another line of questioning, the narrative in Genesis of the forbidden fruit in the Garden of Eden. Many theologians had long recognized it as a story of symbolism involving moral values in human behavior—a lesson involving the consequences of lies, desire, and shame. But to Bryan, everything in the Bible was literal. There were no exceptions. No allowance could be made for more reasonable interpretations.

"Do you believe the story of the temptation of Eve by the serpent?" Darrow asked.

"I do."

"Do you believe that after Eve ate the apple that God cursed Eve and at that time decreed that all womankind thenceforth and forever should suffer the pains of childbirth in the reproduction of the earth?"

"I believe what it says, and I believe the fact as fully—"

Darrow interrupted, "That is what it says, doesn't it?"

"Yes."

"And for that reason every woman born of woman, who has to carry on the race, the reason they have childbirth pains is because Eve tempted Adam in the Garden of Eden?"

Bryan offered a lame retort: "I will believe just what the Bible says."

"And you believe that came about because Eve tempted Adam to eat the fruit?"

"Just as it says."

"And you believe that is the reason that God made the serpent go on his belly after he tempted Eve?"

"I believe the Bible as it is."

"Have you any idea how the snake went before that time?"

"No, sir."

"Do you know whether he walked on his tail or not?"

"No, sir. I have no way to know," Bryan replied, prompting laughter from the audience.

Bryan was startled by it. He had stumbled and was visibly shaken by the fear that people were once again laughing at him. Is that what was happening? Had Darrow's cynical view of biblical stories and his sarcastic retelling of them turned the audience in his favor and against Bryan, the foremost expert on the Bible?

Sweating profusely now in the scorching temperature, Bryan tried to regain his composure, but Darrow pressed on.

"Now, you refer to the cloud that was put in heaven after the flood, the rainbow. Do you believe in that?"

"Read it," Bryan demanded, his voice now shrill.

"All right, Mr. Bryan, I will read it for you."

Bryan jumped in, looking to cut Darrow off. "Your Honor, I think I can shorten this testimony. The only purpose Mr. Darrow has is to slur at the Bible, but I will answer his question. I will answer it all at once, and I have no objection in the world. I want the world to know that this man, who does not believe in a God, is trying to use a court in Tennessee—"

"I object to that," Darrow interjected.

Bryan simply ignored Darrow as he continued to make his case to Raulston. "To slur at it, and while it will require time, I am willing to take it."

Darrow offered another insult to Bryan. "I object to your statement. I am exempting you on your fool ideas that no intelligent Christian on earth believes."

This finally caused Raulston to try to control the exchange. "Court is adjourned until nine o'clock tomorrow morning," he announced after gaveling Darrow down.

By all appearances, Bryan was badly wounded, if not defeated. His uncompromising insistence that everything in the Bible happened exactly as written had allowed Darrow to sow seeds of doubt that the fundamentalist leader was a reliable authority on the subject. The audience could see what Bryan could not. And so could Judge Raulston. He pounded his gavel several times and abruptly ended the cross-examination to put Bryan out of his misery.

Court was adjourned for the day and the crowd disbursed, with Bryan slumped in the witness chair in emotional shock. He was still clutching his Bible with both hands. Only a single friend stood by his side.[1]

Surrounded by a crowd cheering him for his performance, Clarence Darrow had demolished his nemesis William Jennings Bryan, but Darrow took no pleasure in seeing the fundamentalist leader humiliated on the public stage. Darrow knew that he still faced many challenges. His defense of John Scopes had failed. Both Darrow and Bryan had lost in a strange twist, something of a portent of things to come.

Darrow knew it had not been a fair trial, from beginning to end. By siding consistently with the prosecution on all critical issues, Judge Raulston had prevented Darrow from defending Scopes the way he wanted. All of Darrow's proposed witnesses were excluded from testifying before the jury, including Bryan. While helpful to the defense, the fundamentalist leader's admissions were formally expunged from the record by Raulston. The judge had also misconstrued the law to prevent Darrow from arguing to the jury that Scopes never violated the state statute because the teacher never told his students that the theory of evolution "denies the Story of the Divine Creation of man as taught in the Bible," as the statute prohibited. Instead, Raulston erroneously ruled that any teaching that "man descended from a lower order of animals" was sufficient to find the defendant guilty. Raulston's take was a complete misreading of the law.

Darrow realized that his efforts were being wasted in Dayton. Conferring with his cocounsels, Darrow found the rest of his team had drawn the same conclusion. "We all agreed that the ruling of the court had made it impossible to introduce any evidence, and useless to make any arguments," he remembered. Still, Darrow and Scopes's other attorneys were "satisfied that what we had undertaken, the awakening of the country to what was going on had succeeded beyond our fonder hopes." Darrow was already talking about working on the appeal.[2]

On the other side, Bryan mulled over putting Darrow on the stand to grill him over religion and his thoughts on God. The rest of the prosecution refused to even consider the possibility, and Tom Stewart ensured Raulston struck down that possibility.[3]

Bryan was eager to take the fight back to Darrow. Still reeling from the withering cross-examination he had endured the day before, Bryan was determined to resurrect himself with a spellbinding closing argument that he had spent days preparing. It would rectify all the wrongs visited on him by Darrow. But Darrow wasn't about to allow that to happen. Besides, with his expert witnesses not allowed to testify, Darrow well knew that the prosecution had already won the case. What was the point of handing a soapbox to Bryan? Most of all, Darrow couldn't stomach listening to a Bible-infused stem-winder from the religious crusader who was intent on smearing evolution as an insidious evil force in the world. Darrow could not tolerate an hours-long sermon on morality and the devil's influence. He devised a plan to muzzle Bryan before he could further poison the trial. Darrow was aware that, under Tennessee law, Bryan would be barred from presenting a closing argument on behalf of the prosecution provided that the defense waived its own summation of the case. In a shrewd maneuver, Darrow invoked the rule and swiftly deflated Bryan's hopes of using the courtroom to salvage his reputation. His face red, sweat pouring down his copious frame, Bryan fanned himself in a futile effort to cool off both himself and his rising anger. He would have no further say in the trial of John Scopes outside a brief comment after the decision was rendered.[4]

═══

The epic showdown between Darrow and Bryan had stretched for more than an hour and a half. The swollen crowd had followed every word, each question, gauging the responses and movements of the two opponents. Since their hero had largely been put on the defensive, many of Bryan's supporters seemed to think he had failed to display his usual magic on the stump. Darrow left the platform like a boxer who had won a title fight. His supporters and well-wishers quickly surrounded him to congratulate him on his performance. Even Darrow seemed surprised by the response. "They seemed to have changed sides in a single afternoon," he wrote, looking back at the event. The crowd ushered Darrow off the courthouse square, while Bryan was left alone to ponder the day's events.[5]

While the press pool had diminished over the weekend as several other journalists followed Mencken out of Dayton, a handful of reporters remained to cover the trial. Some of the Tennessee reporters painted the confrontation as a draw, but almost all of the national journalists painted it as an astonishing win for Darrow. The *New York Times* dismissed Bryan's efforts as "an absurdly pathetic performance, with a famous American the chief creator and butt of a crowd's rude laughter." Other papers across the nation followed suit, declaring Darrow the victor and mocking Bryan.[6]

More important, many papers across the country carried the transcript of the exchange between Darrow and Bryan. Taking advantage of quicker modes of communication, media outlets promptly reproduced the examination, letting readers judge the clash of the two titans for themselves. Bryan's supporters could cheer their man for defending the Bible against a prominent agnostic such as Darrow. But many more Americans read the transcript and saw Bryan's faith leading him to offer overly simple answers to complex questions. Darrow had exposed some of the problems of religion dictating how science was taught in the classroom.[7] With his questions, Darrow had trapped Bryan, who could not contradict the Bible or biology. Whatever his merits as a Sunday school

teacher and a defender of religion in the public square, Bryan was
no learned theologian—and Darrow had made Bryan look foolish
upon examining him on that hot afternoon.[8]

Sitting in the shade, the defendant, who had attended church
the day before, realized that Darrow elicited "astonishing answers" from Bryan. "When Bryan admitted the earth had not
been made in six days of twenty-four hours, the Fundamentalists
gasped," Scopes recalled. "It seemed incredible that William Jennings Bryan, the Fundamentalist knight on the white charger, had
betrayed his cause by admitting to the agnostic Darrow that the
world hadn't been made in six days!"[9]

Looking back at his exchange with Bryan some seven years later,
when he wrote his autobiography, Darrow laid out how he'd prepared for the examination: "These questions were practically the
same that I had prepared and had published in a Chicago paper
two years earlier. These questions were prepared because Mr. Bryan
had submitted a list of questions through the press to the President
of Wisconsin University, which appeared in the *Chicago Tribune* in
July 1923. My questions were presented in the same month, in reply
to Mr. Bryan's." By pressing Bryan on questions about the Bible,
Darrow stressed that he got his opponent "twisted and dodged and
floundered," which hurt the "Great Commoner" with "the thinking
element, and even his own people."

Darrow also recognized how important the transcripts included in
newspapers across the country were in shaping how the public viewed
the case. "My questions and Bryan's answers were printed in full, and
the story seems to have reached the full world," Darrow wrote. Whatever Raulston's final ruling, Darrow knew he had made his point and
could leave Dayton with a win. Nestled in with his wife, Ruby, at the
house on Second Avenue they'd rented from banker Luther Morgan,

whose son had sat in the class when Scopes taught evolution, Darrow ended that hot Monday night with success already ensured.[10]

On Tuesday, July 21, 1925, on what turned out to be the final day of the trial, the session opened as the Reverend Doctor R. C. Camper from Chattanooga offered a prayer, urging "each and every one do the thing that is good and right here today." After that, Raulston struck Bryan's testimony from the record, despite Darrow's objections.

"I am not at all sure that Mr. Bryan's testimony would aid the Supreme Court or any other human being," Darrow noted dryly. "But he testified by the hour there and I haven't gotten through with him yet."

Stewart quickly rose to push back, doubling down on his efforts to keep Bryan from doing any more damage to the prosecution's case. Despite that, Bryan kept pushing for a rematch. He reminded the court that Darrow had "stated that if I was to take the witness stand, I would ask that the others take the witness stand also, that I might put certain questions to them." Now that Bryan was off the stand, he wanted Darrow on it. Raulston shot down the objections from both sides, and the trial moved to its final phase.[11]

Raulston summoned the jurors. As a matter of custom and courtesy, the judge permitted Darrow to briefly address the jury to disclose why the defense had not put on a case in earnest, thanks largely to Raulston's refusal to let the expert witnesses testify.

The renowned lawyer slowly rose, walked to the jury box, and, in something of a concluding statement, soberly explained that his client could not, in good conscience, deny that he had taught evolution— because he had, in fact, taught it. Darrow would make no apologies for that. Evolution was widely accepted in the scientific world. So much so, it was printed in school textbooks everywhere, including the ones handed out to students and teachers in Dayton. Scopes was obligated to teach biology from the very book that was provided by the public schools.

"My statement that there was no need to try this case further, and for the court to instruct the defendant is guilty under the law, was not made as a plea of guilty or an admission of guilt," Darrow told the jury. "We claim that the defendant is not guilty, but as the court has excluded any testimony, except as to the one issue as to whether he taught that man descended from a lower order of animals, and we cannot contradict that testimony."

Darrow also set the stage for an appeal. "There is no logical thing to come except that the jury find a verdict that we may carry to the higher court, purely as a matter of proper procedure. We do not think it is fair to the court or counsel on the other side to waste a lot of time when we know this is the inevitable result and probably the best result for this case."

Looking over to the prosecution, Darrow made eye contact with Tom Stewart, who nodded. "I think so; yes," Stewart agreed.[12]

After Raulston charged the jury, he allowed Darrow to address its members again.

"Gentlemen of the jury, we are sorry to have not had a chance to say anything to you. The court has held under the law that the evidence we had is not admissible." After repeating his plans to appeal the decision, Darrow reached out to the jurors once again. "I do not want any of you to think we are going to find any fault with you as to your verdict. I am frank to say, while we think it is wrong, and we ought to have been permitted to put in our evidence, the court felt otherwise, as he had a right to hold. We cannot argue to you gentlemen under the instructions given by the court—we cannot even explain to you that we think you should return a verdict of not guilty. We do not see how you could. We do not ask it. We think we will save our point and take it to a higher court and settle whether the law is good, and also whether the judge should have permitted our evidence. I guess that is plain enough."[13]

With that, Darrow, showing dejection for the first time in the trial, sat down. For the moment, he had lost. But he vowed to continue his battle on appeal before a panel of judges who could more objectively see that Tennessee's statute was egregiously unconstitutional.

The jury was hastily escorted from the courtroom to deliberate and vote. It didn't take long. And why should it have? In Judge Raulston's instructions to the jurors, in which he flagrantly contorted the plain language of the law, His Honor had all but directed them to convict Scopes.

Just nine minutes later, at 11:23 a.m., before counsel scarcely had a chance to pack up the legal briefs spread out on their respective tables, the jurors filed back into the courtroom and sat down.

"Mr. Foreman, will you tell us whether you have agreed on a verdict?" Raulston asked.

"Yes, sir. We have, Your Honor."

"What do you find?"

"We have found for the state and found the defendant guilty."

Scopes showed no emotion as the verdict was read. The modest schoolteacher had remained silent throughout the trial. He must have felt as if he were a mere ornament hanging obscurely in the shadows of so many capacious personalities who had commanded the courtroom for eight long days.

Summoning Scopes to the bench, Raulston was impatient to dispense with the entire matter. He immediately pronounced his sentence: Scopes would pay a $100 fine. But as soon as the words were out of the judge's mouth, John Neal realized that Raulston had failed to afford the defendant an opportunity to speak before imposing a punishment, as the law required. "He wants to be heard a moment," Neal insisted.[14]

"Oh," said Raulston. "Have you anything to say, Mr. Scopes, as to why the court should not impose punishment upon you?"

There sat John Thomas Scopes, utterly forgotten and relegated to nothing more than an afterthought. He was finally, if belatedly, given a chance to be heard. He rose to his feet and chose his words carefully.

"Because John Neal remembered to remind the judge, I made my first and only speech in court," Scopes later recalled. "It was a spur-of-the-moment thing; I hadn't expected to talk at all and I hadn't prepared anything to say." During their talks throughout the trial, Darrow had also reminded Scopes that he was not, in fact, a science teacher. Darrow thought anything Scopes would say would only hurt their case.[15]

Despite all of that, Scopes handled himself with gravitas in this moment.

"Your Honor, I feel that I have been convicted of violating an unjust statute. I will continue in the future, as I have in the past, to oppose this law in any way I can. Any other action would be in violation of my ideal of academic freedom—that is, to teach the truth as guaranteed in our Constitution, of personal and religious freedom. I think the fine is unjust."

Raulston was unmoved. He restated his sentence of the ceremonial $100 fine. No jail time was imposed.

The defense team remained active in the last minutes of the trial. As courtly as ever, on behalf of the defense team Dudley Field Malone thanked "the people of the state of Tennessee, not only for their hospitality but for the opportunity of trying out these great issues here." After the thunderous applause for Malone, Arthur Garfield Hays, wrapping up his duties as one of Scopes's attorneys, jumped in to ask for a new trial and records of the one that had just closed.[16]

As things seemed to be over, Bryan rose one last time, to state that the trial had garnered global attention since it was about a "great cause" and to insist it would be "settled right" through the democratic process.

"The people will determine this issue. They will take sides upon this issue, they will state the question involved in this issue, they will examine the information—not so much at what has been brought out here, for very little has been brought out here, but this case will stimulate investigation, and investigation will ring out information, and the facts will be known." Bryan closed with an appeal to prayer. "We ought not only desire, but pray, that that which is right will prevail."[17]

While the crowd applauded for Bryan, Darrow asked if he could say a word, and Raulston recognized him. Taking a page from Malone, Darrow thanked the local residents and even offered some kind words for the judge. But then Darrow's tone grew serious. "I think this case will be remembered because it is the first case of this sort since we stopped trying people in America for witchcraft. We have done our best to turn back the tide that has sought to force itself upon this—upon this modern world—of testing every fact in science by religious dictum."[18]

With that, Darrow closed his case, and Raulston readied to end the trial. The *Baltimore Evening Sun,* the paper that Mencken had made famous across the nation, offered to post a $500 bond for Scopes so that he could pursue his appeal to higher courts. The defense accepted the generous offer. Judge Raulston banged his gavel for the last time and left the bench.

The final reports flew out of Dayton with the news that Scopes had been found guilty.

Journalist Raymond Clapper compared the young teacher to Dred Scott, from the seminal case on slavery that the Supreme Court ruled on in 1857.

"Like the humble Negro slave, who was the instrument through which the chains of human slavery finally were broken, this pleasant young man whose blood comes from the early Anglo-Saxon lovers of liberty, is the medium through which the supreme court of the United States finally will decide whether a state legislature may chain the mind," Clapper predicted.[19]

After the trial ended, Scopes went to the train station to watch most of the remaining reporters leave for home. Scopes headed to the post office and found mail that had been piling up during the trial—some of it in other languages and from across the world—waiting for him. As he went through the mail, Scopes found financial offers, letters from promoters and from pastors praying for his salvation, and even marriage proposals. While he had had his chance to speak to the judge that Tuesday, going through his mail, Scopes increasingly realized that he would never leave behind the trial and the circus that had accompanied it.[20]

While Scopes felt overwhelmed by the future, another of the main figures of the trial readied his next move. Even as reporters filed their last stories from Dayton and informed the public about the decision, William Jennings Bryan, who had lost three presidential elections, looked to bounce back once again, hoping to have his chance to press Clarence Darrow, this time through the media. Despite being humiliated by Darrow, Bryan wanted to show, once again, that he wasn't done yet.

"He Was Not, for God Took Him"

It was over.

The Trial of the Century ended quietly as the crowds in the gallery, the press, tourists, and religious groups disappeared.

If Clarence Darrow, his colleagues on the defense team, and their client, John Scopes, were all despondent over the trial's outcome, William Jennings Bryan was mortified that his reputation had been sullied publicly from the scathing cross-examination. Bryan's situation was all the more humiliating because the leading shepherd of America's fundamentalist movement had been bested in a contest of wits by a renowned agnostic.

Some newspapers and commentators were having a field day at Bryan's expense. H. L. Mencken and other writers mocked Bryan as a symbol of anti-intellectualism and ignorance. Even papers that had traditionally been friendly to Bryan turned against him. The *Memphis Commercial Appeal* reported, "Darrow succeeded in showing that Bryan knows little about the science of the world," while insisting the Great Commoner thought his faith "transcends all the learning of men."[1]

Bryan's eagerness to remedy his embarrassment with a thundering closing argument had been shut down by Darrow's clever move to waive summations, which only added insult to injury. Bryan yearned for an audience to hear his point-by-point refutation of his adversary's arguments, but his support seemed to vanish after the trial. The address Bryan had wanted to give was all over the place, citing Demosthenes, Nietzsche, and the Bible to call for more Christian colleges and stressing that more than half of scientists did not believe in God. Still, even with Bryan's oratorical skills, his speech would probably not have made much of an impact. Bryan, accustomed to drawing an adoring audience, had lost them. He may have won the case, but at what cost?[2]

Even while he remained in a good mood after the trial ended, Bryan physically and mentally appeared to be a broken man. In the days that immediately followed the end of the trial, Bryan was consumed by his desire to restore his diminished stature. Although most of the out-of-town lawyers had departed, Bryan remained in the area. He delivered several speeches in Tennessee. But the crowds were comparatively meager, and their enthusiasm was tepid. He arranged to have his undelivered closing argument published. The precious few reviews of it were largely indifferent. William Jennings Bryan, the once-great statesman, had lost his luster—and he knew it.

On Friday, July 24, Bryan and his wife went to Chattanooga. Once there, he oversaw the publication of the speech he did not deliver in Dayton. The next day, the Bryans drove to Winchester, where they visited with Judge Raulston and Tom Stewart. Looking back on those days, Mary Bryan insisted her husband was "vigorous and smiling" after the trial.[3]

Sitting in the back of the car with his wife as they traveled across southeastern Tennessee, Bryan spoke about his plans for the coming months. Despite the bruises from Dayton, he insisted he would continue to speak out against evolution. "He was trying to do three things," Mary Bryan recalled. "First to establish the right of tax-payers to control what is taught in their schools; second to draw a line between the teaching of evolution as a fact and teaching it as a theory; and third, to see that teachers proven guilty of this offense should be given an opportunity to resign."

Mary Bryan, always her husband's closest confidante and usually his best adviser, pointed to "the narrow margin between this per-fectly legitimate work as touching the public servant, and an en-croachment on individual religious belief, which is a sacred domain." They agreed "that no religious zeal should invade this sacred do-main and become intolerance."

Looking over to his wife, Bryan said, "Well, Mama, I have not made that mistake yet, have I?"

"You are all right so far, but will you be able to keep to this narrow path?"

"I think I can."[4]

Bryan was not the only prominent figure from the trial to escape Dayton and stay in the area. Darrow visited the Great Smoky Moun-tains that weekend to get away from the heat.[5] John Scopes also got out of town, visiting his alma mater, the University of Kentucky. Although he had been thinking about going to law school, Scopes quickly real-ized he could not escape the trial, as everyone from college deans to old professors insisted he could end up as the next Clarence Darrow.

"Soon everyone would expect me to be another Darrow," Scopes realized. "There would be no escape from being compared to the man who defended me." Scopes thought back to the other side at the trial for an example of how someone could be eclipsed in another man's shadow. "I might become another William Jennings Bryan, Jr., walking in the shadow of another man's fame."

Scopes decided he would pursue graduate studies in geology—but he would not do so at the University of Kentucky. "I was beginning to learn that there was no way to remain completely unaffected by the trial," Scopes wrote. "It was a challenge to try."[6]

Still, for the moment, both Darrow and Scopes had eluded the public eye. But the next day, they were confronted with reporters asking unexpected questions.

Bryan was staying in the home of Frederick Richard Rogers— ironically, a pharmacist who worked at Robinson's Drug Store, where Scopes had been recruited to teach about evolution—at the corner of Georgia Avenue and Market Street in Dayton. On the morning of Sunday, July 26, five days after the trial ended, Bryan came into his wife's room, happy with his undelivered speech as the publishers readied to share it with the world. Bryan also talked about how proud he was of William Jr., and how happy he had been to work with him in recent weeks.

Later that morning, Bryan went up the street to attend services at Dayton Methodist Episcopal Church. The famed speaker offered a "beautiful prayer" that addressed God "not as a being far away across worlds, but as a very near and loving Heavenly Father."

At Rogers's house, Bryan talked to his wife about a physical examination he had had the day before and seemed happy with the results: "According to that, Mama, I have several more years to live." After talking about vacationing in the Smoky Mountains, Bryan headed to his room for an afternoon nap.

With evening coming, Mary Bryan sent the chauffeur to wake her husband. But after hearing that Bryan was sleeping peacefully, Mary felt a "sudden foreboding" and urged that he be woken up. The chauffeur searched for a pulse while calls were made to summon doctors— and Mary Bryan could only think back to Enoch's fate in Genesis, the man so beloved by the Lord that he was taken from earth to live in heaven: "He was not, for God took him."[7]

Only a few days after being humiliated by Darrow in Dayton, William Jennings Bryan was dead. With no autopsy performed, reporters wrote that Bryan had died of apoplexy.[8]

News quickly spread of Bryan's death. At the train station in Knoxville, heading from Louisville to Dayton, Scopes ran into Paul Anderson, a reporter for the *St. Louis Post-Dispatch*.

"Are you going back to Dayton for the same reason I am?" Anderson asked.

"I don't know, Paul. What happened?"

"Bryan died a few hours ago."

Looking back at it, Scopes remembered they "were more shocked than surprised" by the news since "Bryan had a diabetic condition and that he was in ill health." Scopes feared that evangelicals would scapegoat him and his attorneys—namely Darrow—for the death of their hero, but the young teacher pointed the blame elsewhere. "Only one man was responsible for Bryan's death and that was Bryan himself," Scopes insisted in his memoirs. "No reasonable man would call his a martyr's death." Remembering Bryan's massive appetite, including devouring foods he should not have touched, Scopes thought the heat and diabetes had done the Great Commoner in.[9]

Darrow was still in the mountains when he heard about Bryan's death, and showing little sympathy for his foe, he thought it was ironic. "A man who for years had fought excessive drinking lay dead from indigestion caused by over-eating," Darrow mused, though he also noted his rival's poor health.[10]

In Baltimore, Mencken dismissed Bryan as an ambitious politician, "broken, furious, and infinitely pathetic." Mencken piled on the dead man, insisting he was "a vulgar and common man, a cad undiluted" who was "ignorant, bigoted, self-seeking, blatant, and dishonest." He found Bryan simply "a peasant come home to the dung-pile" who was "deluded by a childish theology, full of an almost pathological hatred of all learning, all human dignity, all beauty, all fine and noble things." Mencken would continue his attacks on Bryan's legacy in the coming months.[11]

Unlike Mencken, most Americans honored Bryan after his passing, but they praised the earlier part of his political career more than his fundamentalist crusade in his last years. "In all the history of American politics, there are few names which carry the brilliant lustre [*sic*] of spectacular effort which has become part of the memory of William Jennings Bryan," announced the Associated Press. The AP even hyped up the speech Bryan wanted to offer at the Scopes Trial.

Tributes poured in from President Coolidge and Vice President Charles Dawes, a close friend of Bryan's. Darrow and his team quickly expressed their condolences as well.

"I am pained to hear of the death of the Honorable William Jennings Bryan," Darrow told the press. "I have known Mr. Bryan since 1896 and supported him twice for the presidency. He was a man of strong convictions and always espoused his cause with ability and courage." Tom Stewart praised his colleague to the moon, calling Bryan "one of the greatest men of our time" and claiming "the world has lost one of its foremost citizens."[12]

Bryan's death helped ensure his final speech garnered more attention than it would otherwise have. The AP, for example, ran the entire speech on July 28, spreading Bryan's message across the country.[13] With the announcement that Bryan would be buried at Arlington—he had served as a colonel in the Spanish-American War despite his later commitment to pacifism—he seemed to be winning back some of the reputation he lost in Dayton. Crowds gathered for the funeral train, which took Bryan's body up to Washington, with towns across the South honoring their fallen hero.[14]

Darrow picked up on the irony of Bryan's restored reputation. "Mr. Bryan lost his hold in Tennessee when he testified in court, but his tragic end, which came so soon after, restored him to their hearts. I am sincere in saying that I am sorry that he could not have seen all this devotion that followed him to his resting place."[15]

Despite their differences, Scopes proved far kinder to Bryan than his attorney: "No fair man would judge Bryan's place in history by his actions at Dayton alone. He deserves better." While not impressed with Bryan, after four decades Scopes tried to offer a balanced look at him. "Bryan was, like most of us, an individual who had contributed both good and bad and a fair man would pity him for the bad he brought to the world, and love him for the good."[16]

While Darrow chuckled over plans to build a monument to Bryan in Washington, DC, an idea that was never realized, the Great Commoner's legacy continues to live on in the town where he fought his last battle and where he died.

In August 1930, fundamentalist Christians and supporters of Bryan chartered the William Jennings Bryan University in Dayton. The school was launched with the "purpose of establishing, conducting, and perpetuating a university for the higher education of men and women under auspices distinctly Christian and spiritual, as a testimony to the supreme glory of the Lord Jesus Christ, and to the Divine inspiration and infallibility of the Bible."

Time magazine reported on the school's opening: "Matriculating students may be of any race, creed, or sect, but administrative officers and faculty of the college must be firm believers in Old-time Religion." Dr. George E. Guille, a teacher at the Moody Bible Institute in Chicago, became the school's first president.[17]

While construction of the campus began, the first classes at the new university would be held in Rhea County High School—the very building that John Scopes had taught evolution in five years before.

Darrow mocked the new school in his autobiography. When he returned to Dayton to see old friends in 1928, he was not impressed with the first efforts to build the university, insisting it was a "monster project" that did not deserve to succeed. "Bigotry and opposition to learning are not a good foundation for any university in these modern times," Darrow wrote.[18]

But Darrow was wrong. The school survived its slow start and, eventually, flourished. Almost a century after it was launched, the school remains open, perched on a hill and towering over Dayton. The campus is at its best in the fall, with the distant mountains and hills illuminated under clear skies. The college was renamed William Jennings Bryan College in 1958 and finally Bryan College in 1993. With more than fourteen hundred students currently, Bryan College now offers graduate degrees and has been increasingly recognized as one of the region's up-and-coming schools.

Despite its growth, the debate over evolution and creationism continues to shape the college. In February 2014, the administration of Bryan College added a statement of belief to its contracts. "We believe that all humanity is descended from Adam and Eve," the statement read. "They are historical persons created by God in a special formative act, and not from previously existing life forms." The statement led to a decline in enrollment and several faculty members leaving the school. The college president even faced a vote of no confidence on the matter, though that was more about how the statement was added instead of its actual content.[19]

Bryan's death offered far more drama to the already-memorable trial. To what extent the trial, namely Darrow's cross-examination, may have led to Bryan's ultimate demise has often been discussed. Historians have debated it. No clarity has ever emerged.

Bryan died while still in Dayton, just five days after the Scopes Trial ended. As noted, the cause of death was described as "apoplexy," which the medical community attributes to a cerebral hemorrhage or stroke. The informal definition in some dictionaries may be more apt. Apoplexy is described as incapacity or speechlessness caused by extreme anger.

Whether Bryan succumbed to rage, regret, or profound disappointment is unknowable. When defenders claimed that Bryan died of a broken heart, more than a few critics, including Darrow, insisted he died from overeating and his poor health.[20]

Bryan's death was a sad denouement to the Trial of the Century. An incredible clash between religion and evolution ended in the downfall of the man who had won the case. But in the long run, Bryan was not the only loser, and as the coming years would show, many of the main players in the trial lost more than they won from the showdown in Dayton.

"You Can Only Be Free If I Am Free"

History would conclude that Clarence Darrow, the man who lost, is the lawyer who prevailed in his efforts to preserve intellectual freedom and the advancement of science.

But Darrow's win was, at best, a Pyrrhic victory.

Even though evolution has never presented itself as a polemic against the Bible, the tension between the two perspectives still persists. The Trial of the Century never reached a satisfying resolution. The ideas and competing beliefs argued between Clarence Darrow and William Jennings Bryan are just as relevant today as they were in the small town of Dayton, Tennessee, nearly one hundred years ago.

While he won the case, Bryan's reputation never recovered from his role in Dayton. But Bryan was not the only loser at the trial— there were several.

Darrow's strategy for the Scopes Trial appeal did not turn out as he thought it would.

For most of the trial, Darrow assumed his client would lose and the case would be appealed. While the case went to the Tennessee Supreme Court, the drama had been taken out of the case, and attention turned elsewhere. After seven months, with one of the justices having died, the Supreme Court split 2–2, upholding the Butler Act while exonerating Scopes in some exquisitely crafted legal hairsplitting.[1]

Darrow found the appeal frustrating, especially as it continued to drag. "Five judges heard the argument of the case," Darrow remembered. "In the meantime, one had died. The opinion was rendered by four." While applauding the justices for overturning Scopes's conviction, Darrow was unhappy with the final result. "Two of them said that the law was constitutional; one of them held that it was unconstitutional; and one held that it was constitutional but had no application to the Scopes case; that it was only meant to forbid the teaching of materialism." The ruling proved anticlimactic, and Tennessee was glad to finally have the case out of the system.[2]

Darrow did not get all he wanted—but that was typical for almost everyone involved in the case, including Dayton's leadership.

Just as George Rappleyea and other town boosters had anticipated, the Scopes Trial had changed Dayton—but not how they thought it would.

To be sure, William Jennings Bryan University would soon be looming on a hill outside of town and, in 1930, would welcome its first student, Amy Cartwright. A graduate of Rhea Central High School, where John Scopes had once taught, Amy was the granddaughter of Lemuel Cartwright, the Methodist preacher who had opened the trial with a fervent prayer.[3]

But outside of the university, the town continued to struggle. Even with all the attention brought to Dayton from the trial, the coal mines never opened back up the way Rappleyea and others had hoped. Despite all the hype, Dayton failed to grow. By 1940, 1,870 people lived in Dayton—up from 1,701 in 1920, but fewer people than lived there in 1910 when the coal mines were still running.

Even after almost a century, the shadow of the Scopes Trial lingers over Dayton. In 2021, the authors visited Dayton for a few days, meeting with some of the residents and local historians. People who grew up in Dayton never heard about the trial in their classes. Even a recent Rhea County High School graduate, one of the best students in his class, was never made aware of the once-legendary case until he went to college. After the trial and all the various attacks from H. L. Mencken and other reporters, Dayton had been dubbed Monkey Town, and local residents felt embarrassed about their community's moment in the spotlight. This was not at all what Rappleyea and the other business leaders had wanted when they sat around a table at Robinson's Drug Store to pitch their idea to John Scopes.

Like Dayton, most of the participants in the trial did not benefit from their roles in it. Walter White, the Rhea County schools superintendent, ran against Governor Austin Peay in 1926. White hoped that Tennessee voters would overlook their traditional hostility to Republicans and focus on his defense of Christian values, but he garnered only 35 percent of the vote.

Judge John Raulston also hoped his role at the trial would boost his chances for higher office. The trial hurt His Honor's political career more than helped it. Running for reelection in 1926, Raulston went down to defeat. Like White, he ran for governor and lost badly. While he occasionally spoke about the need for more Christian values in public life, Raulston eventually moderated his position on evolution, even asking if the state had the authority to prevent the teaching of scientific theories. Raulston's final years were tragic. He suffered a nervous breakdown in 1950 and injured his legs in a fall. Spending the last six years of his life confined to his home, Raulston died in 1956 at the age of eighty-seven.[4]

Not all of the participants in the trial flopped on the campaign trail. Tom Stewart continued to prosecute cases in the district before being elected to the U.S. Senate in 1938 after a scandal-plagued primary with accusations of ballot stuffing and corruption on all sides. One of the candidates whom Stewart defeated was John Neal, one of the attorneys who had represented Scopes more than a dozen years before.[5] After an undistinguished ten years in the Senate, Stewart lost in the primary to Estes Kefauver.[6]

After the trial, Scopes needed to get out of Dayton. "I had hopes that, once the trial was over, my notoriety would ebb and I would be forgotten," Scopes wrote decades later. "These were false hopes." Scopes went to graduate school at the University of Chicago to study geology, hoping to earn a PhD. But even in the Windy City, Scopes could not escape his fame. Dropping out of school, he headed to Venezuela, taking a job with Gulf Oil and wishing to evade the public eye. "Venezuela was a refuge where notoriety could not easily follow me," Scopes noted. "I would be just another Yankee oil hunter; to the Americans there, I would be another geologist. In many ways it was perfect."[7]

But Venezuela wasn't the panacea Scopes was seeking, despite his best efforts to reinvent himself. In a photo of him taken in Venezuela in 1927, Scopes is almost unrecognizable despite only two years having passed since the trial. Scopes retained his lanky frame, but his clothes, especially his shirt, fell off his wiry body since they were too large. Between his receding hairline, grim expression, thick mustache, and the pipe perched in his mouth, Scopes appeared to have aged fifteen years since his days in Dayton. His health collapsed from infections in South America, and while recuperating back in the States, he met Mildred Elizabeth Walker, a vibrant young woman from South Carolina. Scopes proposed to her and converted to Catholicism upon his marriage to her.[8]

Scopes made one last bid for public attention, running as a Socialist Party candidate for Congress in Kentucky in 1932.[9] After getting routed in that race, he returned to the oil industry, working in Texas and Louisiana and raising two sons. Scopes grappled with depression during the 1930s and 1940s, often trying to bury himself in his work and in the bottle. Despite his best efforts, Scopes could not run from the past, as preachers and students bombarded him with letters, trying to save his soul or ask questions about the trial.[10]

Slowly, Scopes started making peace with his role in history. Thanks to Mildred's prodding, in 1960, Scopes attended the premiere as the popular play *Inherit the Wind* was turned into a film. While the film did not prove to be a hit, Scopes returned to Dayton for the thirty-fifth anniversary of the trial, the first time he had been there since 1931. "The town hadn't changed much," he dryly noted, showing how Rappleyea's plans of transforming Dayton had failed. The few familiar faces included Sue Hicks, who was now a judge. But plenty of the surviving participants from the trial—including Tom Stewart and Rappleyea—were nowhere to be found. Scopes was honored, even getting the key to the city, yet he still drew fire. A local fundamentalist minister hosted a radio show while Scopes was in Dayton and compared him to the devil. Scopes left Dayton convinced that, even in 1960, the verdict would have been the same. He also wrote his autobiography, a self-deprecating and humble account of his life and his role in the trial. In 1970, three years after it was published, Scopes died of cancer at the age of seventy.[11]

Scopes never got the chance to take his case to the U.S. Supreme Court—but he did live to see the highest court in the land rule on teaching evolution in public schools. With the Space Race and the Cold War in full swing, by the 1950s and 1960s America saw a renewed push for teaching science, including evolution. In 1927, Arkansas passed a similar law to the Butler Act, which included a provision dismissing teachers if they taught evolution. Decades later, Susan Epperson, a teacher in Little Rock, challenged that law and took it all the way to the nation's highest court.[12]

In 1968, the Supreme Court unanimously ruled in Epperson's favor, striking down the law. Justice Abe Fortas wrote the high court's opinion: "The law must be stricken because of its conflict with the constitutional prohibition of state laws respecting an establishment of religion or prohibiting the free exercise thereof. The overriding fact is that Arkansas' law selects from the body of knowledge a particular segment which it proscribes for the sole reason that it is deemed to conflict with a particular religious doctrine; that is, with a particular interpretation of the Book of Genesis by a particular religious group."

Fortas insisted that banning the teaching of evolution brought up several issues beyond science and religion. "The antecedents of today's decision are many and unmistakable. They are rooted in the foundation soil of our Nation. They are fundamental to freedom. Government in our democracy, state and national, must be neutral in matters of religious theory, doctrine, and practice. It may not be hostile to any religion or to the advocacy of no religion; and it may not aid, foster, or promote one religion or religious theory against another or even against the militant opposite. The First Amendment mandates governmental neutrality between religion and religion, and between religion and nonreligion."

In the opinion, Fortas also pointed to the Butler Act and invoked the Scopes Trial. "Perhaps the sensational publicity attendant upon the Scopes trial induced Arkansas to adopt less explicit language. It eliminated Tennessee's reference to 'the story of the Divine Creation of man' as taught in the Bible, but there is no doubt that the motivation for the law was the same: to suppress the teaching of a theory which, it was thought, 'denied' the divine creation of man."[13]

Despite the ruling, the debate continues over teaching evolution in the classroom.

"Well, obviously our case did not solve the problem," Epperson said a half century after the Supreme Court decision. "As long as preachers tell their congregations that this is an anti-God idea, then there will be efforts to remove it from classes. I have learned that one cannot debate the validity of evolution with students in class. Evidence that evolution occurred is abundant, so look at the science."[14]

Clarence Darrow could not have agreed more.

More important, through Susan Epperson, almost half a century after he taught at Rhea County High School, John Scopes finally had his day at the Supreme Court—and the highest court in the land ruled in his favor.

Scopes cheered Epperson on, praising her at the end of his autobiography and stressing the importance of their efforts: "By respecting the other man's views and by protecting his liberties, we gain respect for our own views and we protect our own liberties." Fittingly, as he reached the end of his autobiography, his thoughts turned, once again, to his old attorney Clarence Darrow. Scopes offered one last quote from the great lawyer: "You can only be free if I am free. The same thing that would get me may be used to get you, and the government that is not strong enough to protect all its citizens ought not to live upon the face of the earth."[15]

As for Darrow, while he never took the Scopes case to the Supreme Court, the rest of his life was full of honors.

Darrow was sixty-eight when the Scopes Trial ended, and he thought, once again, about retiring from the law. But he could not sit on the sidelines when, after a race riot in Detroit as a white mob attacked a Black family who lived in a primarily white neighborhood, eleven Black men were charged with killing one of the rioters. In front of an all-white jury Darrow defended Dr. Ossian Sweet—one of the men accused of killing the rioter—and his brother Henry. While Henry Sweet confessed to killing the rioter, Darrow successfully led the defense, offering stirring words that showed his commitment to civil rights and equality.

"I speak for a race which will go on and on to heights never reached before," Darrow told jurors. "I speak for a million Blacks who have some hope and faith remaining in the institutions of this land. I speak to you on behalf of those whose ancestors were brought here in chains. I speak to you on behalf of the faces, those Black faces, which have haunted this courtroom since the trial began."

In a seven-hour closing argument, Darrow once again offered a lesson on the importance of justice, of taking on popular opinions. "I ask you on behalf of justice, often maligned and downtrodden, hard to protect and hard to maintain, I ask you on behalf of yourselves, on behalf of our race, to see that no harm comes to them. I ask you gentlemen in the name of the future, the future which will one day solve these sore problems, and the future which is theirs as well as ours, I ask you in the name of the future to do justice in this case."

Darrow's closing argument was so powerful that it left Judge Frank Murphy—later mayor of Detroit, governor of Michigan, Franklin Delano Roosevelt's attorney general, and a Supreme Court justice—in tears.[16]

Financially hurt by the Great Depression, Darrow wrote his autobiography and spent the 1930s giving lectures and taking part in debates on a host of topics. Darrow's health faded as the decade continued, and he passed away from heart disease in 1938 at the age of eighty.[17]

Slowly, Dayton grew to embrace the trial. A statue of Bryan, the same as the one representing Nebraska in Statuary Hall in the Capitol, stood alone in front of the courthouse for many years. Tourists began to visit the town, wanting to see the locations from the famous trial. Tom Davis, who was active with the county historical society, even launched the annual Scopes Festival, giving the town, which now has more than seven thousand residents, a chance to celebrate the trial that put it on the map.[18] Monkey Town, once a phrase dismissing Dayton, has become a term of endearment that the town readily accepts. While Bryan, a supporter of Prohibition, would not approve, on First Avenue, not too far from where Darrow and the Great Commoner clashed, sits Monkey Town Brewing Company, a restaurant that offers a knowing wink at Dayton's past.

Once scornful and ashamed of its legacy, Dayton has started to embrace it. After almost a century, George Rappleyea's gamble has finally paid off—since Dayton was home to one of the most important fights for freedom in American history and the site of the Trial of the Century.

In the Rhea County Courthouse statue of Bryan, he appears buttoned-up and solemn, with a cloak over his suit, dressed for the nineteenth century. It makes the Great Commoner appear more formal than he was in life and trapped in the past. Across from Bryan stands an equivalent likeness of Darrow, his glasses perched precariously on his vest, a finger extended as he makes a point. In 2017, the Freedom From Religion Foundation provided the funds for a replica of Darrow to join the one of Bryan.[19] The dynamic statue, from the passionate look on Darrow's face to the old shoes sticking out from rumpled pants, is far more lifelike than Bryan's—just as the values and arguments Darrow made in Dayton are as relevant now as they were when he made them almost a century ago.

Speaking Freely and Unafraid

Several decades have passed since I first reached for the volume perched on my father's dark walnut bookcase one summer day. But the image of that moment is indelible, still frozen in my mind and will remain so always.

The book has grown old and worn with time. The pages are yellowed and brittle and creased. But the binding still holds together the words that electrified me as a teenager. The ideas are as fresh and durable now as they were on that day when I read the story of an extraordinary man named Clarence Darrow. What inspired me then has never faded.

Darrow shaped my thinking in incalculable ways. The contours of my life were enriched because a lawyer whom I never met inspired me to try to be better than I thought I was capable of being. Darrow was a disciple of charity and justice with a noble character. He brought humanity to the law. His selfless values and the virtues he preached gave me a moral and intellectual road map by which to navigate the challenges that lay ahead. His defiance in the face of incivility, intolerance, and injustice informed me. In a world with too few heroes, Darrow was mine.

The cherished principles that Darrow fought for—academic freedom, scientific acceptance, free speech, civil rights, social equity, and racial justice—are as vital and relevant today as they were a century ago.

Since the Scopes Trial, America has evolved into the most advanced and sophisticated civilization ever known. But the same implacable issues that bedeviled our country at the beginning of the twentieth century still haunt us in the twenty-first.

With new discoveries, it is now impossible to see evolution as anything besides a bedrock scientific principle. Thanks to remarkable achievements in genetics, genomics, and many other fields, our understanding of the wealth of information contained in fossilized records, which continues to be updated, has only expanded. Almost every member—98 percent—of the scientific community fully accepts evolution as the preeminent explanation of the biological process of human development and diversity.[1]

However, even today, in schools across America, comparable acceptance of evolution falls woefully short.

Surprisingly, evolution is still a controversial concept. The teaching of evolution in public schools continues to produce intense dispute, although some progress has been made in the last decade. Fifteen years ago, a slight majority of high school biology teachers emphasized evolution. To the disadvantage of nearly half of all students, the subject disappeared into a black hole. However, by 2019, that emphasis had increased to 67 percent, thanks to a stout set of improved educational standards backed by scientists that were adopted as mandatory in forty-four states.[2] Nevertheless, that leaves a troubling knowledge deficit for far too many students.

Darrow would be gratified that the pitched battle he fought inside a rural Tennessee courtroom almost one hundred years ago led directly to eliminating anti-evolution laws everywhere. No longer are teachers criminally prosecuted. The days of banning instruction on evolution and eliminating textbooks explaining its science are over. But negative pressure from both teachers and parents endures. Darrow would be chagrined that educational recognition of Darwin's theory of biological growth continues to face dissent and opposition from within public institutions themselves.

Roughly 20 percent of teachers inform their students that creationism is scientifically credible.[3] Personal religious beliefs still drive the view that evolution undermines fidelity to God. Perhaps this is not so surprising when you consider that more than 30 percent of American adults believe that "humans and other living things have existed in their present form since the beginning of time."[4]

The numbers of Americans adhering to these beliefs will inevitably change because reliable data shows that younger people are far more willing than older adults to accept that evolution has occurred. And, too, creationists have become less powerful in exerting pressure on school boards. As the population ages and new generations become more educated, skepticism should further recede. As Darrow once said in a different context during the Scopes Trial, "These things take time."

Time has also softened the perspective of religious leaders in many of the world's predominant faiths. Gone is the reflexive assumption that the theories of evolution and Divine Creation are contradictory and inherently incompatible. Quite the opposite has occurred. The Catholic Church and most Protestant denominations now acknowledge the essential tenets of Darwin's theory as a reasonable scientific narrative for the development of life through the passage of millennia. Just as Darrow argued in the Scopes Trial that God may have utilized evolution in Creation as a biological mechanism for progression and change, most Christian religions have come to accept this explanation. Theologians tend to interpret stories of Creation revealed in the Bible as allegorical, not historical; and spiritual, not physical or literal. What the great fundamentalist William Jennings Bryan so vociferously dismissed in 1925 is now conventionally endorsed.

A moment of inflection came in 2014 when Pope Francis spoke candidly about the unity of faith and science in modern culture while addressing the Pontifical Academy of Sciences. He built on the works of previous popes on the matter, including Pius XII and John Paul II. "When we read in Genesis the account of Creation, we risk imagining God as a magician, with a wand able to make everything. But it is not so. He created beings and allowed them to develop," said the pontiff. He added, "The big bang, which nowadays is posited as the origin of the world, does not contradict the divine act of creating, but rather requires it. The evolution of nature does not contrast with the notion of Creation, as evolution presupposes the Creation of beings that evolve."[5]

This was Darrow's thesis all along. Armed with a keen understanding of the Bible learned from his father, a seminarian, and backed by a team of esteemed scientists and eminent scholars in theology whom he convened in Dayton, Darrow endeavored to explain all of this to the Scopes jury. But prosecutors would have none of it. Judge Raulston, blinded by his religious bias, discarded his duty to ensure that the defendant was treated fairly and that justice was done. Raulston summarily disallowed the testimony. Darrow's client was convicted, but the fight for the recognition of science in classrooms and the greater push for academic freedom accelerated.

═══

At present, another battlefront has arisen in education. This fierce and vocal conflict is over a different kind of academic freedom—the teaching of a doctrine known as critical race theory (CRT) within classroom settings. Liberals, conservatives, and others across the political spectrum sharply disagree over its precise definition, which is further complicated by disparate versions deployed in various educational settings. Defenders of CRT insist that it is an effective way for students to understand how historical racism and the legacy of white supremacy have deeply impacted American institutions and shaped public policy. Housing, employment, health care, criminal justice, and education itself have all been affected. Advocates of CRT posit that patterns of racism extend beyond individual prejudice and are still embedded in laws and systems that lend distinct advantages to people born white. Our nation's shameful history of slavery, Jim Crow laws, segregation, and their lingering stain should be more honestly reflected in coursework and classroom conversations. Instruction must be revised, they say, to address these issues forthrightly and with greater accuracy in the teaching of civics, history, and other subjects. Any effort to minimize our country's record of discrimination and the deprivation of civil and human rights is an abdication of educational responsibility to truth.

Opponents adopt a different view. They contend that some forms of CRT instruction are less benign and have gone too far. U.S. history, they say, has been overtly politicized with an inaccurate and arguably poisonous ideology through compelled speech. Some parents and educators lament that students in certain public schools are forced to learn that prejudice in America is so pervasive that we are, without question or dissent, a systemically and irredeemably racist nation. These CRT critics disagree that racial inequity and injustice are inherent and permanent fixtures in every institution and endeavor. Such teaching prompted upset parents to complain vigorously to administrators and ignited protests at school board meetings. They claim that group identity wrongfully takes precedence over individual merit and that, in some instances, their children are divided into either "oppressors" or "oppressed," depending on the color of their skin. Classrooms have reportedly become venues of guilt and shame to advance cultural correctness.

Much like the historic dispute nearly one hundred years ago between creationists and evolutionists, the CRT controversy quickly found its way into our courts. In suburban Chicago, a teacher who was required to undergo antiracist and equity training filed a discrimination lawsuit alleging that white educators were subjected to a hostile work environment. She alleged suppression of free speech and academic freedom over school policies that demand racially segregated antiracist exercises for teachers and students, as well as mandatory pledges to be antiracist.[6] In Pennsylvania, compulsory classroom instruction on white fragility and privilege, systemic racism, and Black Lives Matter triggered a lawsuit citing religious infringements and acts of retaliation for refusing to comply.[7] In Nevada, a biracial student sued because he was allegedly handed a failing grade after he resisted disclosing his racial, gender, and religious identities to designate whether he was an oppressed person or an oppressor.[8] In Virginia, parents filed suit over a school policy that found students guilty of "micro-aggressions" if they declined to agree with the concept of white privilege.[9] Scores of other lawsuits have been brought based on equal protection grounds under the Fourteenth Amendment, the discrimination provisions of the 1964 Civil Rights Act, and freedom of speech guaranteed by the First Amendment.

As plaintiffs pursued these individual legal actions, lawmakers across the United States launched a broader effort to tamp down what they regard as CRT overreach. A majority of states passed legislation or took significant steps to limit schools from utilizing critical race theory instruction that purportedly defies sound educational principles. Bills were passed and signed into law regulating how racism, inequality, and sexism can be discussed by teachers in classrooms.[10]

Oklahoma was among the first to enact a statute that restricts lessons on race and gender in public schools. It prohibits any conversations that people are "inherently racist, sexist, or oppressive, whether consciously or unconsciously." It banned eight racial "concepts," which led teachers to scale back instruction and remove books.[11] The American Civil Liberties Union (ACLU) promptly challenged the new law in federal court, alleging that it violates free speech rights and, therefore, deprives students of vital historical discourse.[12] Irrespective of the trial court's decision, the outcome will likely be appealed and could eventually reach the U.S. Supreme Court as an important test of First Amendment rights and academic freedom.

How would Darrow, who championed such academic freedom, react to today's newly constituted laws imposing severe constraints on probative discussions of race, gender, oppression, colonialism, and historical discrimination? It is impossible to know. However, I suspect he would respond exactly as he did when Bryan and his devout followers pressured states into banning the teaching of evolution. He would probably join forces with his old ally, the ACLU, to fight in favor of our cherished principle of free speech in schools that is foundational to democracy. Consonant with that belief, he would likely oppose any attempt to suffocate diversity of thought. He would reject all efforts to silence speech through state censorship. Just as he waged war against the narrow-minded bigotry of religious fanatics who demanded that Genesis be ordained as the solitary standard of truth in schoolrooms everywhere, Darrow would once again side with the right of educators, not lawmakers, to decide *what* should be taught and *how* to teach it.

Darrow believed that academic freedom is a transcendent value that is self-evident. It should be preserved and safeguarded because classrooms are nothing if not a marketplace of ideas and information that should be freely exchanged. America is a melting pot of diversity. It is rich in cultural, racial, and ethnic backgrounds. Students' understanding of our nation's history—both good and bad—awakens them to essential moral values. It better prepares them to participate effectively and successfully in a heterogeneous society and civic life. It advances their cognitive development. Access to such knowledge is diminished if robust dialogue is stricken from the classroom. Young people are robbed of vital analytical thinking skills whenever discussions are foreclosed. Complex questions about race and gender throughout history must be understood in the context of prior human events. Ignoring them as if they never existed or minimizing them is itself discriminatory. Even worse, it is educationally irresponsible, if not dehumanizing. One can only envision how marginalized students stand to be harmed the most in a less inclusive academic environment where history is being sanitized.

How can we assess what Darrow would do? I am reminded of what he once wrote when fundamentalists "laid siege to state legislatures and school boards" in the 1920s. They endeavor "to modify education to conform to the campaign of ignorance that has overspread the land . . . and they dismiss every teacher who dares to allow intelligence and learning to have anything to do with his mental processes."[13] Darrow, who dared to defend the wonders of science, would once again argue in defense of learning and the right to teach freely the unvarnished truth of America's history. It is not always a comfortable subject. By today's standards, our painful past is hard for young people to assimilate or even comprehend. All the more reason why it must be confronted and reckoned with if students are to gain the knowledge and wisdom that is central to an educated mind. They are capable of engaging in such discussions, even on ideas with which they may disagree. This is an indispensable component of learning. In Dayton, the legendary lawyer knew there was no conflict between science and religion, just as he might know today that there is no conflict when history is informed with truth and the sanctity of free speech.

Might Darrow concede that certain aspects of critical race theory have crossed the boundary from historical accuracy to politically charged indoctrination? Perhaps so. He warned that learning should never be "hampered and measured by dogmas and creeds."[14] Partisan orthodoxy and its corresponding bias cannot be allowed to cast a shroud over classrooms. He would defend teachers and students alike from punitive actions arising from their free speech and opinion rights in CRT controversies. But I suspect that Darrow would also seek common ground, just as he did in the Scopes Trial when he argued that evolution and creation can be viewed as harmonious. He would argue that theoretical and historical perspectives on racism in America should be addressed honestly and candidly but without a divisive social agenda. If cultivation of the human mind is the gift that educators bequeath students, they deserve no less than the unadulterated truth. At the same time, concerned parents play an integral role. They possess a fundamental right under the First Amendment to assemble and petition their local school boards to freely voice their objections if they feel that curriculum is politically driven and not supported by sound academic principles.

Darrow would point out the striking parallel between Tennessee's anti-evolution law of 1925 and Oklahoma's anti-CRT law of today. Both are imprecise and ambiguous, leaving teachers unable to distinguish between content that is permissible or forbidden. Under threat of sanctions, including the loss of their teaching license for violating the new law, teachers are left trapped in a climate of trepidation and potential retaliation. They cannot simply err on the side of caution, they must overcompensate to avoid punishment. As the ACLU lawsuit warns, books by Black or women authors now stand at risk. Should pivotal works such as *To Kill a Mockingbird*, the *Narrative of the Life of Frederick Douglass*, and *A Raisin in the Sun* be discarded by educators out of fear that someone might be offended by the language therein?[15] Are all nonneutral words to be expunged from textbooks and course instruction? Should culturally inclusive curricula be abandoned? Must teachers be forced to wear "intellectual straitjackets" in the classroom to avoid any trenchant examination of the human condition associated with race, gender, and prejudice that is endemic in American history? Should students be muzzled from respectful scholastic debate in what is otherwise protected speech? Does strict obedience to the legislation mean that multiple viewpoints and alternative ideas are repressed in what amounts to an alarming erosion of free speech? Darrow would answer these vexing questions with a resounding "No!"

The Darrow of today would still be animated by his devotion to civil rights. In this regard, he was peerless. He deplored bigotry and racism. He loathed the menace of violent groups such as the Ku Klux Klan. In the early twentieth century, he galvanized the push for racial justice and efforts at equality. Doing more than merely mouthing a slogan, he believed passionately that Black lives matter. He placed his reputation at risk to defend Black victims of a legal system that was biased in its application of laws, discriminatory in its enforcement, prejudiced in its final judgments, and frequently imperiled their freedom. He was an apostle for civil rights in an era when little civility and precious few rights were afforded to people of color.

Darrow worked closely with the ACLU, which was at the vanguard of the struggle for both free speech and causes of racial justice. It still is. Were he alive, the famed lawyer would surely embrace the organization's argument in the Oklahoma lawsuit that "educators cannot adequately teach students about the 1921 Tulsa Race Massacre, the Trail of Tears, the Civil War, World War II, the Holocaust or

any other cultural issue throughout U.S. history by silencing coura-
geous classroom conversations that depict a more inclusive perspective of U.S. history."[16] Darrow would also concur that banishing all
aspects of critical race theory "censors and chills the way Oklahoma
teachers and students discuss fraught topics in state and U.S. history,
particularly regarding racial mistreatment and injustice."[17] Finally,
Darrow would argue—just as he did in the Scopes Trial—that local
educators, faculty, and administrators are best equipped to tailor the
contours of academic instruction and classroom discussions, not state
legislators. This view is echoed by Oklahoma's own State Board of
Education's rule that states, "Do not dictate how teachers should
teach. . . . Do not mandate a specific curriculum. . . . Do not prescribe
all that can or should be taught."[18]

Darrow committed himself to the law with all his might, talent, and soul. With uncommon empathy, he devoted much of his
professional life to helping those who could not help themselves.
When it was unpopular to do so, he challenged conventional wisdom, political correctness, and demagoguery. He labored in favor
of what he called "sanity and humanity against the wave of hatred and malice."[19] Darrow was fond of saying that bigotry and
ignorance were his adversaries. They are relentless and venomous.
Speaking before a large gathering of fellow lawyers, he averred,
"The way to make this world better is to make it kinder. The only
way to cure its evils is to bury hatred."[20]

Darrow was celebrated by some and derided by others as the "attorney for the damned" because he believed with all his heart that
even the despised deserved the fairness of justice. Lost causes needed
defending the most. They were the only ones, he grumbled, that
were worth fighting for. He complained that tolerance and charity
were in short supply. They still are today.

Darrow dreamed of a day when freedom and liberty were not entitlements belonging to the privileged few but existential rights enjoyed by all. He longed for a society where the powerful and the powerless were treated equally both inside and outside courts of law. He regretted how poverty, envy, and despair drove men to desperate acts in desperate times. Greater education was Darrow's remedy for the ills that plagued America's underclass. He saw it not as a panacea but as a path by which the less fortunate could rise from the darkness of their barren circumstances. To the end, he worked sedulously promoting the virtues of literacy and scholarship.

Academic freedom, for which Darrow fought in the Scopes Monkey Trial, was a critical component in his educational crusade. Political, religious, and social beliefs that trended at any given moment should not be imposed by government dictate on students or teachers alike. Both should be permitted to express their views and opinions devoid of restraint. They must be free to engage in intellectual debate without the corrosive fear of censorship or reprisal. Diversity of thought is axiomatic in a free society. Yet these cornerstone values often seem eroded or lost in today's sea of "educational gag orders."[21]

As Darrow neared the twilight of his pilgrimage through a distinguished career, he was a spent man. Looking back, he wrote, "I had grown tired of standing in the lean and lonely front line facing the greatest enemy that ever confronted man—public opinion."[22] Yet, despite his weariness, he soldiered on. He could not desert his intrinsic desire to fight injustices whenever they might knock on his battered door. Darrow feared that those injustices would intensify unless someone courageously stepped forward to stop them. That someone always seemed to be Darrow.

A quote from a book Darrow edited distills his view of the essence of humanity: "All men do the best they can. But none meet life honestly and few heroically."[23] Darrow proved to be the exception. He was far from perfect. He grappled with his mistakes and personal failures, as we all do. But Darrow possessed a glorious intellect and strength of character that one cannot help but admire. More than most, he lived his life valiantly and heroically.

The old warrior came to the aid of a young Tennessee schoolteacher who dared to teach evolution in a time when simple minds and timid men surrendered to the zealousness of public pressure and governmental overreach. Darrow's brilliant and devastating cross-examination of William Jennings Bryan turned the tide in education. It spelled the beginning of the end for the kind of religious intrusion that our Constitution forbids. The wonders and benefits of science were untethered. Generations of Americans became Darrow's beneficiaries.

I can still remember sitting as a teenager by the window of my room absorbing every word in Irving Stone's account of Darrow's intrepid defense in the Scopes Trial—how Darrow openly challenged the judge's bias and was held in criminal contempt, how he lashed out at the idea of a law that inhibited learning, and how he marshaled compelling evidence that evolution in no way undermined creationism. I was incensed at the injustice of it all, just as Darrow was. I admired him as he held sturdy and steadfast in the face of overwhelming odds.

As the shadows of day turned to night, I kept reading. Darrow's cross-examination of Bryan was mesmerizing and bold. With resolute patience and penetrating questions, Darrow began to dismantle the veneer of his adversary's beliefs. The more Bryan fumbled, the more he fanned himself in the searing heat. As sentiment started to shift, derisive laughter from the crowd only inflamed Bryan's panic. Darrow's relentless prodding and inescapable logic destroyed his nemesis. A part of me felt sorry for Bryan. He was thoroughly discredited. Bryan had doggedly clung to a righteous-ness that he mistakenly ascribed to virtue. He forced his religious ideology on others by helping enact a misbegotten law. It became the sad and tragic epitaph of a once-great man.

When court adjourned, Darrow was congratulated and swept away by a throng of admirers. "Looking back, he saw Bryan stand-ing with only one friend by his side," wrote Stone.[24] Bryan was a defeated man. The national press destroyed him further. Bryan died five days later, still in Dayton. And still clinging to the hope that he might somehow survive his epic humiliation and rebound to the kind of triumph he yearned for.

Yes, Clarence Darrow lost the trial. But he won the more import-ant and enduring argument against imposing limits that suffocate in-tellectual independence, frustrate progress, and enervate the birth of new ideas. The human mind is an open canvas of possibilities. We should be free to paint it with our own brushstrokes.

In its day, the Scopes Monkey Trial was widely regarded as the Trial of the Century. It remains so not for the obsessive worldwide attention it garnered but because it advanced the indispensable propo-sition that no one should be told how to think.

Acknowledgments

My being reluctant to write another book, my literary agent and friend, David Vigliano, suggested a coauthor to share the workload. Veteran writer and author Don Yaeger proved to be an excellent choice. My sincere thanks to him for digging deep into the history of Dayton and the many remarkable characters involved. Don was instrumental in bringing back to life a long-ago trial. His colleague, Kevin Derby, provided thoughtful editing along the way.

Three incredible Dayton residents generously gave us their time and access to information. This led to great nuggets of content crucial to our success. They are Tom Davis, Jacob Ellis, and Rhea County historian Pat Guffey. Their kindness is much appreciated.

The challenge and the gift of writing a book about an event that occurred one hundred years ago is finding new turf to plow when so many others have written on pieces of the story. To that end, we studied the works of many journalists, authors, and historians, including William F. McComas, Anthony Horvath, Edward J. Larson, Timothy C. Curver, Janet M. Curver, Marvin Olasky, John Perry, Randy Moore, Donald McRae, Irving Stone, Geoffrey Cowan, Michael Kazin, Louis William Koeing, Lawrence Levine, and Robert W. Cherny.

Gratitude is owed to Kevin W. Woodruff, Research Literacy Librarian at Bryan College, for locating and making available the collection of historical photographs of Dayton, Tennessee, in 1925 and the events of the Scopes Trial that are published with permission herein.

I'd like to thank the entire team of people at Threshold Editions of Simon & Schuster. From the outset they were enthusiastic about the book and offered important ideas on how the story should be crafted. Specific thanks to Natasha Simons, Mia Robertson, Jennifer Long, and Stephen Rubin.

Finally, thank you to my wife and two daughters, who, as always, offered their encouragement and support. This book is dedicated to my late father, Joseph W. Jarrett, who gave me his love of the law and its navigating principles.

Notes

CHAPTER ONE: "HELL IS GOING TO POP NOW"

1. Randy Moore and William F. McComas, *The Scopes Monkey Trial* (Charleston, SC, 2016), 55.
2. Clarence Darrow, *The Story of My Life* (New York, 1932), 265.
3. Anthony Horvath, ed., *The Transcript of the Scopes Monkey Trial* (Greenwood, WI, 2018), 441–47.
4. Brian Farmer, *American Conservatism: History, Theory and Practice* (Cambridge, UK, 2005), 213.
5. *Public Acts of the State of Tennessee Passed by the Sixth-Fourth General Assembly* (Nashville, 1925), chap. 127, House Bill no. 185. *Normals* here refers to teacher-training institutions.
6. This look at Bryan draws from Paolo E. Coletta, *William Jennings Bryan*, 3 vols. (Lincoln, NE, 1964–69); Michael Kazin, *A Godly Hero: The Life of William Jennings Bryan* (New York, 2006); Louis William Koenig, *Bryan: A Political Biography of William Jennings Bryan* (New York, 1971); and Lawrence W. Levine, *Defender of the Faith: William Jennings Bryan: The Last Decade, 1915–1925* (Oxford, UK, 1965).
7. This take on Darrow draws from Darrow, *Story of My Life*; Donald McRae, *The Last Trials of Clarence Darrow* (New York, 2009); and Irving Stone, *Clarence Darrow for the Defense* (Garden City, NY, 1941).
8. Horvath, 1–2.
9. Darrow, 259.
10. Darrow, 256.
11. Horvath, 8.
12. Horvath, 4.

13. Darrow, 265.
14. Edward J. Larson, *Summer for the Gods: The Scopes Trial and America's Continuing Debate over Science and Religion* (New York, 1997), 170–76.
15. Larson, 176–83.
16. Timothy C. Curver and Janet M. Curver, eds., *You Be the Judge: Scopes Trial* (Dayton, TN, 2000), 134.
17. John T. Scopes and James Presley, *Center of the Storm: Memoirs of John T. Scopes* (New York, 1967), 161.
18. H. L. Mencken, *A Religious Orgy in Tennessee: A Reporter's Account of the Scopes Monkey Trial* (Brooklyn, 2006), 89.

CHAPTER TWO: CHAMPION OF THE UNDERDOG
1. Clarence Darrow, *The Story of My Life* (New York, 1932), 11.
2. Darrow, 11.
3. Darrow, 12–15; Irving Stone, *Clarence Darrow for the Defense* (Garden City, NY, 1941), 7.
4. Darrow, 12–13; Stone 5–7.
5. Darrow, 12–21, 361; Stone 7–9; Donald McRae, *The Last Trials of Clarence Darrow: The Landmark Cases of Leopold and Loeb, John T. Scopes, and Ossian Sweet* (New York, 2009), 128–29.
6. Darrow, 16; Geoffrey Cowan, *The People v. Clarence Darrow: The Bribery Trial of America's Greatest Lawyer* (New York, 2003), 12–13.
7. Darrow, 22–25.
8. Darrow, 25–28.
9. Darrow, 29–30.
10. Cowan, 16–17; Stone, 10–12.
11. Darrow, 40–41.
12. Stone, 12–17.
13. Darrow, 57–58.
14. Cowan, 32. For an excellent account of the Harrison murder and its importance in Chicago's history, see Erik Larson, *The Devil in the White City: Murder, Magic, and Madness at the Fair That Changed America* (New York, 2013); and 2003. Darrow, 426.
15. For the strike, see Almont Lindsey, *The Pullman Strike: The Story of a Unique Experiment and of a Great Labor Upheaval* (Chicago, 1943); and David Ray Papke, *The Pullman Case: The Clash of Labor and Capital in Industrial America* (Lawrence, KS, 1999). For Debs, see Nick Salvatore, *Eugene V. Debs: Citizen and Socialist* (Urbana, IL, 1984); and Ray Ginger, *The Bending Cross: A Biography of Eugene Victor Debs* (New Brunswick, NJ, 1949).

16. Darrow, 66–67.
17. Cowan, 35–37.
18. Darrow, 90–92.
19. Darrow, 92–93.
20. Darrow, 93–95.
21. Cowan, 42–43. For more on the strike, see Robert J. Cornell, *The Anthracite Coal Strike of 1902* (Washington, DC, 1957).
22. Cowan, 47–50.
23. Edward J. Larson and Jack Marshall, eds., *The Essential Words and Writings of Clarence Darrow* (New York, 2007), 51–61.
24. Darrow, 16–17.

CHAPTER THREE: "A PASSION FOR LOST CAUSES"

1. Donald McRae, *The Last Trials of Clarence Darrow: The Landmark Cases of Leopold and Loeb, John T. Scopes, and Ossian Sweet* (New York, 2009), 34–36; Geoffrey Cowan, *The People v. Clarence Darrow: The Bribery Trial of America's Greatest Lawyer* (New York, 2003), 3–5.
2. For more on the bombing, see Lee Irwin, *Deadly Times: The 1910 Bombing of the* Los Angeles Times *and America's Forgotten Decade of Terror* (Guilford, CT, 2013).
3. Clarence Darrow, *The Story of My Life* (New York, 1932), 179–83.
4. Cowan, 235–42.
5. Darrow, 186–87.
6. For an excellent overview of how biographers and historians have weighed Darrow's guilt or innocence on the matter, see John A. Farrell, "Clarence Darrow: Jury Tamperer?," *Smithsonian*, December 2011.
7. McRae, 44–51.
8. Darrow, 203–4; Irving Stone, *Clarence Darrow for the Defense* (Garden City, NY, 1941), 220–26.
9. Darrow, 210–13.
10. Darrow, 69–73.
11. This account draws from McRae, 51–63; Simon Baatz, *For the Thrill of It: Leopold, Loeb and the Murder That Shocked Chicago* (New York, 2008); and Hal Higdon, *Leopold and Loeb: The Crime of the Century* (New York, 1975).
12. "Statement of Nathan F. Leopold made in the office of the State's Attorney of Cook County on Sat. May 31," McRae, 56–57.
13. Darrow, 232.
14. Darrow, 236–37.
15. Darrow, 237; McRae, 68–69.

16. McRae, 54–55.
17. Stone, 262–63.
18. Arthur Weinberg, ed., *Attorney for the Damned: Clarence Darrow in the Courtroom* (Chicago, 1957), 19–87.
19. McRae, 130.
20. Darrow, 231–32, 241–43.
21. Russell Owen, "Darrow Likes to Fight for Lost Causes," *New York Times*, July 25, 1925.
22. McRae, 147–49.

CHAPTER FOUR: "A TOWN OF HOPES AND NIGHTMARES"

1. For a good look at the early history of Dayton and Rhea County, see Bettye J. Boyles, *History of Rhea County, Tennessee* (Dayton, TN, 1991).
2. Henry Gannett, *The Origin of Certain Place Names in the United States* (Washington, DC, 1905), 101.
3. *San Francisco Call* 87, no. 179 (May 28, 1901).
4. *Chattanooga Times*, May 27, 1901.
5. John T. Scopes and James Presley, *Center of the Storm: Memoirs of John T. Scopes* (New York, 1967), 35.
6. Scopes and Presley, 35.
7. Scopes and Presley, 35; Clarence Darrow, *The Story of My Life* (New York, 1932), 247.
8. Scopes and Presley, 35–39.

CHAPTER FIVE: THE CRUSADE AGAINST TEACHING EVOLUTION

1. For an excellent account of the era, see Michael E. Parrish, *Anxious Decades: America in Prosperity and Depression, 1920–1941* (New York, 1994).
2. Richard Hofstadter, *Social Darwinism in American Thought, 1860–1915* (Philadelphia, 1944).
3. For an excellent look at Victorian opposition to Darwin, see David L. Hull, *Darwin and His Critics: The Reception of Darwin's Theory of Evolution by the Scientific Community* (Chicago, 1983).
4. William Trolinger, *The Anti-Evolution Pamphlets of William Bell Riley* (New York, 1995), xix.
5. Matthew Avery Sutton, *Aimee Semple McPherson and the Resurrection of Christian America* (Cambridge, MA, 2007), 52.
6. For an excellent look at Sunday's baseball career, see Wendy Knickerbocker, *Sunday at the Ballpark: Billy Sunday's Professional Baseball Career, 1883–1890* (Lanham, MD, 2000).

7. Sunday has been the subject of several good biographies, including Roger Burns, *Preacher: Billy Sunday and Big-Time Evangelism* (New York, 1992); Robert F. Martin, *Hero of the Heartland: Billy Sunday and the Transformation of American Society, 1862–1935* (Bloomington, 2002); and William G. McLoughlin, *Billy Sunday Was His Real Name* (Chicago, 1955).

8. Edward J. Larson, *Summer for the Gods: The Scopes Trial and America's Continuing Debate over Science and Religion* (New York, 1997), 52–53.

9. Ruth C. Stern and J. Herbie DiFonzo, "Dogging Darwin: America's Revolt against the Teaching of Evolution," *Northern Illinois University Law Review* 33 (2016): 35.

10. William E. Ellis, "Frank LeRond McVey: His Defense of Academic Freedom," *Register of the Kentucky Historical Society* 67, no. 1 (January 1969): 37–54.

11. Larry O'Dell, "Anti-Evolution Movement," *The Encyclopedia of Oklahoma History and Culture*, https://www.okhistory.org/publications/enc/entry?entry=AN011.

12. "Governor Vetoes Evolution and Board Cuts Out Books," *Raleigh News and Observer*, January 24, 1924, 1, 2.

13. Clarence Darrow, *The Story of My Life* (New York, 1932), 247.

14. Kenneth K. Bailey, *Southern White Protestantism in the Twentieth Century* (New York, 1964), 78–86.

15. *New York Times*, July 18, 1925, 1–2.

16. *Scopes v. State*, 154 Tenn. 105, 126, 289 S.W. 363, 369 (1927).

17. *New York Times*, July 18, 1925, 1–2; Ray Ginger, *Six Days or Forever?: Tennessee v. John Thomas Scopes* (Oxford, UK, 1958), 3–4.

18. Larson, 52–59.

19. Donald McRae, *The Last Trials of Clarence Darrow: The Landmark Cases of Leopold and Loeb, John T. Scopes, and Ossian Sweet* (New York, 2009), 158.

20. McRae, 158.

21. Joseph MacPherson, "Democratic Progressivism in Tennessee: The Administrations of Governor Austin Peay, 1923–1927," *East Tennessee Historical Society Publications* 40 (1968): 50–61.

22. Phillip Langsdon, *Tennessee: A Political History* (Franklin, TN, 2000), 303–9.

23. Larson, 48–49.

24. Larson, 56–59.

25. Darrow, 247.

26. Larson, 79–81.

27. *New York Times*, July 18, 1925, 1–2.

CHAPTER SIX: "WE'VE JUST ARRESTED A MAN FOR TEACHING EVOLUTION"

1. John T. Scopes and James Presley, *Center of the Storm: Memoirs of John T. Scopes* (New York, 1967), 36–37.
2. Scopes and Presley, 36; Marvin Olasky and John Perry, *Monkey Business: The True Story of the Scopes Trial* (Nashville, 2005), 7–9.
3. Olasky and Perry, 7–9.
4. For some excellent looks at the early years of the ACLU, see Peggy Lamson's *Roger Baldwin: Founder of the American Civil Liberties Union* (New York, 1976); and Samuel Walker's *In Defense of American Liberties: A History of the ACLU* (Oxford, UK, 1990).
5. Edward J. Larson, *Summer for the Gods: The Scopes Trial and America's Continuing Debate over Science and Religion* (New York, 1997), 61–83.
6. Larson, 87–89; Scopes and Presley, 60.
7. Scopes and Presley, 61.
8. Scopes and Presley, 56–57.
9. Scopes and Presley, 57–58.
10. Larson, 90.
11. Scopes and Presley, 57–60.
12. Olasky and Perry, 16.
13. Scopes and Presley, 61.
14. Randy Moore and William F. McComas, *The Scopes Monkey Trial* (Charleston, SC, 2016), 26.

CHAPTER SEVEN: "AN ORDINARY YOUNG MAN COMES TO DAYTON"

1. John T. Scopes and James Presley, *Center of the Storm: Memoirs of John T. Scopes* (New York, 1967), 3.
2. Scopes and Presley, 8–9.
3. Scopes and Presley, 53.
4. Scopes and Presley, 17–18.
5. Scopes and Presley, 18–19.
6. Scopes and Presley, 22–27.
7. Scopes and Presley, 28–30.
8. For McVey's leadership at the university, see Eric A. Moyen, *Frank L. McVey and the University of Kentucky: A Progressive President and the Modernization of a Southern University* (Lexington, 2011).
9. William E. Ellis, "Frank LeRond McVey: His Defense of Academic Freedom," *Register of the Kentucky Historical Society* 67, no. 1 (January 1969): 37–54.

10. Scopes and Presley, 29–30.

11. Scopes and Presley, 33–34.

12. "Rhea Central High School through the Years," August 17, 2020, https://yester dayindayton.net.

13. Scopes and Presley, 35–44.

14. Randy Moore, *A Field Guide to the Scopes Trial* (Dayton, TN, 2016), 32.

15. Scopes and Presley, 37.

16. Moore and McComas, 31.

17. Scopes and Presley, 42–44.

18. Scopes and Presley, 34–41.

19. Scopes and Presley, 39–40.

20. Scopes and Presley, 40–41.

21. Scopes and Presley, 44.

CHAPTER EIGHT: "THE PRINCIPLES OF OUR GOVERNMENT AND THE PRINCIPLES OF CHRISTIAN FAITH"

1. Louis W. Koenig, *Bryan: A Political Biography of William Jennings Bryan* (New York: 1971), 24.

2. Robert W. Cherny, *A Righteous Cause: The Life of William Jennings Bryan* (Boston, 1985) 56.

3. This take on Bryan draws from Paolo E. Coletta, *William Jennings Bryan*, 3 vols. (Lincoln, NE, 1964–69); Michael Kazin, *A Godly Hero: The Life of William Jennings Bryan* (New York, 2006); and Koenig, *Bryan*.

4. Clarence Darrow, *The Story of My Life* (New York, 1932), 92.

5. Kazin, 245.

6. Koenig, 351–55.

7. Kazin, 131–41.

8. William Jennings Bryan, *The Prince of Peace* (New York, 1914), 3–63.

9. Kazin, 270–71.

10. Koenig, 605–7.

11. Koenig, 607–8.

12. Koenig, 613.

13. William Jennings Bryan and Mary Baird Bryan, *Memoirs of William Jennings Bryan* (Chicago, 1925), 459.

14. Kazin, 262–67.

15. For a vivid account of the 1924 convention and the Bryan brothers' role in it, see Robert K. Murray, *The 103rd Ballot: The Incredible Story of the Disastrous Democratic Convention of 1924* (New York, 1976).

16. Bryan and Bryan, 459–60.

17. Koenig, 632–33; Bryan and Bryan, 481–82.
18. Bryan and Bryan, 483.

CHAPTER NINE: "I WANT DARROW"

1. For an excellent history of the ACLU, see Samuel Walker, *In Defense of American Liberties: A History of the ACLU* (Oxford, UK, 1990). For Baldwin, see Peggy Lamson, *Roger Baldwin: Founder of the American Civil Liberties Union* (New York, 1976).
2. Clarence Darrow, *The Story of My Life* (New York, 1932), 249; John T. Scopes and James Presley, *Center of the Storm: Memoirs of John T. Scopes* (New York, 1967), 66–67.
3. Darrow, 250–51.
4. Edward J. Larson, *Summer for the Gods: The Scopes Trial and America's Continuing Debate Over Science and Religion* (New York, 1997), 100–101.
5. Darrow, 249.
6. Marvin Olasky and John Perry, *Monkey Business: The True Story of the Scopes Trial* (Nashville, 2005), 28.
7. Scopes and Presley, 70–71.
8. Donald McRae, *The Last Trials of Clarence Darrow: The Landmark Cases of Leopold and Loeb, John T. Scopes, and Ossian Sweet* (New York, 2009), 164.
9. Scopes and Presley, 72–73.
10. Scopes and Presley, 73–74.
11. Larson, 102–3.
12. Scopes and Presley, 75–76; McRae, 168.
13. Timothy C. Cruver and Janet M. Cruver, eds., *You Be the Judge: Scopes Trial* (Dayton, TN, 2000), 8.
14. Scopes and Presley, 77–78.
15. Scopes and Presley, 78–82; Darrow, 248.
16. Larson, 103; "Dudley F. Malone Dies in California," *New York Times*, October 6, 1950.
17. Darrow, 251.
18. McRae, 168–69.
19. Scopes and Presley, 83–84.

CHAPTER TEN: THE CIRCUS COMES TO DAYTON

1. John T. Scopes and James Presley, *Center of the Storm: Memoirs of John T. Scopes* (New York, 1967), 77.
2. Marvin Olasky and John Perry, *Monkey Business: The True Story of the Scopes Trial* (Nashville, 2005), 33.
3. Randy Moore and William F. McComas, *The Scopes Monkey Trial* (Charleston, SC, 2016), 38–41, 50.

4. Timothy C. Cruver and Janet M. Cruver, eds., *You Be the Judge: Scopes Trial* (Dayton, TN, 2000), 15–17.
5. Scopes and Presley, 94–95.
6. For Mencken, see Carl Bode, *Mencken* (Carbondale, 1969); Fred Hobson Jr., *Mencken: A Life* (New York, 1994); and Terry Teachout, *The Skeptic: A Life of H. L. Mencken* (New York, 2002). Fred Hobson's *Serpent in Eden: H. L. Mencken and the South* (Baton Rouge, 1974) continues to offer excellent insights into his take on that region.
7. Edward J. Larson, *Summer for the Gods: The Scopes Trial and America's Continuing Debate over Science and Religion* (New York, 1997), 157–58.
8. H. L. Mencken, *A Religious Orgy in Tennessee: A Reporter's Account of the Scopes Monkey Trial* (Brooklyn, 2006), 27–33.
9. Cruver and Cruver, 23–24, 27–28.
10. Cruver and Cruver, 30, 33–35; Randy Moore, *A Field Guide to the Scopes Trial* (Dayton, TN, 2016), 43–45.
11. Cruver and Cruver, 30–31.
12. Scopes and Presley, 85–87; Cruver and Cruver, 33.
13. Cruver and Cruver, 35–37.
14. Moore, 66; Scopes and Presley, 84.
15. Cruver and Cruver, 38–40.
16. Cruver and Cruver, 40.
17. Cruver and Cruver, 40–41.
18. Cruver and Cruver, 42.
19. Clarence Darrow, *The Story of My Life* (New York, 1932), 251–52.
20. Moore, 35.
21. Darrow, 251–53.
22. Scopes and Presley, 88–90.
23. Scopes and Presley, 90.
24. Cruver and Cruver, 42.
25. Darrow, 253–55.
26. Scopes and Presley, 96.
27. Scopes and Presley, 98–99.
28. Moore and McComas, 68–69.
29. Moore and McComas, 71–72.

CHAPTER ELEVEN: DARROW IN THE LION'S DEN

1. Anthony Horvath, ed., *The Transcript of the Scopes Monkey Trial* (Greenwood, WI, 2018), 1–2.
2. John T. Scopes and James Presley, *The Center of the Storm: Memoirs of John T. Scopes* (New York, 1967), 105.

3. Horvath, 4–6.
4. Clarence Darrow, *The Story of My Life* (New York, 1932), 263.
5. Horvath, 7.
6. Horvath, 148–50.
7. Horvath, 20–21.
8. Darrow, 260.
9. Scopes and Presley, 106.
10. H. L. Mencken, *A Religious Orgy in Tennessee: A Reporter's Account of the Scopes Monkey Trial* (Brooklyn, 2006), 42–43.
11. Darrow, 254.
12. Horvath, 92–93.
13. Horvath, 110–14.
14. Marvin Olasky and John Perry, *Monkey Business: The True Story of the Scopes Trial* (Nashville, 2005), 49–50.
15. Horvath, 87–90.
16. Horvath, 99–101.
17. Horvath, 101.
18. Horvath, 103.
19. Scopes and Presley, 111.
20. Horvath, 128–46.
21. Scopes and Presley, 112.
22. Mencken, 61–64.

CHAPTER TWELVE: THE PROSECUTION MAKES ITS CASE

1. Anthony Horvath, ed., *The Transcript of the Scopes Monkey Trial* (Greenwood, WI, 2018), 184–85.
2. Horvath, 185–86.
3. Horvath, 186–88.
4. John T. Scopes and James Presley, *The Center of the Storm: Memoirs of John T. Scopes* (New York, 1967), 126–27.
5. Scopes and Presley, 127.
6. Horvath, 184–90.
7. Horvath, 192.
8. Horvath, 192–93.
9. Horvath. 203–5.
10. Scopes and Presley, 132.
11. Horvath, 258.
12. Horvath, 205–11.

13. Scopes and Presley, 132–33.

14. Horvath, 211–13.

15. Clarence Darrow, *The Story of My Life* (New York, 1932), 260–61.

16. Scopes and Presley, 134.

17. Horvath, 212–19.

18. Horvath, 220.

19. Scopes and Presley, 127.

20. Timothy C. Curver and Janet M. Curver, eds., *You Be the Judge: Scopes Trial* (Dayton, TN, 2000), 141–43.

CHAPTER THIRTEEN: "ARE WE ENTITLED TO SHOW WHAT EVOLUTION IS?"

1. Anthony Horvath, ed., *The Transcript of the Scopes Monkey Trial* (Greenwood, WI, 2018), 221.

2. Clarence Darrow, *The Story of My Life* (New York, 1932), 265.

3. Horvath, 221–37.

4. H. L. Mencken, *A Religious Orgy in Tennessee: A Reporter's Account of the Scopes Monkey Trial* (Brooklyn, 2006), 78–79.

5. Horvath, 238–40.

6. Horvath, 269–73.

7. Horvath, 273–75.

8. John T. Scopes and James Presley, *Center of the Storm: Memoirs of John T. Scopes* (New York, 1967), 142.

9. Mencken, 79.

10. Scopes and Presley, 143.

11. Horvath, 277–84.

12. Horvath, 285–88.

13. Horvath, 288–94.

14. Scopes and Presley, 143–44.

15. Scopes and Presley, 146–47.

16. Horvath, 296–97.

17. Horvath, 298–99.

18. Horvath, 296–300.

19. Horvath, 300–303.

20. Scopes and Presley, 154–55.

21. Mencken, 81–83.

22. Timothy C. Curver and Janet M. Curver, eds., *You Be the Judge: Scopes Trial* (Dayton, TN, 2000), 119.

23. Horvath, 303–6.
24. Horvath, 306–20.
25. Mencken, 77.

CHAPTER FOURTEEN: THE RULING ON EXPERT WITNESSES

1. Anthony Horvath, ed., *The Transcript of the Scopes Monkey Trial* (Greenwood, WI, 2018), 321–24.
2. Clarence Darrow, *The Story of My Life* (New York, 1932), 262.
3. Horvath, 329–30; John T. Scopes and James Presley, *Center of the Storm: Memoirs of John T. Scopes* (New York,1967), 160.
4. Scopes and Presley, 160–61.
5. H. L. Mencken, *A Religious Orgy in Tennessee: A Reporter's Account of the Scopes Monkey Trial* (Brooklyn, 2006), 89.
6. Timothy C. Curver and Janet M. Curver, eds., *You Be the Judge: Scopes Trial* (Dayton, TN, 2000), 143–55.
7. Horvath, 334.
8. Scopes and Presley, 162.
9. Horvath, 356–57.
10. Scopes and Presley, 163.
11. Horvath, 358–59.
12. Scopes and Presley, 163.
13. Scopes and Presley, 164.
14. Horvath, 338.
15. Horvath, 338–39.
16. Horvath, 362–436.

CHAPTER FIFTEEN: "I HAVEN'T GOTTEN THROUGH WITH HIM YET"

1. Anthony Horvath, ed., *The Transcript of the Scopes Monkey Trial* (Greenwood, WI, 2018), 441–77.
2. Clarence Darrow, *The Story of My Life* (New York, 1932), 268–69.
3. Louis W. Koenig, *Bryan: A Political Biography of William Jennings Bryan* (New York, 1971), 652–53.
4. Darrow, 267–69; Donald McRae, *The Last Trials of Clarence Darrow* (New York, 2009), 220–22; John T. Scopes and James Presley, *Center of the Storm: Memoirs of John T. Scopes* (New York, 1967), 187.
5. Edward J. Larson and Jack Marshall, eds., *The Essential Words and Writings of Clarence Darrow* (New York, 2007), 121–23.
6. Marvin Olasky and John Perry, *Monkey Business: The True Story of the Scopes Trial* (Nashville, 2005), 154.

7. Larson and Marshall, 202–203.
8. Michael Kazin, *A Godly Hero: The Life of William Jennings Bryan* (New York, 2006), 293.
9. Scopes and Presley, 178.
10. Larson and Marshall, 122–23.
11. Horvath, 479–83.
12. Horvath, 483.
13. Horvath, 487–88.
14. Scopes and Presley, 187.
15. Scopes and Presley, 187–88.
16. Horvath, 491–93.
17. Horvath, 495–96.
18. Horvath, 497.
19. Timothy C. Curver and Janet M. Curver, eds., *You Be the Judge: Scopes Trial* (Dayton, TN, 2000), 185.
20. Scopes and Presley, 192–93.

CHAPTER SIXTEEN: "HE WAS NOT, FOR GOD TOOK HIM"

1. Anthony Horvath, ed., *The Transcript of the Scopes Monkey Trial* (Greenwood, WI, 2018), 500–525.
2. Michael Kazin, *A Godly Hero: The Life of William Jennings Bryan* (New York, 2006), 294.
3. Horvath, 500–525.
4. William Jennings Bryan and Mary Baird Bryan, *Memoirs of William Jennings Bryan* (Chicago, 1925), 484–86.
5. Clarence Darrow, *The Story of My Life* (New York, 1932), 269.
6. John T. Scopes and James Presley, *Center of the Storm: Memoirs of John T. Scopes* (New York, 1967), 194–96.
7. Bryan and Bryan, 485–87.
8. Louis W. Koenig, *Bryan: A Political Biography of William Jennings Bryan* (New York, 1971), 658.
9. Scopes and Presley, 196–98.
10. Darrow, 270.
11. H. L. Mencken, *A Religious Orgy in Tennessee: A Reporter's Account of the Scopes Monkey Trial* (Brooklyn, 2006), 109.
12. Timothy C. Curver and Janet M. Curver, eds., *You Be the Judge: Scopes Trial* (Dayton, TN, 2000) 229–45.
13. Curver and Curver, 277–309.
14. Bryan and Bryan, 488–91.

15. Darrow, 271.

16. Scopes and Presley, 217.

17. *Time* 16, no. 7 (August 18, 1930).

18. Darrow, 272–73.

19. "Faculty leaving Bryan College after change in beliefs," Associated Press, May 4, 2014.

20. Koenig, 658.

CHAPTER SEVENTEEN: "YOU CAN ONLY BE FREE IF I AM FREE"

1. Donald McRae, *The Last Trials of Clarence Darrow: The Landmark Cases of Leopold and Loeb, John T. Scopes, and Ossian Sweet* (New York, 2009), 320–24, 328–30.

2. Clarence Darrow, *The Story of My Life* (New York, 1932), 273–75.

3. Randy Moore and William F. McComas, *The Scopes Monkey Trial* (Charleston, SC, 2016), 103.

4. "John T. Raulston, Jurist, 87, Dead," Associated Press, July 12, 1956.

5. "Tennessee: Surprise Ending," *Time*, August 15, 1938.

6. "The Rise of Senator Legend," *Time*, March 24, 1952.

7. John T. Scopes and James Presley, *Center of the Storm: Memoirs of John T. Scopes* (New York, 1967), 233–43.

8. Scopes and Presley, 255–59.

9. " 'Monkey Trial' Figure Named for Congress; John Thomas Scopes, Convicted of Teaching Evolution, Will Run as Kentucky Socialist," *New York Times*, August 13, 1932, 17.

10. Scopes and Presley, 263–67.

11. Scopes and Presley, 267–73.

12. "Looking Back with Epperson, Fifty Years Later," *Reports of the National Center for Science Education* 38, no. 4 (November 5, 2018).

13. 393 U.S. 97, *Susan Epperson et al., Appellants, v. Arkansas, no. 7*, Supreme Court of the United States, November 12, 1968.

14. "Looking Back with Epperson."

15. Scopes and Presley, 277.

16. McRae, 227–92.

17. McRae, 332–39.

18. "At Site of Scopes Trial, Darrow Statue Belatedly Joins Bryan's," *New York Times*, July 14, 2017.

19. "At Site of Scopes Trial."

EPILOGUE: SPEAKING FREELY AND UNAFRAID

1. David Masci, "For Darwin Day, 6 Facts about the Evolution Debate," Pew Research Center, February 11, 2019.

2. Glenn Branch and Ann Reid, "Evolution Education in the U.S. Is Getting Better," *Scientific American*, September 12, 2020.

3. Glenn Branch, "Evolution Education: What a Difference a Dozen Years Makes," National Center for Science Education, September 9, 2020.

4. Pew Research Staff, "Chapter 4: Evolution and Perceptions of Scientific Consensus," Pew Research Center, July 1, 2015.

5. CNA Staff, "Francis Inaugurates Bust of Benedict, Emphasizes Unity of Faith, Science," Catholic News Agency, October 27, 2014.

6. Douglas Belkin and Jacob Gershman, "Federal Lawsuits Say Antiracism and Critical Race Theory in Schools Violate Constitution," *Wall Street Journal*, July 1, 2021.

7. Michelle Merlin, "East Penn Parents Sue District, Alleging Conversations about Race, Racism Are Anti-Christian Discrimination," *Morning Call*, June 16, 2021.

8. April Corbin Girnus, "Las Vegas Charter School Sued for Curriculum Covering Race, Identity," *Nevada Current*, January 21, 2021.

9. Sam Dorman, "Virginia Parents Sue School District over Alleged Racial Discrimination, Free Speech Violations," Fox News, June 2, 2021.

10. Sarah Schwartz, "Map: Where Critical Race Theory Is Under Attack," *Education Week*, September 28, 2022.

11. Oklahoma Statute, title 70, section 24-157 (2021), https://legiscan.com/OK/text/HB1775/id/2387002.

12. Tyler Kingkade and Antonia Hylton, "Oklahoma's Anti–Critical Race Theory Law Violates Free Speech Rights, ACLU Suit Says," NBC News, October 20, 2021; Alia Wong, "Is Banning Critical Race Theory in Schools Unconstitutional? Lawsuit in Oklahoma Seeks to Prove It," *USA Today*, October 19, 2021.

13. Clarence Darrow, *Closing Arguments: Clarence Darrow on Religion, Law, and Society*, ed. S. T. Joshi (Athens, OH, 2005), 22–23.

14. Darrow, ed. Joshi.

15. *Amended Complaint, Black Emergency Response Team vs. John O'Connor, U.S. District Court for the Western District of Oklahoma*, Case No. 5:21-cv-1022-G, filed November 9, 2021, https://www.aclu.org/sites/default/files/field_document/eb3c4178-ce02-4740-8c82-e6bf2ad42b9a.pdf.

16. Lauren Camera, "Federal Lawsuit Poses First Challenge to Ban on Teaching Critical Race Theory," *US News and World Report*, October 20, 2021.

17. Oklahoma State Department of Education, Oklahoma Academic Standards, July 22, 2021, https://sde.ok.gov/oklahoma-academic-standards.

18. Clarence Darrow, *The Story of My Life* (New York, 1932), 232.
19. *Darrow, Closing Arguments*, 153.
20. Donald McRae, *The Last Trials of Clarence Darrow: The Landmark Cases of Leopold and Loeb, John T. Scopes, and Ossian Sweet* (New York, 2009), 130.
21. Steven Lubet, "The Fragility of Academic Freedom," *Hill*, December 1, 2021.
22. Darrow, *The Story of My Life*, 232.
23. Clarence Darrow and Walter Rice, *Infidels and Heretics: An Agnostic's Anthology* (Boston, 1929), 206.
24. Irving Stone, *Clarence Darrow for the Defense* (Garden City, NY, 1941), 462.

Index